THE
SHAKESPEAREAN CIPHERS
EXAMINED

> so prove it,
> That the probation bear no hinge nor loop
> To hang a doubt on. . . .
>
> *Othello*, Act III, sc. III

THE SHAKESPEAREAN CIPHERS EXAMINED

AN ANALYSIS OF CRYPTOGRAPHIC
SYSTEMS USED AS EVIDENCE THAT
SOME AUTHOR OTHER THAN
WILLIAM SHAKESPEARE
WROTE THE PLAYS COMMONLY
ATTRIBUTED TO HIM

BY

WILLIAM F. FRIEDMAN
&
ELIZEBETH S. FRIEDMAN

CAMBRIDGE
AT THE UNIVERSITY PRESS
1957

PUBLISHED BY
THE SYNDICS OF THE CAMBRIDGE UNIVERSITY PRESS

Bentley House, 200 Euston Road, London, N.W. 1
American Branch: 32 East 57th Street, New York 22, N.Y.

First edition 1957
Reprinted 1957

Printed in Great Britain at the University Press, Cambridge
(Brooke Crutchley, University Printer)

PREFACE

For almost two hundred years the authorship of the plays commonly attributed to Shakespeare has been disputed; and a good many writers, in contesting the attribution, have made specific claims for someone else as author. Some of these writers have supported their claims with cryptographic proofs: that is, with evidence derived from the solution of ciphers or other cryptographic systems incorporated, they believe, in the writings themselves.

The late Dr Logan Clendening, reviewing Charles Allen's *Notes on the Bacon-Shakespeare Question* in *The Colophon* of September 1939, said that Allen dealt 'clearly and soberly with all the arguments except the cipher and cryptography allegations'; and added, 'a book by an unbiased cryptographer is badly needed'. In a letter written in 1941 to one of the authors of this book, Dr Clendening said: 'I wish you had time to do a study of the cryptographic work on the Bacon-Shakespeare controversy....I am...a thorough skeptic about the Baconian authorship of Shakespeare, but in all my studies I have never been able to evaluate critically the cryptographic literature, including Mrs Gallup's biliteral cipher, and old Ignatius Donnelly's work of long ago.'

Even among the anti-Stratfordians, a writer like A. W. Titherley, with a scientific and impartial attitude (to this question at any rate), could say in his *Shakespeare's Identity*: 'as to the validity of "signatures" decoded by modern Baconians, the present writer is not competent to judge'.

We have long intended to present a full-scale appraisal of the cryptographic arguments from the point of view of the professional cryptanalyst. We have both been interested in the problem for many years; that we also have some personal or 'inside' knowledge will appear in later chapters. The preparation of the study has been delayed by our professional duties during and since the Second World War; meanwhile

Elizabethan scholars in America—Stratfordians and anti-Stratfordians—have encouraged us to complete it.

An earlier version was awarded one of the two Folger Prizes in 1955; that more detailed study has been deposited in typescript in the Folger Shakespeare Library in Washington, for consultation by professional scholars and those most closely interested. This version has been revised for general publication, in the belief that the ordinary reader is interested in the controversy. Certainly this seems likely, if one is to judge by the attention paid in the Press to almost anyone presenting a new theory of 'Shakespeare's identity'. Whether the public is willing to pay the more sober kind of attention needed to follow a careful examination of arguments is another matter—particularly if the examination leads to what might be called sedative results. None the less we believe it is useful to present conclusions which we feel our professional colleagues would accept, and to suggest standards and employ arguments and methods which future examinations of cryptograms allegedly present in Shakespeare's plays ought not to ignore.

ACKNOWLEDGMENTS

It is a pleasure to acknowledge our debt to all writers from whom we have quoted, anti-Stratfordians and Stratfordians alike. In addition, it is our pleasant task to thank those who have specifically helped us in the preparation of this book.

For the original suggestion that this material (much of which had first been embodied in a lecture) be made into a book-length manuscript we are indebted to Dr James G. McManaway, editor of *The Shakespeare Quarterly*, who also gave us much encouragement throughout its preparation. To the Director of the Folger Shakespeare Library, Dr Louis G. Wright, and the principal members of his technical staff, Dr McManaway, Dr E. E. Willoughby, Dr Giles E. Dawson, Miss Dorothy Mason and others, we are grateful for assisting our access to and study of the Library's collection of Shakespeareana and, even more important, its anti-Stratfordiana, the largest collection of its type in the United States. We are indebted to

Mr Frederick Goff, Head of the Rare Book Room of the Library of Congress, and his staff, for providing access to the Fabyan and Goudy Collections; and to Mr Angus Wilson, until recently Superintendent of the Reading Room in the British Museum, for much time-saving assistance.

To Dr Fred E. Miller, and to Dr Charlton Hinman, we owe thanks for technical assistance on important typographical questions concerning the most intriguing of the ciphers we studied.

To Mr Frank Woodward, Jr, former Chairman, Cmdr Martin Pares, Chairman, and Captain William W. Aspden, Secretary, of the Bacon Society of England, we are especially grateful for their courtesy to Colonel Friedman when in 1953 and 1954 he visited Canonbury Tower, headquarters of the society.

We acknowledge also our debt to Mr Ronald Mansbridge, Manager of the American Branch of the Cambridge University Press, for his determined faith and encouragement in the project of making a book from our prize-winning manuscript; to Dr Sidney Kramer, bibliographer turned bookseller, for his continuing exhortations to us to continue when our faith in the project lagged; to Rear-Admiral Dwight M. Agnew, USN, Retired, for a valuable suggestion relating to the manner in which we deal with some of our material; and most particularly are we indebted to Mr M. H. Black and Mr R. A. Becher, of the Cambridge office of our publishers, for their skilled aid in the condensation and revision of our manuscript.

Finally, despite our critical remarks on the part played by the late Colonel George Fabyan, we acknowledge with gratitude our debt to him for introducing us to Elizabeth Wells Gallup, whose work on the question of Shakespearean authorship aroused our life-long interest in the subject.

W. F. F.
E. S. F.

Washington, D.C.
February 1957

CONTENTS

LIST OF ILLUSTRATIONS

PLATES

FIGURES

INTRODUCTION

SHAKESPEAREAN SCHOLARS have often had to deal with arguments that Shakespeare did not have the birth, breeding or education necessary to write the plays. The evidence brought forward by both sides in this particular argument is necessarily conjectural, and must therefore always be inconclusive. On the other hand, claims based on cryptography can be scientifically examined, and proved or disproved. In this book we examine the cryptographic evidence used to support the thesis that someone other than Shakespeare wrote the plays.

Many of the anti-Stratfordians who use cryptography to support their arguments have two aims: they wish to prove that Shakespeare did not write the plays, and they also wish to prove that someone else—usually Bacon—did. Of course other claimants have been brought forward; and there is even one subtle sceptic who, while not accepting Shakespeare, has found in the First Folio cryptographic evidence which has convinced him that there are hidden messages proving the writer to be a man whose Christian name was Will and whose surname began with 'Shake' (see ch. VI). There are also those who find that Shakespeare, like Homer, was a syndicate—or, to use the current jargon of American scholarship, a 'project'.

At the outset we must make two things clear. First, the science of cryptology (which concerns itself with secret writing by means of codes and ciphers) is a branch of knowledge which goes back far into the past—certainly beyond Elizabethan times. In the sixteenth century it was abundantly used. It is also certain that Francis Bacon (the leading contender for the authorship of the plays) gave a brief account of cryptography, and invented a unique and admirable cipher system which we shall later describe. So it is clear that ciphers could quite certainly have been used, and by Bacon in particular, to conceal a claim to the true authorship of any work. The question of course— as Prof. E. R. Vincent pointed out in the parallel case of

Dante[1]—is not whether ciphers could have been used, but whether they were used.

Second, the authors of this book have no professional or emotional stake in any particular claim to the authorship of Shakespeare's plays. We have no bias for or against any Elizabethan or Jacobean writer or writers as contenders for the title. It is true that for three-and-a-half centuries most scholars have accepted the attribution to Shakespeare; but it is also true that for a great part of that time the attribution has been challenged by many people on many grounds, and some anti-Stratfordians have been learned and distinguished. The argument has spread to all countries where the plays are known; it cannot be simply dismissed without examination.

Anyone interested in English literature must know of the dispute, but few know anything of its history; it is therefore useful to summarize it before going on to the cryptographic arguments themselves. Our first chapter touches on the chief stages, the chief writers and the most important publications since 1728, and a selection of the arguments advanced by anti-Stratfordians. We do not attempt to mention everything which librarians place in the category *Baconiana*. This term itself is elastic, and really means *anti-Shakespeareana*, since it covers many different claims to the authorship of Shakespeare's works. The word 'deviationist', at one time used by a number of scholars, has since been usurped by the contestants in another no less bitter dispute, and we shall not use it here.

The stages which we list below are only the more significant ones in a long series which shows no sign of ending. In 1950 the British Broadcasting Corporation transmitted on its Third Programme a talk by Dr Giles E. Dawson, curator of rare books at the Folger Shakespeare Library. It was called 'Who wrote Shakespeare?' The Council of the Francis Bacon Society asked the B.B.C. for equal time in which to present their own view. The request was denied, and there followed a storm of protest from anti-Stratfordians who felt their case had been damaged without the chance to make it good. The record of this incident is to be found in *Baconiana* for October 1950. Since then, there

[1] Gabriele Rossetti claimed that *The Divine Comedy* contained a cipher.

has been the much publicized claim of Mr Calvin Hoffman, that Christopher Marlowe was author of the plays. And no doubt before long there will be another nominee.

Most scholars ignore or slight the theories of anti-Strat-fordians, who feel, understandably, all the more aggrieved. They must be given something better than derision, if only to reassure them that they are not the victims of a merely emotional reaction on the part of those who often have a material interest in the affair. They are entitled to a courteous and—wherever possible—a scientific examination of their arguments. It is in the case of cryptographic systems that this can most easily be done.

CHAPTER I

THE GREAT CONTROVERSY

IT seems that the first man to question Shakespeare's sole authorship of the plays was a certain 'Captain' Goulding. In a small book called *An Essay against Too Much Reading*, published in 1728, he hinted at one of the anti-Stratfordian arguments. The plays, he said, are so superlative that '*Shakespear* has frighten'd three parts of the World from attempting to write; and he was no Scholar, no Grammarian, no Historian, and in all probability cou'd not write *English*'. Goulding then introduces the first ghost:

> Although his Plays were historical...the History Part was given him in concise and short, by one of those Chuckles that could give him nothing else....I will give you a short Account of Mr. *Shakespear's* Proceeding; and that I had from one of his intimate Acquaintance. His being imperfect in some Things, was owing to his not being a Scholar, which obliged him to have one of those chucklepated Historians for his particular Associate...and he maintain'd him, or he might have starv'd upon his History. And when he wanted anything in his Way...he sent to him....Then with his natural flowing Wit, he work'd it into all Shapes and Forms, as his beautiful Thoughts directed. The other put it into Grammar....

One may see here the germ of much future ingenuity; there is also a probable reference back to Jonson's remarks about Shakespeare's scholarship, Heminge and Condell's testimony to his facility, and Shakespeare's own comment on the poetic imagination ('The poet's pen, Turns them to shapes, and gives to airy nothing A local habitation and a name'). The trouble is that it is difficult to decide whether Goulding is in earnest; some scholars have declared the Essay to be an exercise in early eighteenth-century deflationary anti-heroics.

In 1769—some forty years later—there was published in England a curious little allegory with a historical framework, called *The Life and Adventures of Common Sense*. It is anonymous, but has been ascribed to one Herbert Lawrence. A copy of the book came up for sale in New York in 1916; when attention was drawn to a certain passage in it, the bidding shot up from a trifling sum to $1825—a lot of money in those days for a book of seemingly little importance. The passage contains what has been considered to be one of the first references to Bacon as Shakespeare.

In the allegory, *Common Sense*, his father *Wisdom*, and his companions *Genius* and *Humour* arrive in London together; they meet on their arrival a *Stranger*,

a Person belonging to the Playhouse; this Man was a profligate in his Youth, and, as some say, had been a Deer-stealer....This Man... took the first opportunity...to rob them of every Thing he could lay his Hands on....Amongst my Father's Baggage, he presently cast his Eye upon a common place Book, in which was contained, an Infinite Variety of Modes and Forms, to express all the different Sentiments of the human Mind, together with Rules for their Combinations and Connections upon every Subject or Occasion that might Occur in Dramatic Writing....With these Materials, and with good Parts of his own, he commenced Play-Writer, how he succeeded is needless to say, when I tell the Reader that his name was *Shakespear*.

Bacon kept a commonplace book, which has survived. Some Baconians have therefore inferred that Bacon is represented by *Wisdom*, 'my Father', in the allegory.

The first writer to come out firmly for Bacon was the Rev. James Wilmot, D.D. He made the attribution in about 1785, but it seems not to have attracted attention at the time; his priority was recorded and authenticated in 1805 and 1813.[1]

Another allegorical work referred to the authorship of the plays in 1786; this was *The Story of the Learned Pig*, by 'An Officer of the Royal Navy'. It is a small step from the notion of a learned pig to that of the learned Bacon; some readers have been eager to make it. The Pig as he describes himself is a Protean figure—the cliché is justified, for he was successively greyhound, deer and bear. By p. 35 he can state:

I am now come to a period in which, to my great joy, I once more got possession of a human body....I was early in life initiated in the

[1] See Lord Sydenham of Combe (George Sydenham Clarke), 'The First Baconian', in *Baconiana* (3rd series, Feb. 1933), vol. XXI, pp. 143–50.

profession of horseholder to those who came to visit the playhouse, where I was well known bv the name of 'Pimping Billy'. . . .I soon after contracted a friendship with that great man and first of geniuses, the 'Immortal Shakespeare', and am happy in now having it in my power to refute the prevailing opinion of his having run his country for deer-stealing, which is as false as it is disgracing. . . . With equal falsehood has he been father'd with many spurious dramatic pieces. 'Hamlet, Othello, As you like it, the Tempest, and Midsummer's Night Dream', for five; of all which I confess myself to be the author.

The tempo now begins to quicken. In 1848 the New York publishers Harper and Brothers issued *The Romance of Yachting* by Joseph C. Hart, a former American consul at Santa Cruz, who had often given it as his opinion that 'the money-lending actor could not have been the author of the plays'. His book has little to say about yachting; it is 'a kind of horn-book of digression'; but it displays a good deal of anti-Stratfordian scepticism. While it proposes no one specific author, by impli- cation it favours Jonson. Soon afterwards, in 1852, the August issue of Chambers' *Edinburgh Journal* carried an anonymous article called 'Who Wrote Shakespeare?' Again no specific author is named; it is merely suggested that Shakespeare 'kept a poet'.

Bacon was really launched as Shakespeare in 1856. *Putnam's Monthly* published in January an article on 'Shakespeare and His Plays: An Inquiry Concerning Them'. The author, 'D. Bacon', was an American woman, and, as she said, no relation. Delia Bacon wrote more articles; and in 1857 she published a 543-page volume called *The Philosophy of the Plays of Shakespeare Unfolded*. She believed in several authors, but this contention tended to be overlooked as Baconians grew more numerous and more convinced. It is worth noting that both Mark Twain and Nathaniel Hawthorne gave countenance if not support to anti-Stratfordianism. Hawthorne, then consul in Liverpool, was sought out by Miss Bacon and asked to help find a publisher. Instead he wrote a Preface; recording in his *English Notebooks* that she was 'a remarkable woman', and in the Preface the equally judicious remark 'it is for the public to judge whether or not my country woman has proved her theory'.

3   I-2

James Russell Lowell is reputed to have said that Delia Bacon had opened a question that would never be closed. It seemed also as if she had opened a giant valve: the books, the articles, the journals now appeared in a gathering spate: some 'for', but most 'against' Shakespeare.

In the same year, 1857, another book came out in England. William Henry Smith in *Bacon and Shakespeare: An Inquiry Touching Players, Play-Houses and Play-Writers in the Age of Elizabeth* developed a doubt which he had first suggested in an open letter. By the end of 1857 there had arrived the first defender: George Henry Townsend with his *William Shakespeare Not an Impostor*, published in England and the United States.

It was in 1882 that the cryptographic argument was first put forward. A Mrs Windle was the author, and her work bore this strange majestic title:

REPORT TO THE BRITISH MUSEUM
on behalf of the
ANNALS OF GREAT BRITAIN
and
THE REIGN OF HER MAJESTY, QUEEN VICTORIA
Discovery and opening of
THE CIPHER
— of —
Francis Bacon, Lord Verulam,
Alike in his prose writings and in the
'SHAKESPEARE' DRAMAS
proving him the author of the dramas.
by Mrs. C. F. Ashmead Windle
(Letters Patent of England to be Procured)
San Francisco.
Jos. Winterbourn & Co.,
Book and Job Printers and Electrotypers.
1882.

The Windle 'Cipher' was concerned to find significance (or at least a kind of hazy support) in puns on words, names and titles. *The Winter's Tale* became a sequence of near-homophones: The wind us tail; the win tears tail; the vent us tail;

4

the venture's tail, the venturous tale; the wondrous tale. A Windle's tale, one may be excused for thinking. This is not really a cipher; and we see no need to discuss it further.

Fairly late in the history of the arguments for Baconian authorship, in 1888, there appeared Ignatius Donnelly's *The Great Cryptogram*, discussed in ch. III. This was the earliest of the many attempts to find a true cipher as evidence for a belief about the authorship; all over the world dogged and ingenious heads now pored over the texts themselves—not for their beauty or their significance, but for the hidden simple acrostic, acrotelestic, numerologic or other concealed messages.

But this is to anticipate: we deal with the various cryptographic studies in later chapters. Meanwhile, of course, writers in almost every country where the plays are read have produced works on their authorship which do not use cryptography as a support; more will have appeared by the time this book is published. Two of the most recent books of this kind are *This Star of England*,[1] a volume of 1282 pages by Dorothy and Charlton Ogburn, supporters of Edward de Vere, 17th Earl of Oxford, and *The Man who was Shakespeare*,[2] by Calvin Hoffman, who supports Marlowe. One can best indicate the magnitude of the literature by pointing out that the late Prof. Joseph S. Galland of Northwestern University had completed a bibliography just before his death in 1947. It had more than 1500 pages of manuscript; no one could afford to publish it.[3]

Though Edward de Vere comes a strong second, most of this vast literature is devoted to proving that Bacon was Shakespeare; the prevalence of the term 'Baconian' indicates the measure of support given to him. The Bacon Society was founded in England in 1885; in the following year it began to publish the *Journal of the Bacon Society*, which still appears, though it changed its name to *Baconiana* in January 1891. The Bacon Society of America was founded in 1922, and from 1923

---

[1] New York: Coward-McCann Inc. 1952.

[2] New York: Julian Messner, 1955; London: Max Parrish, 1955.

[3] Microfilm copies of his *Digesta Anti-Shakespeareana: An historical and analytical bibliography of the Shakespeare authorship and identity controversies* have been deposited in various libraries. We are grateful for the use of a carbon copy of the original given us by Prof. Burton S. Milligan of the University of Illinois.

until 1931 it produced its own journal, *American Baconiana*. Baconian theories caught on in Germany, and from 1930 to 1932 there was published at Frankfurt a journal called *Deutsche Baconiana: Zeitschrift für Bacon-Shakespeare Forschung*—a title with a fine solid ring about it. All these Bacon Societies claim that their first aim is the study of the life and works of Francis Bacon, Lord Verulam, and their second the investigation of his supposed authorship of certain other works 'including the Shakespeare dramas and poems'.

There are of course yet other contenders. In the first year of publication of the *Journal of the Bacon Society* of Great Britain there appeared a pamphlet, *Who Wrote Shakespeare?*, whose author signed himself 'Multum in Parvo'. He was an American, a Mr M. L. Hore, who maintained that Robert Burton was Shakespeare. Hore pondered and searched for twenty-five years; and he gained one notable recruit—George Parker of the Bodleian Library.

In 1888, the year when Donnelly published his Baconian cipher, an Englishman, F. Scott Surtees, proclaimed Sir Anthony Sherley as the real author. He pointed out (and it is a matter which deserves notice and is capable of extension) that Donnelly's work did not contradict him, it 'backed him up'; much of it 'might fit Sherley as well as Bacon'—and he showed it might. In 1912 the Belgian professor, Célestin Demblon, nominated Roger Manners, Earl of Rutland, in a book called *Lord Rutland est Shakespeare. Le plus grand des mystères dévoilé*. In 1914 an American retorted with Sir Walter Raleigh (Henry Pemberton, Jr., in *Shakespeare and Sir Walter Raleigh*). In 1916 John M. Maxwell of Indiana proposed Robert Cecil, Earl of Salisbury, in a book called *The Man behind the Mask*.

The initiative passed back to Europe. Prof. Abel Lefranc adopted the idea of the mask, but put behind it the face of William Stanley, Earl of Derby. After years of work he produced two big books: *Sous le masque de 'William Shakespeare'* and *Secret de William Stanley*. Stanley's authorship had first been proposed by an Englishman, James Greenstreet, in a series of articles in *The Genealogist*. The thesis has recently (1952) been defended by another Englishman, A. W. Titherley.

Edward de Vere, Earl of Oxford, was first proposed as recently as 1920; his rise to favour has been spectacular. His first sponsor was an English schoolmaster, J. T. Looney, who was able to gather a considerable following. Among the more notable are the Ogburns (see p. 5). Perhaps the most active partisan in England was Mr Percy Allen, who engaged in public debate with Baconians. In America an Oxfordian, Mr Gelett Burgess, has said about Baconians the sort of thing usually said by Stratfordians: 'The Baconian auctorial theory has long since exploded in a kind of spontaneous combustion of its own fantastic symbolism, numerology and cryptographia which proved anything, everything and nothing.'[1] Mr Burgess' evidence for the Oxford theory was not, however, of the sort which could be scientifically examined.

In 1937 a former Harvard instructor, Alden Brooks, challenged Shakespeare's authenticity in his *Will Shakspere: factotum and agent*; in 1943, in *Will Shakspere and the Dyer's hand*, he introduced his own nominee, Sir Edward Dyer. He felt, however, that 'without Kyd we should never have had *Hamlet*, without Marlowe no *Richard II* or *III*'.

The first commoner (apart from Shakespeare) was introduced into this distinguished gathering when Marlowe was proposed. Mr Calvin Hoffman claims to have 'ironclad evidence' that Marlowe wrote the plays. Scholars are still in process of finding chinks in it, and his own excavations in the Walsingham tomb have so far met with no success. Another plebeian, Daniel Defoe, was suggested by Mr George M. Battey (no more fortunately named than Mr Looney; and, quite properly, no more deterred by it). Marlowe and Defoe give the chronological extremes, having been born in 1564 and 1659 respectively.

The longest-odds contender was Michele Agnolo Florio, an Italian, who may have been the John Florio who lived in London, translated Montaigne, was tutor to the Countess of Pembroke, secretary to the Earl of Southampton ('Shakespeare's' patron) and knew almost everyone worth knowing. At any rate, Michele Agnolo Florio was found to have published verses which ten years later appeared in *Hamlet*—or so

[1] *Washington* (D.C.) *Post*, July 1948.

it was claimed by Signor Santi Paladino, as reported in the *Literary Digest* in 1927 and 1930. The theory is supported only in Italy.

The *group, proprietary, synthetic,* or *editorial theory* of authorship is commonly held, but there is great diversity in claims about the composition of the group. Perhaps the most conservative and scholarly advocate of the *disintegrationist* theory (as it is also called) was Appleton Morgan, for many years president of the Shakespeare Society of New York. He held that Shakespeare was 'stage editor', and that he set down in writing the plays which were to be acted; 'as copyist his wits led him to interpolate and change'.

Disintegrationists have proposed syndicates which between them include almost all the well-known Elizabethan writers and many obscure ones as well. It has been urged that Bacon acted as Secretary to the Syndicate, or as editor in chief, or as 'polisher and reconstructor'. It was a businesslike arrangement, and for convenience we set out below in a businesslike way some forms of the theory:

Delia Bacon in *The Philosophy of the Shakespeare Plays Unfolded* (1857) suggested: chief editor: Bacon; collaborators: Raleigh, Lord Buckhurst, Lord Paget, the Earl of Oxford.

James Appleton Morgan in *The Shakespeare Myth* (1881): Shakespeare as stage manager and editor 'rewrote for the stage what his unknown poet, poets, or friends composed'. Bacon and Raleigh are possible authors. (Morgan modified his views in later years, and was despised as a turncoat.)

Thomas William White in *Our English Homer* (1892): Bacon editor and 'Secretary General'; on the board: Greene, Marlowe, Nash, Peele, Daniel, Lodge.

John Hawley Stotsenburg in *Impartial Study of the Shakespeare Title* (1904): Bacon as 'polisher and reconstructor'; writers: Drayton, Dekker, Heywood, Webster, Middleton, Porter, Anthony Munday, Henry Chettle.

Gilbert Slater in *Seven Shakespeares* (1931): Bacon *primus inter pares* with the Countess of Pembroke, Raleigh, Shakespeare, Oxford, Derby, Marlowe.

Wallace McCook Cunningham and Maria Bauer in *Tragedy of Sir Francis Bacon* (Cunningham, 1940); *The Great Virginia Vault* and *Foundations Unearthed* (Bauer, 1939–40): Bacon as the Great

Architect to a body of about seventy, including Lancelot Andrewes, the three brothers Bodley, Raleigh, Jonson, Drake, Thomas More, Spenser, Marlowe and others. (A fine body of men, but hard perhaps to bring together.)

The group theory has been buttressed by evidence from the spirit world. The American press agency, United Press, produced the following report from London in January 1948:[1]

> Drama critic Percy Allen reported today he had contacted William Shakespeare, the Earl of Oxford and Sir Francis Bacon in the spirit world and had asked them bluntly: 'Who wrote the plays attributed to William Shakespeare?' Shakespeare admitted he was not the sole author of his famous plays and poems and that Edward de Vere, seventeenth Earl of Oxford, was his collaborator, Allen said.

To sum up: it has been estimated that by 1950 more than 4000 separate books and articles, in six languages, support and dispute the claims presented for seventeen possible authors. There are also the disintegrationists, and finally a group of anti-Stratfordians who claim that not only did Bacon, or some other contender, write Shakespeare, but that he produced a good portion of the rest of Elizabethan literature as well. This kind of claim usually results from extending the methods of those who pursue cryptographic evidence, and we examine the phenomenon later.

We have given only a brief account of the rise of anti-Stratfordian investigations. The reader may well wonder how it all came about; what is wrong with Shakespeare that so many people are unwilling to accept him as author of the plays; what kind of dissatisfaction, what kind of hint, what kind of evidence has kept the controversy going?

Again we can give only the shortest summary. In general it can be said that the anti-Stratfordian position is supported by three kinds of argument: historical, stylistic, and cryptographic. The rest of this book deals with the cryptographic arguments. Stylistic questions are best left to literary historians and critics. 'Historical' matters seem to be everyman's stamping ground,

[1] *Washington Post*, 6 January 1948.

and the term covers a wide range of considerations. We list a few below. Against Shakespeare's authorship it has been argued:

That much more should surely be known about the author of works as remarkable as the plays; but that very little is known about the historical William Shakespeare.

That whoever wrote the plays must have been a highly cultured man, learned in many studies, versed in the classics, knowing several languages. It is not known that Shakespeare ever went to a university, and the records of his schooling are dubious and uncertain.

That the plays must have been written by a much-travelled man, who knew Spain, France, Italy, Denmark, Navarre, Scotland (and presumably the sea-coast of Bohemia). Yet there is no record that Shakespeare ever left England; his only travels were with his company of players.

That *Hamlet* must be the autobiographical record of a born nobleman; no plebeian could have written it. But Shakespeare was a common man.

That the author of the plays must have moved on terms of easy intimacy with the great, that he must have known from the inside what the life of the aristocracy was like; what it was to live in courts, palaces, castles and great houses. There is no record that Shakespeare moved freely in this society, and it is inherently unlikely.

That the plays show a professional knowledge of the Law, but Shakespeare was a layman.

That the author of the greatest works in the language would have been recognized as such by his contemporaries and amply described, his plays discussed, and his death more widely noted and lamented.

That the handwriting in the known Shakespeare signatures is that of an illiterate; and that it is crabbed and illegible (while his editors stated they had received his papers from him with 'scarce a blot').

On behalf of the various contenders for authorship it has been said:

That Bacon (Oxford/Rutland/Derby/Sherley/Dyer) was the author because he was eligible by his birth, breeding and travels, his learning and languages and his place at Court.

That de Vere (Oxford) used the pseudonym Shakespeare because his coat of arms as Lord Bulbeck—another of his titles—was a lion shaking a spear.

That de Vere was 'obsessed with the theatre', that he owned two companies of actors—one a travelling company—and used them as the performers of his plays.

That in *Measure for Measure* de Vere recorded his own love affair with Anne de Vavasour.

That de Vere wrote the plays because the urge to exteriorize the conflicts of his own childhood would naturally lead to the writing of *Hamlet*, *Macbeth* and *Othello* (at least). His childhood dilemma was that of Hamlet.

That de Vere's death coincided with Shakespeare's retirement to Stratford—that is, the mouthpiece had to withdraw when the voice was gone.

That Roger Manners, Earl of Rutland, had known an actual Rosenkrantz and Guildenstern at the University of Padua.

That by the time they appeared Shakespeare was too old to have written *Venus and Adonis* or *Love's Labour's Lost* (he was twenty-nine and thirty-four at these times, while Rutland was seventeen and twenty-two).

That Rutland's childhood was mirrored in *Hamlet*; and he visited Elsinore in 1603 on a state mission.

That according to indisputable family records the Rutland device, which also provided the pseudonym 'Shakespeare', was designed by the historical Shakespeare, and painted by the actor Burbage.

That the evident interest in magic of William Stanley, Earl of Derby, suggests that he wrote the plays. (Derby was a friend and pupil of Dr John Dee the astrologer.)

That the first[1] and the last of the plays, *Love's Labour's Lost* and *The Tempest* both have a Ferdinando as a leading character. This is the name of the brother whom William Stanley succeeded as Earl of Derby.

That Derby visited Navarre in 1583, and could therefore have written *Love's Labour's Lost*; and *A Midsummer Night's Dream* is claimed to have been written by him to celebrate his marriage to Elizabeth de Vere.

That Bacon alone among the Elizabethans knew Navarre well enough to write *Love's Labour's Lost*.

That only Bacon commanded sufficient knowledge of the Law to write the plays.

That Sir Walter Raleigh or Sir Francis Drake must have written the plays, since the author shows so much knowledge of ships and the sea.

These claims are just a representative selection, showing the main lines of approach. Rejoinders have come from the

---

[1] That *Love's Labour's Lost* was the earliest play is not admitted by the scholars.

scholars, directly and indirectly. The compilation of *The Shakespeare Allusion-Book*, for instance, provided thousands of references to Shakespeare, and decisively refuted the argument that Shakespeare, the obscure actor, was never mentioned by his contemporaries. It is typical of the controversy that anti-Stratfordians could retort, with obvious point, that all these references are not conclusive; the plays were put out as Shakespeare's, even though they were not written by Shakespeare; the references in the *Allusion-Book* were made by honest souls who had no reason to know of the deception, or by those who enjoyed furthering it.

In historical arguments, then, the Stratfordian is reduced sometimes to an inversion of anti-Stratfordian arguments. It can be said that the qualities which must have been found in the author of the plays were certainly to be found in many other writers. It is thus no use to say that because the author must have been well educated, nobly born, and much travelled, therefore he was *A*; he could equally have been *B*, *C*, or *D*; indeed, by that criterion he could have been almost anybody—even a woman. Was not Elizabeth herself. . .(and one may well dread that at this point in the argument some dedicated soul will spring up and say 'I was coming to that. Elizabeth I was, of course, a first-rate scholar. . .'. This thesis has been ironically anticipated by Stratfordians, so it has lost some of its force).

Nor is it much use pointing out that the Elizabethan and Jacobean periods were peculiarly rich in literary talent, yet many of the foremost writers were without a university education— and this applied to at least one-fifth of the men proposed by the disintegrationists as members of the Shakespeare panel. They were sons of tailors, drapers, dyers; they lived by their pens; we know little or nothing about the lives of many of them; yet nobody has so far thought to challenge their authorship of *their* works. In the *Dictionary of National Biography* either the date of birth or death is often given with a question mark; some just 'flourished 1599'. One might well think that given the disinclination of the age for superfluous records, what is known about Shakespeare's life is almost extravagantly detailed.

As for legal knowledge, it is a commonplace that it was a

litigious age. A court of law was a thing to attend as a spectacle, to enjoy. Manuals like Littleton's *Tenures* were widely read; many young men were educated at the 'third university', the Inns of Court. And Shakespeare's father was a Justice of the Peace; what better proof could there be of the popular concern with the Law than the institution in the Tudor period of a lay magistracy?

Court life was in a manner accessible to the writer and the artist, because an author looked naturally for a patron: a man who gave protection, countenance and in some cases even friendship. It was a nobleman's duty to cultivate the arts and one quick way of doing it was to cultivate an artist. More specifically the companies of players were often in a nobleman's household, wore his livery, entertained his guests, celebrated the great events of his life in his home. It is usually assumed that Shakespeare's patron was the Earl of Southampton.

That Shakespeare's name rarely appeared on printed plays in his lifetime, and that few of the plays were printed (and then in 'stolen and surreptitious copies') is in no way remarkable. Copyright was obtained by entering a title in the Register of the Stationers' Company; yet it has been reckoned that at least one in every five of the printed books of the time was never registered. Eight of Shakespeare's plays and the two poems are registered—a good proportion. The manuscript, the acting copy, was what mattered in the playhouse; it was the property of the manager who bought or commissioned it; it might or might not also be bought by a printer for sale to the reading public. But really a play was a thing to be seen, it was not thought of as a book; and in so far as it existed in manuscript it was as a prompt-book, not the precious life-blood of a master spirit.

The argument of the textual scholar that the printed text 'merely records the conditions of the last performance before printing was taken in hand' (J. Dover Wilson), that plays were freely retouched, even recast, can be, and is, seized on by anti-Stratfordians. So of course can the admission that in some plays the work of a second hand is discernible. Shakespeare, they contend, may have had a trifling hand in the work of some greater man: conversely some greater man may have put into their present state some crude efforts by the 'playhouse hack', William Shakespeare.

For example, in *The Complete Peerage* it is said of Edward de Vere that 'early in 1580 he took over Lord Warwick's company of actors. In the face of the prejudices of his day, which held literature and the drama—Oxford's main interests—to be beneath the dignity of a great noble, his work was mostly anonymous, or issued under the names of others'. If you are looking for a hint, that one will do better than most. From a hint it is a small step to a certainty—a few coincidences are too much to be ignored. By the time one has argued oneself to a certainty the counter-arguments against the original hint can probably be inverted to buttress the certainty.

In fact the historical argument can never produce certainty either way: there is always a counter-argument, always an appeal to the lack of evidence, a counter-interpretation of what evidence there is, much inference, some coincidence and, despite Mr Percy Allen, no voice from the grave.

It is with relief that we turn to the more certain ground of cryptology. That may seem a strange claim, but we hope to uphold it. We cannot agree with F. P. Gervais, who, while grateful to Baconians for some things, said 'no man would spend his time in such a profitless occupation as ciphers'. He was thinking perhaps of the way people have sometimes mis-spent their time on unsystematic cipher-hunting; properly handled, it is a matter on which great things are decided.

Nor can we agree with Prof. Frederick E. Pierce, who once said, 'Even if genuine ciphers could be found...the authorship of the dramas would still be awarded to the man of Avon.... Even an unquestionable hidden message would probably mean a false claim or a type-setter's practical joke, and would simply add to the backstairs gossip of literature.' To be convinced that the authenticity of a literary idol could never be impugned even by a genuine cipher is an arbitrary attitude, and we do not share it. The question is: has a genuine cipher been found?

CHAPTER II

CRYPTOLOGY AS A SCIENCE

THE term 'cryptology' covers cryptography, the art of writing ciphers, and cryptanalysis, the science of solving them. A cipher is different from a code; we shall not discuss codes in this book, but since the word 'code' is often used by laymen (including some of the anti-Shakespeareans) in contexts where they clearly mean 'cipher', it is worth drawing the technical distinction between the two, so as to avoid confusion.

The difference is a simple one, and can be put quite briefly. In code systems, the units or symbols to be translated can be of different lengths: a letter, a syllable, a word, a sentence, or just a string of letters or numbers is agreed to stand for a particular word or a whole phrase in the message (for example, 'A cat may look at a King' might be agreed to mean 'Oil shares steady', or 'JAZYN' to be the code sign for 'Come home—all is forgiven—Mother'). In contrast, the units in cipher systems are of uniform length and bear a uniform relationship to the units of the plain text. Usually one letter in the cipher corresponds to one letter in the message, though in some systems groups of two or even three letters are used in a cipher to stand for one letter in the message.

In this chapter we shall be discussing the conditions which any cipher has to satisfy if it is to count as a valid cryptogram. The principles of cryptology are based on common sense, but this is no guarantee that they will be observed; the most obvious things are often the easiest to overlook. So we had better begin at the beginning.

Ciphers are basically of two types: *transposition*, in which the letters of the original or plain-text message are rearranged; and *substitution*, in which they are replaced by other letters, by numbers, or symbols. In transposition the letters retain their identities but their relative positions are changed; in substitution the letters retain their relative positions but their identities are changed. In both types the operations are usually controlled by what is called the *key*, an element concerning which more must be said later. Some writers on cryptography include *concealment ciphers* as a third type of ciphers; and these, too, will play a prominent role in our studies. They really do not constitute a third category because practically all examples can be reduced to one or the other of the two basic types mentioned above, or to a combination of them.

What ciphers are used for is also a basic question. If somebody wants to hide his meaning from all but a few, he might employ an unusual language, or he might invent a special language and teach it only to selected people; but, more conveniently, he might put his information into cipher. In any case, he would be unlikely to put himself to the trouble of saying something in a covert way unless what he said was directed at some audience: someone in a distant country, perhaps, or in a later generation.

Of course, the recipient might be nearer home. The message might be one the writer means for himself alone; something he wants to record secretly, and decipher on a later occasion. Cryptic writing appears quite often in diaries. It is less risky, if more troublesome, than keeping them locked away—the key to a lock is easily lost, or gets into the wrong hands; but a key to a cipher can be carried in one's head, where not even the brain surgeon can dig it out. Samuel Pepys and William Byrd come to mind here: their diaries are written in a kind of private shorthand, not in cipher, but neither of them left any indication of the system he used, and in a sense what they wrote had to be 'deciphered' by a later generation. (Pepys used a modified form of the system Thomas Skelton set out in 1641, in his *Tachygraphy*, though this was not discovered until fifty years after the diary had been deciphered; Byrd used a fairly common system called 'The Flying Pen'.)

Cryptograms have also been used to establish priority in scientific discovery. Galileo used one in a letter to Kepler, recording his discovery that the planet Venus imitates the phases of the moon. While Huygens made his confirmatory investigations, he sent to a friend a cryptic note of his finding

16

one of Saturn's rings; in this way he deposited a record of his priority without prematurely announcing the discovery. Roger Bacon, the thirteenth-century scientist (not to be confused with the Bacon who might have written Shakespeare), wrote out part of his recipe for making explosives in cryptic form. It is worth digressing to look at the examples provided by Huygens and Galileo.

Huygens' cryptogram was simply a list, in alphabetical order, of the sixty-two letters used in the sentence announcing his discovery.

aaaaaaa	ccccc	d	eeeee	g	h	iiiiiii	llll	mm
(7)	(5)	(1)	(5)	(1)	(1)	(7)	(4)	(2)

nnnnnnnnn	oooo	pp	q	rr	s	ttttt	uuuuu
(9)	(4)	(2)	(1)	(2)	(1)	(5)	(5)

When these letters are properly arranged, each letter being used once, and no letter being omitted, they spell out 'Annulo cingitur tenui plano, nusquam cohaerente, ad eclipticam inclinato' (It is girdled by a thin flat ring, nowhere touching, inclined to the ecliptic). In a case like this, it is unlikely that anyone apart from the originator of the message can easily rearrange the letters to get the correct solution; there are no rules, and an enormous number of possible arrangements. Without a key, re-combining sixty-two letters to form a coherent sentence is a tedious business (if you have any doubts try it out on your friends; or, better, on your enemies).

Galileo had already gone a stage further: he rearranged the letters of his original message to make other Latin words, and the cryptic version he sent to Kepler read: 'Haec immatura a me jam frustra leguntur, O.Y.' (These unripe things are now read by me in vain); the letters 'O.Y.' left over at the end spoil the effect a bit, but it was a brave attempt. When the letters are rearranged in their proper order, they read 'Cynthiae figuras aemulatur mater amorum' (The mother of love [Venus] imitates the phases of Cynthia [the moon]).

Returning to our general discussion, the main point to stress is that any message put into cipher must be meant for someone's benefit. We have mentioned cases where this is the writer himself; but, of course, far more often the message is meant for someone else. We do not speak always in soliloquies; no more do cryptographers for ever compose private memoranda. It follows that there must be a direct and rigid relationship between the plain message and the cryptic version, however disguised this relationship is; the procedure must admit no doubts, for doubts lead to ambiguities, and ambiguities to errors, and errors perhaps to disaster. To be sure that the message originally enciphered is the same as the one eventually deciphered and that there is no possible alternative, the process, like any other organized activity, must have its rules. This is true even where a cipher message is written for posterity. It is only by discovering that there are such rules that the future decipherer can be sure he is right in suggesting that there is a hidden message. It is only by discovering what the rules are, and methodically employing them, that he can be sure he is right in his version of the message.

Usually the rules are of two kinds. The first lays down a basic general procedure (e.g. each cipher unit is formed of one letter of the English alphabet, and each such letter corresponds to one and only one unit in the plain text); technically, these rules are said to belong to the *general system*. The second kind is more specific. It operates within the general system, and deals with its application in a particular cryptogram (e.g. 'in this cipher, Z corresponds to the letter A in plain text; N to the letter B', etc.). In technical jargon it constitutes the *specific key* which deals with the *variable elements*. This is quite a familiar distinction: bridge players, for example, are well aware of the difference between the laws of the game (which lay down the general procedure) and the rules governing a particular convention of bidding (which set out one specific way of acting in accordance with the laws).

Cryptograms of the type used by Huygens and Galileo are *anagrams*; they are in reality examples of what may be called unkeyed transposition ciphers. Because a key is not used in transposing the letters of the original message to form the cryptogram, rearranging the letters of the cryptogram to recover the original message is difficult, especially if there are many letters. Even when the anagram has only a few letters there may be more than one 'solution'; and when it has many letters there can be many 'solutions'—all equally valid.

In cryptography used for serious purposes, such as secret communication, the rules which make up the general system and those which comprise the specific keys may be few or many, simple or complicated. But whatever they are like, they must have one thing in common: they must be unambiguous. Once the rules are known, it must be possible to apply them precisely and inflexibly; otherwise the decipherer may get the wrong answer when he tries to do in reverse what the encipherer has already done.

In the face of strange or extravagant claims, it is sometimes appropriate to offer platitudes. We shall meet a number of such claims in this book, and here, in readiness, is a suitable pair of platitudes. If, in any system, there are several keys, or several elements in the key, and if their selection is at any point dubious or arbitrary, then the solution itself is open to doubt. If, in any system, one of the keys is such that the decipherer has to make a decision for himself, and if this decision involves a judgment upon factors which are not themselves conclusive and certain, then the solution is again open to doubt.

Now very many of the cipher systems used by government departments and business organizations do, in fact, have a number of different specific keys. There is good reason for this. Clearly, the more particular applications there are of a general system, the more difficult it is to break down the cipher. If one always used the same key, it would be easily discovered; if one alternated it with another, discovery would be harder; and so on. In systems of this kind the encipherer can exercise his judgment; if one key has been used quite frequently, he will reject it in favour of one which has not. But once the key to be used in a given cryptogram is decided, the rest of the process must follow automatically. The decipherer must be told unambiguously, either in the message itself or in some other way, which key is actually being used; and unlike the encipherer he must not be allowed to exercise his judgment at all. In all practical systems this is an inflexible rule, and common sense is behind it—an enormous amount of time and trouble would be wasted if anyone deciphering a message had to try each of a large number of possible keys in turn.[1] It is worth noting that transposition ciphers of the unkeyed variety have been much more favoured than have substitution ciphers in the many attempts to find cryptographic proofs that somebody other than Shakespeare wrote the works attributed to him by history. The reason for this favouritism may become clear later.

You need not be a spy-story addict nowadays to know that there are experts skilled in breaking down cryptograms without already having the key. How can they ever be sure they have the right answer? If they build up for themselves a kind of skeleton key, how do they know it fits? After all, with ordinary physical locks and keys, there is a click, and the hinges swing open. But in a cipher there are no clicks and no hinges.

Nevertheless, there are ways of knowing whether one has found the solution. The experienced cryptologist looks for two things, and they are equally important. First, the plain-text solution must make sense, in whatever language it is supposed to have been written; it must be grammatical ('Hearts green slow mud' would not do) and it must mean something ('Pain is a brown Sunday' would not do either). It does not matter whether what the solution says is true or not; it may be a pack of lies, but that is not the cryptologist's business. The important thing is that it must say something, and say it intelligibly.

This is perhaps obvious; the second demand the cryptologist makes is less so. Not only does the answer have to obey the rules of grammar and the laws of logic; the cipher system and the specific key also have to obey certain rules. We have already mentioned a few of the basic requirements of cipher systems, and we are still discussing cipher systems, so they still apply. Without reassuring himself that the system he has been using is a valid one, the cryptanalyst cannot be sure he has found the right answer. Without checking that the key or sequence of

---

[1] A machine could of course be built to do part of the work; it could even be made to distinguish between a possible, probable or correct answer. But this would be taking gadget-mindedness to extremes.

keys he has reconstructed can be used reasonably, precisely and without ambiguity, there is still room for doubt.

But if there is rhyme and reason about the way he has reached the solution, if the system really is a rational and consistent system, the keys really keys, and if when they are rigorously applied they produce a plain text which is really a text, he can begin to take himself seriously. The point must be reached where he begins to feel that the whole thing did not and could not happen by accident. But it is not simply a matter of his *feeling* this; the assessment can be far more rigorous. The mathematical theory of probability can be applied, and the chances calculated exactly. If the cryptanalyst finds a certain key and (on the basis of the way it is built up) he calculates that the chances of its appearing by accident are one in one thousand million, his confidence in the solution will be more than justified. On the other hand, if he thinks he has found a key, and then works out that it can turn up by accident fifty times in a hundred, his confidence ought to be shaken. For then he can no longer be sure that the key was put there by anybody at all; it is just as likely to have happened by chance.

Getting a correct solution is not a matter of the cryptanalyst's thinking he has done the trick; it is not a question of opinion, but a question of proof. No solution can be taken as valid simply because the cryptanalyst says it is; he must in addition be able to show others that it is the right one. His demonstration must be unbiased, systematic and logically sound; it must be free from appeals to insight, clear of guesswork, and should avoid imponderables like the plague; in a word, it must be scientific.

This is not perhaps often enough realized by laymen, so it is worth drumming home. There is an art in devising ciphers, and an art in breaking them down. But in setting out his results, a cryptologist is above all a man of science. The validity of his solutions depends on the same kind of objective tests as other scientists use, and the steps in his reasoning are subject to the same criteria. He, like them, goes through the whole process of observation, hypothesis, deduction and induction, and confirmatory experiment. And in cryptanalysis, as in all science, there is the basic demand that if two suitably qualified investi-gators get to work independently on the same material they will reach identical results in the end. Just as there is only one valid solution to a scientific or mathematical problem, so there is only one valid solution to a cryptogram of more than a very few letters which involves the use of a real key; to find two quite different but equally valid solutions would be an absurdity.

Notice the qualification in the last sentence, though. The cryptogram must be keyed and of a reasonable length before it is safe to assume that it has a unique solution; obviously, one can find a large number of 'answers' to a 'cryptogram' made up of just a few units. For instance the nine-letter 'cryptogram' ABCDDEFGE could be 'deciphered' in a number of ways. Even assuming that repetitions in the cipher must correspond to repetitions in the plain text, CHALLENGE, BY OFFENSE, IS TO ORDER and HE SOON CAN are among the various possible solutions. And if we remove the limitation about repeated letters, the range of possibility is enormous (in fact there are as many answers as there are recognizable words or word groups among all the combinations and permutations of the letters of the alphabet, taken in sets of nine at a time).

We have still to settle what length is a reasonable one: how many letters are needed before we can be sure that there will be only one solution. A good deal of theoretical work has been done on this question. In particular, there is an interesting paper by Claude E. Shannon on 'Communication Theory of Secrecy Systems',[1] in which he concludes that (in a system where one letter in cipher corresponds to one letter in text and only one alphabet is involved) if a cryptogram has only about fifteen letters or less, there will be more than one solution; if it has about fifty letters or more, only one solution can possibly be obtained. Now this result is a purely mathematical one, and practical experience does not altogether agree with it: the estimate that fifty letters are needed before a solution can be trustworthy seems to us rather high. In a more recent paper,

---

[1] *Bell System Technical Journal*, vol. XXVIII, no. 4 (October 1949), pp. 656–715. Only section 16 (pp. 698–9) is directly relevant, but mathematically inclined readers will gain something from reading the article as a whole.

however, Shannon has revised his calculations and reached a different answer.[1] In the case of ordinary English, he now puts the minimum length at twenty-five letters; our own experience suggests that this is about right. In other words, about twenty-five letters are needed before the cryptanalyst can be sure that his solution of a mono-alphabetic substitution cipher is the only possible solution.

Of course, this is not a hard and fast rule; one could produce much longer cryptograms where the solution is still open to doubt. For instance, some of the cryptographic problems in newspapers are made up to contain letters which are normally seldom used, and to exclude the more common letters. Here is an example, taken from a book of cryptographic puzzles[2]: 'Jmoud vag, Mhow gipsy, stalk mohr nth time. Mpongwe gunboy aims nickt khnum. Unfed, knab, jhum, ngapi.' This is actually the correct solution of a cipher: the solution is in English; all of its words can be found in an unabridged English dictionary. The letter E, which usually occurs more frequently than any other, is used only three times. If all messages had texts of this kind, all cryptologists would be in the madhouse by now; but luckily most of the messages they have to deal with are less exotic, and though the minimum of twenty-five letters is not a rigid minimum it is quite a reliable guide.

We remarked earlier that two cryptanalysts working independently should always be able to reach identical answers. If this does not happen, it is usually found that the method lacks precision and that the rules are not straightforward and cannot be applied consistently; the decipherment often involves some arbitrary decision on the part of the solver. Often, too, it turns out that an unprofessional cryptanalyst has changed a large number of letters (or, as he would put it, corrected the errors) in order to make his solution intelligible. Sometimes a novice may produce a plain text which is so odd that it makes no sense

[1] 'Prediction and Entropy of Printed English', *Bell System Technical Journal*, vol. xxx, no. 1 (January 1951), pp. 50–64.
[2] *The Cryptogram Puzzle Book*, by Buranelli, Hartswick and Petherbridge (Simon and Schuster, 1928), p. 120.

to anyone else, even if he claims that it does make sense to him. Sometimes he offers a complicated explanation, expanding groups of letters which he says are abbreviations, or claiming that the text is quaint because it is written in an old-fashioned style. Now things which are old-fashioned may often seem quaint, but it hardly follows that everything which is quaint is necessarily old-fashioned. And more often than not, it simply turns out that he is misleading himself. In effect he has produced a solution which no one else would reach, and which cannot be substantiated.

Suppose someone produces an answer to a simple cipher which assumes a fifty per cent error in the cryptic version (in other words, he claims that because of mistakes by the encipherer, bad transmission, bad reception and so on, one letter in two is wrong). In a case like this, the corrections he makes are likely to be based on what he thinks or hopes the message is about. Someone else working on the same problem may make corrections in different places and produce a quite different plain text. And they might both be working on the wrong assumptions about the cipher system itself. Even if a cipher is there, it may be more complicated than they think; an experienced cryptanalyst may be able to analyse it correctly, and show that the number of errors is actually quite small. When the correction is excessive, one is right to doubt the validity of the solution.

The most important thing to remember is that for a solution to be valid it must be possible to show that it is the only solution. In practice, one has to make allowances for a few mistakes here and there; and certainly, occasional errors may lead to *minor* differences in the solutions offered by different cryptanalysts working independently (though where a correction or insertion may make a difference to the meaning of a plain text it is usual to show the various possible alternatives). But the validity of the rest of the text is not affected by a few doubtful letters.

How many letters are there in a 'few'? Would a solution be considered invalid if ten per cent of the letters were doubtful? Or twenty per cent? or twenty-five per cent? Again, there can be no hard and fast rule. Obviously, as we get near fifty per cent, the business becomes more and more implausible. But there are cases in which quite convincing solutions have been offered with as many as half the cipher letters missing. As a rule, these involve ciphers in which a pair of letters or more in the cipher stand for each plain-text letter. In the case of Bacon's biliteral cipher, which we shall come to later, each letter in the plain text is represented by five characters in the cipher, and here it is sometimes possible to find a plausible solution even if a large number of the cipher elements are missing or doubtful or erroneous. However, in ciphers where one letter in the cipher represents one in the text, the situation is different. Each case must be treated on its merits, but in practice the allowable error is seldom more than five to ten per cent at the outside. Very occasionally it may be higher; but then the solution can only be taken as valid if the errors can be shown to be systematic in some way, or if their presence can be explained objectively.

In general, it can be said that any cipher system, or any method which claims to follow valid cryptographic procedures, must yield unique solutions. If in any system two different investigators applying the same key or keys to the same basic material get inconsistent answers, the system is self-refuting. In other words, it can be used to show its own invalidity: with ingenious use, it can be made to produce any answer you like. Of course, the systems used by cryptologists in practice are quite rigorous, and it is impossible to juggle with them in this way. But when we come to examine the cipher systems set out in the following chapters, we shall see whether the methods themselves can be shown to be invalid, or their practical application open to doubt, by applying this test.

Turning now to our main theme, the so-called cryptographic proofs of authorship, it is not of course necessary that we should be able to find any recorded evidence of the systems used. If cryptograms do exist in Shakespeare's works, the keys for deciphering them might possibly have been written down and carefully preserved, but so far none has been discovered. No more, indeed, have original manuscripts in Shakespeare's hand (apart from the brief portions in *Sir Thomas More*, which are generally accepted by Stratfordians), for all the digging that has gone on; but that is another matter.

Nor is it reasonable to expect that, if cryptic messages actually were inserted in the text, they would be clearly signalled in some way. One does not put something in a secret hiding-place and then put up a sign saying 'Notice: Secret hiding-place'. The Baconians are well aware of this argument in their favour, and in fact they can cite an appropriate reference to it in Bacon's *Advancement of Learning*: 'The vertues of cyphars whereby they are to be preferred are three; that they be not laborious to write and reade; that they be impossible to decypher; and in some cases, that they be without suspicion.' An apparently innocent text containing within it a secret text should 'be without suspicion'; the presence of the cipher should not be suspected by those who have no business to know about it. There must be no external clues.

Crypto-systems of this sort are, and have always been, widely used; as already noted they are technically known as 'concealment systems'. All the cases we shall be dealing with come under this heading. We shall not therefore demand any external guide to the presence of the secret texts. We shall only ask whether the solutions are valid: that is to say, whether the plain texts make sense, and the cryptosystem and the specific keys can be, or have been, applied without ambiguity. Provided that independent investigation shows an answer to be unique, and to have been reached by valid means, we shall accept it, however much we shock the learned world by doing so.

CHAPTER III

IGNATIUS DONNELLY
AND
'THE GREAT CRYPTOGRAM'

I GNATIUS DONNELLY (1831–1901)[1] was a Minnesotan, a lawyer, pioneer, entrepreneur and politician. Before he became a Baconian and cryptographer he had already published two books, *Atlantis: the Antediluvian World*, and *Rögnarok: The Age of Fire and Gravel*, titles on which the eye of a sceptic could hardly be expected to dwell with enthusiasm. It is not certain when Donnelly first became convinced that Bacon wrote Shakespeare; but he announced in 1884 that he thought there were ciphers in the plays, and in 1888 he produced a huge book of two volumes and 998 pages: *The Great Cryptogram*, published by R. S. Peal and Co. of New York, Chicago and London. It was the result of years of persistent work. It has three parts: Book I, *The Argument*; Book II, *The Demonstration*; Book III, *Conclusions*. Book II deals with 'The Great Cryptogram' itself, in 392 pages.

In his introduction Donnelly says: 'For a long time before I conceived the possibility of a Cipher in the Shakespeare Plays, I had been at work collecting proofs from many sources to establish the fact that Francis Bacon was the real author of those works.' Given this interest in Bacon, it is perhaps strange that Donnelly was for a long time unaware that Bacon had described a useful kind of cipher. He seems to have discovered it by accident, and in a curiously unlikely source. In his chapter 'How I came to look for a Cipher', he says:

One day I chanced to open a book belonging to one of my children, called *Every Boy's Book*...a very complete and interesting work of its kind, containing over eight hundred pages. On page 674 I found a

---

[1] Biographical details are given by Henry W. Wack, in 'Ignatius Donnelly, Recollections of a Great Baconian', *American Baconiana*, 1, 50–62.

chapter devoted to 'Cryptography' or cipher writing, and in it I chanced upon this sentence:

The most famous and complex cipher perhaps ever written was by Lord Bacon. It was arranged in the following manner:

aaaaa	stands for a	abaaa	stands for i, j	baaaa	stands for r
aaaab	,,	,, b	abaab	,,	,, k	baaab	,,	,, s
aaaba	,,	,, c	ababa	,,	,, l	baaba	,,	,, t
aaabb	,,	,, d	ababb	,,	,, m	baabb	,,	,, u , v
aabaa	,,	,, e	abbaa	,,	,, n	babaa	,,	,, w
aabab	,,	,, f	abbab	,,	,, o	babab	,,	,, x
aabba	,,	,, g	abbba	,,	,, p	babba	,,	,, y
aabbb	,,	,, h	abbbb	,,	,, q	babbb	,,	,, z

Now suppose you want to inform someone that 'All is well'. First place down the letters separately according to the above alphabet: aaaaa ababa ababa abaaa baaab babaa aabaa ababa ababa. Then take a sentence five times the length in letters of 'All is well'—say it is 'We were sorry to have heard that you have been so unwell'. Then fit the sentence to the cipher above like this:

```
a a a a a a b a b a a b a b a a b a a a b a a a b b
w e w e r e s o r r y t o h a v e h e a r d t h a t
```

```
                    a b a a a a b a a a b a b a a b a b a
                    y o u h a v e b e e n s o u n w e l l
```

marking with a dash every letter that comes under a *b*. Then put the sentence down on your paper, printing all marked letters in italics and the others in the ordinary way, thus We were *sorry to have* heard th*at* y*ou* have *been* s*o* un*we*ll. The person who receives the cipher puts it down and writes an *a* under every letter except those in italics; these he puts a *b* under. He then divides the cipher obtained into periods of five letters, looks at his alphabet and finds the meaning to be: 'All is well.'

That description sets out quite clearly and accurately the principles of Bacon's biliteral cipher. Bacon first mentioned it briefly in his *Of the Advancement of Learning* in 1605. The account given there is itself only a few cryptic words; it is doubtful if anyone not fully conversant with the history and techniques of cryptology would be able to divine what Bacon had in mind. But fortunately he later set down a more detailed description of how to write OMNIA PER OMNIA in the *De Augmentis Scientiarum* of 1623. We give here the English translation (1857) by James Spedding. Bacon's original woodcut illustrations reproduced in Figs. 1 and 2 overleaf are from Gilbert Wats' translation (1640):

Let us proceed then to Ciphers. Of these there are many kinds: simple ciphers; ciphers mixed with non-significant characters; ciphers containing two different letters in one character; wheel ciphers; key-ciphers; word ciphers; and the like. But the virtues required in them are three; that they be easy and not laborious to write; that they be safe...; and lastly that they be if possible such as not to raise suspicion....Now for this elusion of inquiry, there is a new and useful contrivance for it, which as I have it by me, why should I set it down among the desiderata, instead of propounding the thing itself? It is this: let a man have two alphabets, one of true letters, the other of non-significants; and let him infold in them two letters at once; one carrying the secret, the other such a letter as the writer would have been likely to send, and yet without anything dangerous. Then if any one be strictly examined as to the cipher, let him offer the alphabet of non-significants for the true letters, and the alphabet of true letters for non-significants. Thus the examiner will fall upon the exterior letter; which finding probable, he will not suspect anything of another letter within. But for avoiding suspicion altogether, I will add another contrivance, which I devised myself when I was at Paris in my early youth, and which I still think worthy of preservation. For it has the perfection of a cipher, which is to make anything signify anything; subject however to this condition, that the infolding writing shall contain at least five times as many letters as the writing infolded: no other condition or restriction whatever is required. The way to do it is this: First let all the letters of the alphabet be resolved into transpositions of two letters only. For the transposition of two letters through five places will yield thirty-two differences; much more twenty-four, which is the number of letters in our alphabet. Here is an example of such an alphabet.

Example of an Alphabet in two letters

A	B	C	D	E	F	G
Aaaaa.	aaaab.	aaaba.	aaabb.	aabaa.	aabab.	aabba.
H	I	K	L	M	N	O
aabbb.	abaaa.	abaab.	ababa.	ababb.	abbaa.	abbab.
P	Q	R	S	T	V	W
abbba.	abbbb.	baaaa.	baaab.	baaba.	baabb.	babaa.
X	Y	Z
babab.	babba.	babbb.

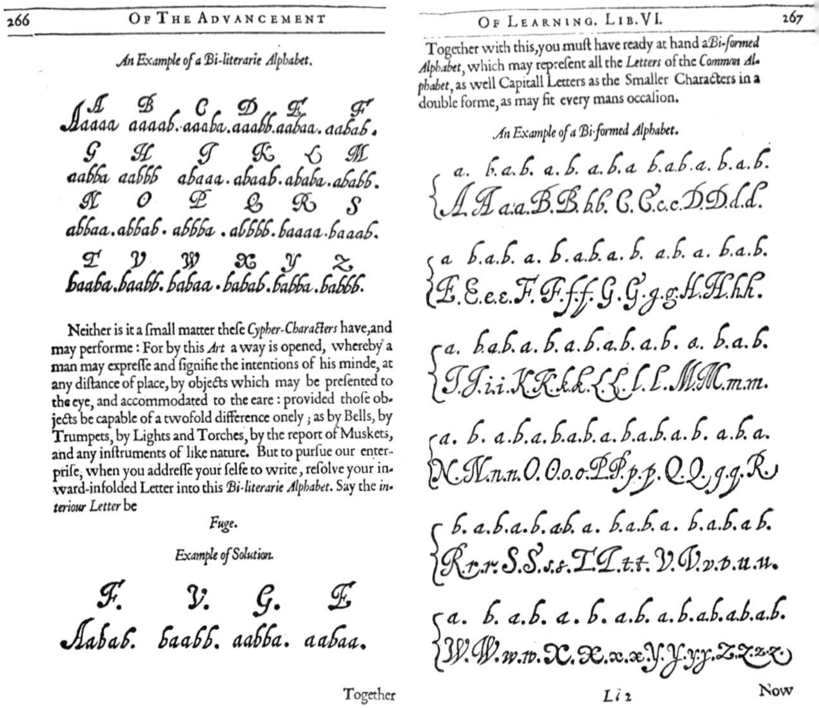

266 OF THE ADVANCEMENT

An Example of a Bi-literarie Alphabet.

A B C D E F
aaaaa aaaab. aaaba. aaabb. aabaa. aabab.
G H I K L M
aabba aabbb abaaa. abaab. ababa. ababb.
N O P Q R S
abbaa. abbab. abbba. abbbb. baaaa. baaab.
T V W X Y Z
baaba. baabb. babaa. babab. babba. babbb.

Neither is it a ſmall matter theſe *Cypher-Characters* have, and may performe: For by this *Art* a way is opened, whereby a man may expreſſe and ſignifie the intentions of his minde, at any diſtance of place, by objects which may be preſented to the eye, and accommodated to the eare: provided thoſe objects be capable of a twofold difference onely; as by Bells, by Trumpets, by Lights and Torches, by the report of Muskets, and any inſtruments of like nature. But to purſue our enterpriſe, when you addreſſe your ſelfe to write, reſolve your inward-infolded Letter into this *Bi-literarie Alphabet*. Say the *interiour Letter* be

Fuge.

Example of Solution.

F. V. G. E.
aabab. baabb. aabba. aabaa.

Together

OF LEARNING. LIB. VI. 267

Together with this, you muſt have ready at hand a *Bi-formed Alphabet*, which may repreſent all the *Letters* of the *Common Alphabet*, as well Capitall Letters as the Smaller Characters in a double forme, as may fit every mans occaſion.

An Example of a Bi-formed Alphabet.

a. b. a. b. a. b. a. b. a b. a. b. a. b. a. b.
A. A. a. a. B. B. b. b. C. C. c. c. D. D. d. d.

a. b. a. b. a. b. a. b. a. b. a. b. a. b. a. b.
E. E. e. e. F. F. f. f. G. G. g. g. H. H. h. h.

a. b. a. b. a. b. a. b. a. b. a. b. a. b. a. b.
I. I. i. i. K. K. k. k. L. L. l. l. M. M. m. m.

a. b. a. b. a. b. a. b. a. b. a. b. a. b. a. b. a.
N. N. n. n. O. O. o. o. P. P. p. p. Q. Q. q. q. R.

b. a. b. a. b. a. b. a. b. a. b. a. b. a. b.
R. r. r. S. S. s. s. T. T. t. t. V. V. v. v. u. u.

a. b. a. b. a. b. a. b. a. b. a. b. a. b. a. b.
W. W. w. w. X. X. x. x. Y. Y. y. y. Z. Z. z. z.

Li 2 Now

Fig. 1.

Nor is it a slight thing which is thus by the way effected. For hence we see how thoughts may be communicated at any distance of place by means of any objects perceptible either to the eye or ear, provided only that those objects are capable of two differences; as by bells, trumpets, torches, gunshots, and the like. But to proceed with our business: when you prepare to write, you must reduce the interior epistle to this biliteral alphabet. Let the interior epistle be

Fly.

Example of reduction.

F L Y

aabab. ababa. babba.

Have by you at the same time another alphabet in two *forms*; I mean one in which each of the letters of the common alphabet, both

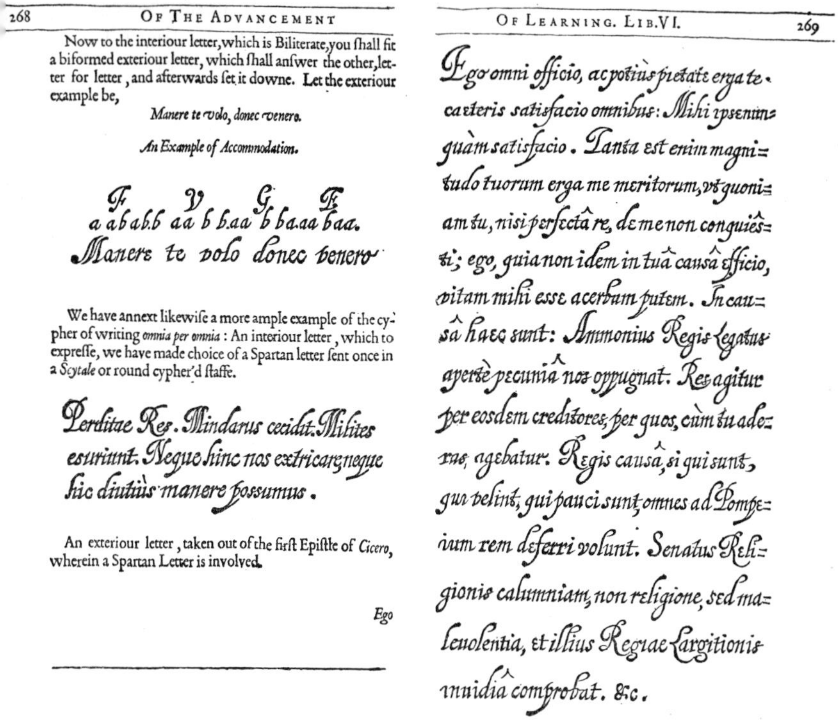

268 OF THE ADVANCEMENT

Now to the interiour letter, which is Biliterate, you ſhall fit a biformed exteriour letter, which ſhall anſwer the other, letter for letter, and afterwards ſet it downe. Let the exteriour example be,

Manere te volo, donec venero.

An Example of Accommodation.

F V G F
a ab ab.b aa b b.aa b ba.aa baa.
Manere te volo donec venero

We have annext likewiſe a more ample example of the cypher of writing *omnia per omnia*: An interiour letter, which to expreſſe, we have made choice of a Spartan letter ſent once in a *Scytale* or round cypher'd ſtaffe.

Perditae Res. Mindarus cecidit. Milites esuriunt. Neque hinc nos extricare, neque hic diutiùs manere possumus.

An exteriour letter, taken out of the firſt Epiſtle of *Cicero*, wherein a Spartan Letter is involved.

Ego

OF LEARNING. LIB.VI. 269

Ego omni officio, ac potiùs pietate erga te caeteris satisfacio omnibus: Mihi ipse nunquàm satisfacio. Tanta est enim magnitudo tuorum erga me meritorum, vt quoniam tu, nisi perfectâ re, de me non conquiêsti; ego, quia non idem in tuâ causâ efficio, vitam mihi esse acerbam putem. In causâ haec sunt: Ammonius Regis legatus apertè pecuniâ nos oppugnat. Res agitur per eosdem creditores, per quos, cùm tu aderas, agebatur. Regis causa, si qui sunt, qui velint, qui pauci sunt, omnes ad Pompeium rem deferri volunt. Senatus Religionis calumniam, non religione, sed maleuolentia, et illius Regiae largitionis inuidiâ comprobat. &c.

Fig. 2.

capital and small, is exhibited in two different forms,—any forms that you find convenient.

Example of an Alphabet in two forms.

a	b	a	b	a	b	a	b	a	b	a	b
A	*A*	*a*	*a*	B	*B*	*b*	*b*	C	*C*	*c*	*c*
D	*D*	*d*	*d*	E	*E*	*e*	*e*	F	*F*	*f*	*f*
G	*G*	*g*	*g*	H	*H*	*h*	*h*	I	*J*	*i*	*i*
K	*K*	*k*	*k*	L	*L*	*l*	*l*	M	*M*	*m*	*m*
N	*N*	*n*	*n*	O	*O*	*o*	*o*	P	*P*	*p*	*p*
Q	*Q*	*q*	*q*	R	*R*	*r*	*r*	S	*S*	*s*	*s*
T	*T*	*t*	*t*	U	*U*	*u*	*u*	*v*	*v*		
W	*W*	*w*	*w*	X	*X*	*x*	*x*	Y	*Y*	*y*	*y*
				Z	*Z*	*z*	*z*				

Then take your interior epistle, reduced to the biliteral shape, and adapt to it letter by letter your exterior epistle in the biform character; and then write it out. Let the exterior epistle be,

Do not go till I come.

Example of Adaptation.

F L Y.

aa	*bab.*	*ab*	*aba.b*	*a*	*bba.*
Do	*not*	*go*	*till*	*I*	*come.*

I add another larger example of the same cipher,—of the writing of anything by anything.

The interior epistle; for which I have selected the Spartan despatch, formerly sent in the *Scytale.*

All is lost. Mindarus is killed. The soldiers want food. We can neither get hence, nor stay longer here.

The exterior epistle, taken from Cicero's first letter, and containing the Spartan despatch within it.

In all duty or rather piety towards you I satisfy every body except myself. Myself I never satisfy. For so great are the services which you have rendered me, that seeing you did not rest in your endeavours on my behalf till the thing was done, I feel as if life had lost all its sweetness, because I cannot do as much in this cause of yours. The occasions are these: Ammonius the King's ambassador openly besieges us with money: the business is carried on through the same creditors who were employed in it when you were here, &c.

[This passage is actually set in two closely related founts (Garamond and Imprint are the names by which the printer knows them; they are both descended from sixteenth-century originals). The reader probably finds it hard to pick out more than a letter here and there which strikes him as obviously an intruder from another fount; imagine the greater difficulty when for the mechanical smoothness of modern paper and the evenness of machine-impression are substituted the rough paper and uneven inking of poor seventeenth-century printing. Here is the same passage set in two more obviously contrasting forms (roman and italic):

In all duty *or* rather *piety* towards *you* I *satisfy every* body *except* myself. *Myself* I *never satisfy. For* so *great are* the *services* which *you* have *rendered* me, *that* seeing *you* did *not* rest *in* your *endeavours on* my *behalf* till *the* thing *was done,* I *feel as if* life *had* lost *all its* sweetness, *because* I *cannot* do *as* much *in* this *cause* of *yours.* The *occasions* are *these:* Ammonius *the* King's *ambassador openly* besieges *us* with *money: the* business *is* carried *on* through *the* same *creditors* who *were* employed *in* it *when you were here, &c.*]

32

The doctrine of Ciphers carries along with it another doctrine, which is its relative. This is the doctrine of deciphering, or of detecting ciphers, though one be quite ignorant of the alphabet used or the private understanding between the parties: a thing requiring both labour and ingenuity, and dedicated, as the other likewise is, to the secrets of princes. By skilful precaution indeed it may be made useless; though as things are it is of very great use. For if good and safe ciphers were introduced, there are very many of them which altogether elude and exclude the decipherer, and yet are sufficiently convenient and ready to read and write. But such is the rawness and unskilfulness of secretaries and clerks in the courts of kings, that the greatest matters are commonly trusted to weak and futile ciphers.

The similarity of intention between this passage and the one which Donnelly quoted from *Every Boy's Book* which he 'chanced to open' is plain. We quote now a further passage from Donnelly's introduction. He is speaking of his own decipherments:

As to the actuality of the Cipher there can be but one conclusion. A long continuous narrative, running through many pages, detailing historical events in a perfect symmetrical, rhetorical, grammatical manner, and always *growing out of the same numbers employed in the same way, and counting from the same or similar starting points, cannot be otherwise than a prearranged arithmetical cipher.*

The italics are Donnelly's, and though one may detect a possible weakening of principle in 'the same or similar', the passage as a whole shows that Donnelly accepts the prime necessity for system, order, precision and the refusal to make arbitrary decisions in cryptological work. Yet it also shows, and this is more important, that in spite of his careful quotation from *Every Boy's Book* he seems to have completely misunderstood the nature of Bacon's biliteral cipher; he has not understood the explanation he himself quotes. For Bacon's was not a 'prearranged arithmetical cipher', in spite of the arithmetical relationship of the 'infolding' innocent text to the 'infolded' significant message. The essential part of the method is the use of slightly different letter-shapes (in the case given in *Every Boy's Book*, roman and italic letters: in the more sophisticated versions, different founts, where the dissimilarity between the letter shapes is slight and not easily apparent). One is almost inclined to believe that the passage describing the cipher in *Every*

Boy's Book was cited by someone else, who understood it, while the rest of the introduction was by Donnelly, who did not.

Donnelly says that he became convinced that the last of Bacon's desiderata for perfect ciphers (that they be if possible such as not to raise suspicion) was Bacon's way of hinting that he had 'injected a cipher narrative, an "interior epistle", into the Shakespeare plays'. Donnelly goes on:

How subtle and cunning all this is! Note the use of the word *alphabet*. Note too the excuse that he gives for discussing the cipher: 'he has it by him'—lest anyone might suppose he was furnishing a key to some other writings. Observe his rule, that the cipher 'must not raise suspicion' as to its existence; it must be '*infolded*' in something else; so that the reader, falling upon the exterior writing, will not suspect another writing within.

On p. 509 he gives a long quotation repeating Bacon's exposition in the *De Augmentis*, concluding with some words of his own:

But to proceed with our business: When you prepare to write, you must reduce the interior epistle to this biliteral alphabet. Let the interior epistle be—

FLY.

Example of reduction.

F	L	Y
aabab	ababa	babba

Have by you at the same time another *alphabet* in two *forms*—I mean one in which each of the letters of the common alphabet, both capital and small, is exhibited in two different forms—any forms that you find convenient.

Example of an alphabet in two forms [Donnelly uses roman and italic]:

A	B	A	B	A	B	A	B	A	B	A	B
A	*A*	a	*a*	B	*B*	b	*b*	C	*C*	c	*c*
D	*D*	d	*d*	E	*E*	e	*e*	F	*F*	f	*f*
G	*G*	g	*g*	H	*H*	h	*h*	I	*I*	i	*i*
K	*K*	k	*k*	L	*L*	l	*l*	M	*M*	m	*m*
N	*N*	n	*n*	O	*O*	o	*o*	P	*P*	p	*p*
Q	*Q*	q	*q*	R	*R*	r	*r*	S	*S*	s	*s*
T	*T*	t	*t*	U	*U*	u	*u*	V	*V*	v	*v*
W	*W*	w	*w*	X	*X*	x	*x*	Y	*Y*	y	*y*
				Z	*Z*	z	*z*				

Then take your interior epistle, reduced to the biliteral shape, and adapt to it letter by letter your exterior epistle in the biform character; and then write it out. Let the exterior epistle be:

Do not go till I come.

Example of adaptation.

F   L   Y

aa	bab	ab	abab	a	bba
Do	not	go	till	I	come.

I add another large example of the same cipher—of the writing of anything by anything.

The interior epistle, for which I have selected the Spartan dispatch, formerly sent in the *Scytale*:

All is lost. Mindarus is killed. The soldiers want food. We can neither get hence nor stay longer here.

The exterior epistle, taken from Cicero's first letter and containing the Spartan dispatch within it:

In all duty or rather piety towards you I satisfy everybody except myself. Myself I never satisfy. For so great are the services which you have rendered me, that, seeing you did not rest in your endeavors on my behalf till the thing was done, I feel as if my life had lost ALL its sweetness, because I cannot do as much in this cause of yours. The occasions are these: Ammonius the King's ambassador openly besieges us with money, the business IS carried on through the same creditors who were employed in it when you were here, etc.

I have capitalized the words *all* and *is*, supposing them to be part of the sentence, 'All is lost', but I am not sure that I am right in doing so. The sentence ends as above and leaves us in the dark.

Now this plainly shows Donnelly's incomprehension. Mechanically he reproduced the table giving the two forms of the letters. Yet neither in the short cipher message (FLY in 'Do not go till I come') nor in the long one did he make use of the alternative letter-forms—which are the key to the whole system. All he did, as he says, was to capitalize ALL and IS, because these two words happen by coincidence to be in the exterior message as well as the interior one. 'But I am not sure that I am right in doing so', he says lamely. Could there be a plainer confession that he was totally in the dark, but had seized, none the less, on a chance correspondence? Moreover the word 'ALL' appears twice. It first occurs as the second word in the external text; but the second occurrence, which

Donnelly capitalized, is the fifty-fourth word. 54 is one of the numbers which plays a significant part in Donnelly's work, and we shall come across it again later; it is this chance which led him perhaps to seize on the second occurrence.

To sum up: Donnelly's book gives two explanations of the biliteral cipher. The first is correct, and shows an understanding of the principles. The second is a complete misunderstanding. What his misunderstanding and his introduction point to is a disposition to seize on whole significant words in the 'enfolding' text, a vague preoccupation with mathematics, and a totally wrong impression that in explaining his invention Bacon 'seems to leave the subject purposely obscure'. Having decided that there was a cipher, Donnelly

reread the Shakespeare Plays...with my eyes directed singly to discover whether there is or is not in them any indication of a cipher. And I reasoned thus: if there is a cipher in the Plays, it will probably be in the form of a brief statement that 'I, Francis Bacon, of St Albans, son of Nicholas Bacon, Lord Keeper of the Great Seal of England, wrote these Plays, which go by the name of William Shakespeare'. The things to be on the lookout for in my reading were the words *Francis*, *Bacon*, *Nicholas*, and such combinations of *Shake* and *Speare*, or *Shakes* and *peer* and would make the word *Shakespeare*.

His next chapter is called 'A vain search into the Common Editions' and he tells there of his attempts to find the outlines of a cipher story in the plays, using these significant words as clues, and testing Act II of *I Henry IV*, where some of them happen to occur. So far as the biliteral cipher is concerned, the reader will already have seen that this was bound to be a vain search; that cipher could only be detected in the first printings of the plays; it would have to have been inserted by a printer who was specifically directed to use the alternative letter-forms in his type-setting operation. But Donnelly was acting on other principles; he goes on:

I did so using an ordinary edition of the Plays. For days and weeks and months I toiled over those pages. I tried in every possible way to establish some arithmetical relation between these significant words. It was all in vain. I tried all the words on page 53, on page 54, on page 55. I took every fifth word, every tenth word, every twentieth word, every fiftieth word, every hundredth word. But still the result was incoherent nonsense. I counted from the top of the pages down, from the bottom up, from the beginning of acts and scenes and from the ends of acts and scenes, across the pages, and hop, skip and jump in every direction; still it produced nothing but dire nonsense....

After many weary months of this self-imposed toil, trying every kind and combination of numbers that I could think of, I gave it up in despair. I did not for one instant doubt that there was a cipher in the Plays. I simply could not find it.

This shows first of all the 'mathematical' turn of Donnelly's mind. It also shows naïveté and a depressing lack of thought. For how could Bacon have known in his day how the pagination of the ordinary editions of Donnelly's day would fall? How could Bacon have foreseen how later editors of the plays would divide them into acts and scenes? As for the kind of cipher which takes words at regular intervals as significant, it is so unsophisticated that it is only found in children's books and the communications of the humbler kind of criminal. Though a similar device has since been used to convey a claim to authorship (see p. 100), in that case only individual letters were used, and never entire words.

Donnelly cannot be criticized merely for beginning with the assumption that a cipher was there, somewhere, to be found, or for assuming that certain specific words would be likely to occur in the message. That is a legitimate assumption, and sometimes quite fruitful; the cryptologist calls it 'the probable word method'. When one feels with reasonable certainty that a specific word (or phrase) is actually present in the plain text, it can be used as a crib to break down the message. On the other hand if a cipher is being used, significant words of the text are most unlikely to appear 'in clear' (i.e. not enciphered); and we have already pointed out that in the case of the biliteral cipher the finding of whole words which are identical in the vehicle and the message which it carried would be a mere coincidence.

Donnelly concluded, somewhat late, that he would have to work on the First Folio itself, or a facsimile. He got a copy of the Staunton facsimile; and his first appreciation of the accidents of pagination and certain 'signatures' or 'tokens' of the printers strengthened his suspicion that secrets were imbedded in the text. His fifth chapter, called—without irony—'Lost in the Wilderness', relates first his agonized pursuit of the elusive goal, then his astonishment when a certain 'arithmetical method' led him to the words he wanted to be led to. On p. 53 of the Histories (he was still at work on *I Henry IV*) he counted the number of words before 'Bacon'; it was the 371st. That number can be divided by 53: result 7. Now there are exactly 7 italic words in that column on p. 53 (*not* counting stage directions, names of speakers, etc.). But this, he thought, must have been brought about by a 'method'; for 'there are 459 words in this column, and there was, therefore, only one chance in 459 that the number of italic words would agree with the quotient obtained by dividing 371 by 53'. This is the kind of remark which may well reduce the reader to a silence more stunned than admiring.

'Computations' on pp. 53–5 of *I Henry IV*, counting backwards and forwards, using both columns, starting from various 'breaks' in the column if not from the top, occasionally adding the counts in two columns, in part or in total, produce this evidence:

$53 \times 6 = 318 =$ Francis	2nd col., p. 55
$53 \times 7 = 371 =$ Bacon	1st col., p. 53
$54 \times 12 = 648 =$ Nicholas	2nd col., p. 53
$54 \times 11 = 594 =$ Bacons	2nd col., p. 54
$53 \times 9 = 477 =$ son	1st col., p. 54

'All these things', Donnelly says, 'tended to make me more and more certain that there was a cipher in the Plays, and that it depended on the paging of the Folio.' They make the reader more and more certain that he found the word first and then tried to bolster his find by his arithmetic. It seems odd that 'Francis' is on p. 55, and is obtained by a multiple of 53; while 'Bacon' on p. 53 is also found by multiplying 53, Nicholas on p. 53 by multiplying 54 and 'son' on p. 54 by multiplying 53. And what was the starting point for the counting in each case?

Donnelly seems to have had in mind a purely theoretical example of a trick cryptogram in which the Lord's Prayer was supposed to have been inserted in an exterior text, successive words of the prayer being the 10th, 18th and 27th words of the external text in a continuous series; thus:

10th	18th	27th	10th	18th	27th	10th	18th	27th
word	word	word	word	word	word	word	word	word
our	father	which	art	in	Heaven	hallowed be		thy etc.

Donnelly's comment on this postulated example is

> If the cipher narrative moves through the text...10, 18, 27, 10, 18, 27, etc....does it not amount to an absolute demonstration if this series of numbers or any other series of numbers extends through many pages of narrative, from the beginning of one play to the end of another? Instead of the cipher story in these plays being...a mere hop-skip-and-jump allocation of words, it will be found to be purely arithmetical, and as precisely regular as...the examples given above.

That is precisely what one doubts; for what is the 'Francis Bacon, Nicholas Bacon's son' sequence but a hopping back and forth over three pages, justified by retrospective coincidences which are by no means a regular mathematical series, and which are in any case obtained by varying the point at which one begins counting and the direction in which one counts? What is 'precisely regular' about that?

The system was complicated; it was made more so by Donnelly's discovery that brackets 'have significance', by the introduction of 'multipliers' deduced for no explicit reason from p. 75 col. 1; by the development (by a secret process from the 'multipliers') of 'root numbers'; and the later introduction of 'modifying' numbers. All these mathematical conscripts serve Donnelly by helping him to get to points he wishes to reach. Hyphenated words prove as useful as bracketed words; he uses a small b or h to show when he is counting them in, though he admits with pleasant candour 'we sometimes counted in the bracketed and additional hyphenated words...and sometimes we did not'.

Among the 'root numbers' are 505, 513, 516 and 523; these are 'products' of the 'multipliers' 7, 10, 11 and 18, in Donnelly's private use of the word 'product' (the result of some process). 'Modifiers' are 30 and 50; but 197, 198, 218 and

Observe, here, how precisely the same number brings out *seas* and *ill;* compare the numbers in groups; — 516—516; — 167—167; — 349—349; — 22 *b* & *h*—22 *b* & *h*; — 327—327: — and going up the first column of page 76 with 327, we find *seas;* while going up the first column of page 75 with 327 brings us to *ill.*

	Word.	Page and Column.	
516—167=349—22 *b* & *h*=327—284=43. 447—43 =404+1=405+3 *b*=408.	408	75:1	that
516—167=349—22 *b* & *h*=327—254=73--15 *b* & *h*= 58. 448—58=390+1=391.	391	76:1	More
516—167=349—22 *b* & *h*=327—50=277—50 (74:2) =227—1 *h*=226.	226	74:1	low
516—167=349—22 *b* & *h*=327—254=73—50 (76:1) =23—1 *h*=22.	22	76:1	or
516—167=349—22 *b* & *h*=327—30=297—254=43 —15 *b* & *h*=28.	28	75:2	Shak'st
516—167=349—22 *b* & *h*=327—248=79. 193--79 =114+1=115+ *b* & *h*=(121).	(121)	75:1	spur
516—167=349—22 *b* & *h*=327—254=73—15 *b* & *h* = 58. 498—58=440+1=441.	441	76.1	never
516—167=349—22 *b* & *h*=327—50=227—7 *b* & *h*=	220	76:2	writ
516—167=349—22 *b* & *h*=327.	327	76:1	a
516—167=349—22 *b* & *h*=327—145 (76:2)=182. 498—182=316+1=317.	317	76:1	word
516—167=349—22 *b* & *h*=327—193=134. 248— 134=114+1=115.	115	74:2	of
516—167=349—22 *b* & *h*=327—254=73—15 *b* & *h* =58—5 *b*=53.	53	74:1	them.

I will ask the skeptical reader to examine the foregoing three remarkable combinations of words : *seas-ill* (Cecil), *more-low* (Marlowe), and *shak'st-spur* (Shakspere). Remember they are *all derived from the same root-number, and the same modification of the same root-number:* 516—167=349—22 *b* & *h* (167)=327; — and that they *are all found in four columns!* Are there four other columns, on three other consecutive pages, in the world, where six such significant words can be discovered? And, if there are, is it possible to combine them as in the foregoing instances, not only by the same root-number, but by the same modification of the same root-number? If you can indeed do this in a text where no cipher has been placed, then the age of miracles is not yet past.

And here, confirmatory of this opinion, thus bluntly expressed by Cecil, as to the authorship of the Shakespeare and Marlowe Plays, we have — *growing out of precisely the same root-number and the same modification of the same root-number* — still other significant words:

516—167=349—22 *b* & *h*=327—198=129. 447—129 =318+1=319.	319	75:1	It
516—167=349—22 *b* & *h*=327—237 (73:2)=90.	90	74:1	is
516—167=349—22 *b* & *h*=327—198 (74:2)=129— 11 *b* & *h*=118.	118	74:1	plain
516—167=349—22 *b* & *h*=327—198 (74:2)=129— 90 (73:1)=39.	39	73:2	he

Fig. 3. A page from Donnelly's *The Great Cryptogram* (1888).

219 are added later. In one tight corner he discovers 'sub-ordinate root numbers'. All these are the basic implements, the elements which combine, when judiciously used, to indicate a certain word in the text. We show in Plate II one of Donnelly's work sheets with its bewildering computations; in Fig. 3 a page of his book giving his conclusions from a page of computations.

Below we give a sequence of the 'cipher'. Here, according to Donnelly, the Bishop of Worcester is talking to Cecil. The starting point is the root 523, from which is subtracted the modifier 218, yielding a 'product' of 305. Two computations lead him to 'enough', yet sometimes as many as eight are needed to lead him to the other words of his secret text, which is extracted from pp. 76–81 of Act I of *II Henry IV*, following the Staunton reproduction of the First Folio.

	Word	Page and Column	
$305-32=273-50=223-5\,b=218-50$ $(76:1)=168.\;\;468-168=300+1=$ $301+10\,b$ col.$=311.$	311	78:1	We
$305-31=274-30=244-162=82-$ $13\,b$ & b col.$=$	69	78:2	know
$305-32=273-50=223-5\,b=218-$ $50=168-146=22-3\,b\;(146)=19.$ $420-19=401+1=402.$	402	81:2	him
$305-32=273-50=223-30=193-$ $162=31.$	31	77:2	as
$305-32=273-50=223-5\,b=218-$ $50=168-146$	22	81:2	a
$305-31=274-50=224-5\,b=219.$	219	78:2	butcher's
$305-31=274-30=244-5\,b=239.$ $610-239=371+1=372.$	372	72:2	rude
$305-31=274-50=224-5\,b=219-50$ $(76:1)=169-146=23.\;\;162-23=$ $139+1=140.$	140	78:1	and
$305-31=274-30=244-162=82.$ $462-82=380+1=381+5\,b$ col.$=$ $386.$	386	78:2	vulgar
$305-32=273-50=223-5\,b=218-50$ $(76:1)=168-4\,b$ & b col.$=164.$	164	81:2	'prentice,
$305-31=274-50=224.$	224	78:2	and

	Page and Word	Column	

$305-32=273-50=223-5\ b=218-$
$50=168-50=118.\ 162-118=$
$44+1=45.$ 45   78:1   it

$305-32=273-50=223-50=173-$
$50=123.\ 468-123=345+1=346.$ 346   78:1   was,

$305-31=274-193=81-49\ (76:1)=32.$ 32   76:2   in

$305-31=274-50=224-5\ b=219-50$
$(76:1)=169-146=23-5\ b\ \text{col.}=18.$ 18   79:1   our

$305-31=274-50=224-5\ b=219-$
$50=169-146=23+162=185.$ ...   185   78:1   opinions,

$305-32=273-50=223-50=173+$
$162=335.$ 335   78:1   not

$305-31=274-30=244+162=406-2\ b$
$\text{col.}=404.$ 404   78:1   likely

$305-32=273-50=223-193\ (75:1)=$
$30.\ 462-30=432+1=433.$ ...   433   78:2   that

$305-31=274-193=81-49\ (76:1)=$
$32.\ 457+32=$ 489   76:2   he

$305-31=274-50=224-4\ b\ \text{col.}=220.$ 220   76:2   writ

$305-32=273-50=223-5\ b=218-$
$146=72.\ 448-72=376+1=377.$ 377   76:1   them;

$305-31=274-193\ (75:1)=81-50$
$(76:1)=31.\ 458+31=489.$ ...   489   76:2   he

$305-31=274-254\ (75:1)=20.$ ...   20   78:1   is

$305-32=273-50=223-5\ b=218-$
$50=168-51=117-1\ b\ \text{col.}=116.$ 116   76:2   neither

$305-31=274-193=81-50=31.$ ...   31   76:2   witty

$305-31=274-254=20-15\ b\ \&\ h=5.$
$448-5=443+1=$ 444   76:1   nor

$305-31=274-50=224-5=219-50=$
$169-50\ (76:1)=119.\ 577-119=$
$458+1=459+11\ b=470.$ ...   470   77:1   learned

$305-32=273-50=223.$ 223   78:1   enough.

$305-31=274-30=244-50=194-$
$162=32.$ 32   78:2   The

$305-31=274-50=224-50=174-$
$145=29-3\ b\ (145)=$ 26   79:1   subjects

$305-31=274-50=224-5\ b=219-$
$145=74.$ 74   79:1   are

$305-32=273-50=223-5\ b=218-$
$58\ (80:1)=160.\ 468-160=308+$
$1=309.$ 309   78:1   far

	Word	Page and Column	
$305 - 32 = 273 - 162 = 111.$	111	78:2	beyond
$305 - 31 = 274 - 162 = 112.$	112	78:2	his
$305 - 31 = 274 - 50 = 224 - 5 \; b = 219 -$ $50 \; (76:1) = 169 - 145 = 24.$ ...	24	78:2	ability.
$305 - 32 = 273 - 50 = 223 - 5 \; b = 218 -$ $50 = 168 - 50 = 118 - 2 \; b \; \text{col.} = 116.$	116	78:2	It
$305 - 31 = 274 - 50 = 224 - 5 \; b = 219 -$ $50 \; (76:1) = 169 - 146 = 23. \; 318 -$ $23 = 295 + 1 = 296.$	296	79:1	is
$305 - 31 = 274 - 50 = 224 - 50 = 174 -$ $146 = 28 - 1 \; b \; \text{col.} =$	27	81:2	even
$305 - 31 = 274 - 50 = 224 - 50 = 174 -$ $146 = 28 - 3 \; b \; (146) = 25. \; 317 -$ $25 = 292 + 1 = 293.$	293	79:1	thought
$305 - 31 = 274 - 30 = 244 - 50 = 194 -$ $162 = 32 + 32 =$	64	79:1	here
$305 - 32 = 273 - 50 = 223 - 5 \; b = 218 -$ $50 = 168. \; 489 - 168 = 321 + 1 =$ $322 + 1 \; b \; \text{col.} = 323.$	323	81:1	that
$305 - 31 = 274 - 50 = 224 - 50 = 174 -$ $146 = 28 + 317 =$	345	79:1	your
$305 - 31 = 274 - 30 = 244 - 50 = 194 -$ $162 = 32. \; 610 - 32 = 578 + 1 = 579.$	579	77:2	cousin
$305 - 31 = 274 - 50 = 224 - 5 \; b = 219 -$ $50 = 169 - 145 =$	24	81:2	of
$305 - 31 = 274 - 5 \; b = 269 - 162 = 107.$	107	81:2	St. Albans
$305 - 32 = 273 - 50 = 223 - 38 \; (80:1) =$ $185.$	185	81:1	writes
$305 - 31 = 274 - 30 = 244 - 50 = 194.$ ...	194	82:1	them.

The cipher messages which emerge are indicated in the chapter titles: Cecil tells the story of Marlowe; The story of Shakespeare's youth; Shakespeare incapable of writing the plays; Shakespeare carried to prison; Shakespeare's aristocratic pretensions; Sweet Ann Hathaway; Bacon overwhelmed; Shakespeare's sickness. The story 'takes control' now and again; as when the Queen is referred to as 'the old jade'—not a loyal remark. Donnelly explains that it would of course have provoked suspicion if the word *Queen* had been dotted all over the Plays.

What is the point of it all? Did Bacon write the plays solely so that he could insert in them messages about his authorship? Donnelly has his answer:

Why. . .have men in all ages performed great intellectual feats?. . . Bacon probably enjoyed the exercise of his vast ingenuity. . . . We can imagine him, rising to go to the task he loved, the preparation of the inner history of his times, in cipher, which. . .must, he knew, live forever. . .as one of the supreme triumphs of the human mind: as one of the wonders of the world.

Modesty no doubt forbade him to add that if it was one of the wonders of the world to invent the cipher, how much greater must be the glory of its decipherment.

But it is not by the magnitude of the labour and ingenuity involved that a cipher method is to be judged. Let us apply our twofold test to Donnelly's cipher and its results. First, as far as the linguistic validity of the deciphered texts is concerned, we can, with the exercise of charity, say that they come up to standard. The spelling, syntax and intelligibility pass the test. Take the statement: 'Seas ill (Cecil) said that More low (Marlowe) or Shak'st spurre (Shakespeare) never writ a word of them.' As cryptologists we must say that the sentence is a valid one—grammatically correct, in normal syntax, intelligible. We can accept Donnelly's contention that the spelling of the names is the necessary consequence of the limitations of the method; since the Folio does not (and could not without arousing suspicion) contain the names of the author's distinguished contemporaries, it would be reasonable to expect some such phonetic approximation. We do not therefore question certain strikingly odd spellings. We say that as cryptologists; but we must call to the attention of our readers what other critics have said: that it is unlikely that a man who led a busy public life (and spent his leisure hours writing the works of Bacon and Shakespeare) would go to such extremes to bury a story full of desperate puerilities and trackless garrulity. The 'inner history' of the times turns out to be mainly gossip. Elizabethan scholars have pointed out that the language in which it is written is at best pastiche, but mostly in the rhythm and word-order of the twentieth century.

These points are controversial and outside our province (though one cannot help taking notice of things so obvious). If we apply our second cryptological test, the result is more likely to impress the unbiased mind. What of the keys employed in the decipherment?

The fact is that there is no true key, as a cryptologist would understand the term. There are five basic 'root' numbers, as Donnelly called them; and no rule for selecting any one of them in any given case. There are scores of 'modifiers', which may be added to or taken from the 'root', and no rule for their selection, or to determine whether they should be added or subtracted, or to govern the number of them used in any given computation. Hence only two sums are needed in some cases, and eight in others—as we have noted. The result of the sum is applied to the pages and columns of the Folio; but there is no rule governing the selection of page and column. We have already pointed out that counting can begin from a selection of convenient points, that it can be done forwards or backwards from that point and that brackets and hyphens can be observed or ignored at will.

In fact Donnelly's system is no system; it leaves a scientific-ally unacceptable latitude in the exercise of choice on the part of the decipherer. More plainly, it provides him with the means of justifying retrospectively his selection of words. Donnelly, having described Bacon's own cipher without understanding it, showed a fatal inclination to seize on whole words which happen to be in both the vehicle and the message to be deciphered. The system by which he reached these words was never mentioned by Bacon, its like has never been proposed by a serious writer on cryptography at any time, and it cannot be accepted by any such writer now or in the future.

Donnelly's weakness as a cryptanalyst was only equalled by his confidence. Several times he challenged his readers to con-struct similar or other messages starting from any number which is not one of his 'roots'. He even did some random computations himself, using the numbers 500 and 450; not surprisingly, they produced a series of words which made no sense. But since there is no rule for the selection of his own numbers or for governing the subsequent steps of his computations, how could he be sure that someone else could not evolve messages completely different from his own, using his own numbers and modifiers?

In fact this is just what happened. We said in the last chapter that if the application of the same key to the same basic material by two different investigators produces different results, the system carries its own refutation. In the same year as *The Great Cryptogram*, there appeared a parody of it, *The Little Cryptogram*, by another Minnesotan, Joseph Gilpin Pyle; it was subtitled *A literal application to the plan of 'Hamlet' of the cipher system of Mr Ignatius Donnelly*. Here is a sample of Pyle's 'decipherments':

	Word	Page and Column	
$523 - 273 =$	250	273:2	Don ⎫
$276 \div 6 =$	46	276:2	nill he, ⎬ Donnelly
$523 - 306 = 217 \quad 273 - 217 = 56 +$			
$\quad 30 = 86 - 50 = 36 - 2i =$ ...	34	273:2	the
$523 - 273 = 250 \quad 516 - 250 = 266 +$			
$\quad 2i =$	268	273:2	author,
$523 - 306 = 217 \quad 274 - 217 = 57 -$			
$\quad 2h =$	55	274:2	politician
$523 - 50 = 473 - 273 =$	200	273:2	and
$523 - 397 = 126 + 276 = 402 - 50 =$	352	276:1	mountebanke,
$523 - 274 = 249 + 50 = 299 - 4h =$			
$\quad 295 - 2h =$	293	274:1	will
No. words *p.* 274, col. 1 = ...	395	275:2	worke
$516 + 50 = 566 - 273 = 293 - 30 =$ ...	263	273:2	out
$523 + 50 = 573 - 397 = 176 - 30 =$			
$\quad 146 - 5h =$	141	274:2	the
$516 - 306 = 210 - 198 = 12 + 10i =$	22	274:1	secret
$523 - 397 = 126 - 1 =$	125	274:2	of
$523 - 274 = 249 \quad 306 - 249 = 57 +$			
$\quad 11i + 1 =$	69	274:1	this
$516 - 423 = 93 + 50 = 143 - 2i =$			
$\quad 141 - 1h = 140 - 1 =$ ...	139	276:1	play.
$523 - 274 = 249 - 30 = 219 - 2h - 1 =$	216	274:2	The
$523 + 30 = 553 - 423 =$	130	278:2	Sage
$523 - 397 = 126 + 30 = 156 - 2h =$	154	274:2	is
$523 - 274 = 249 + 5h = 254 - 1 =$ ...	253	274:2	a
$516 - 274 = 243 + 50 = 292 + 5h + 1 =$	298	274:2	daysie.

These calculations are so similar to Donnelly's that the implications ought not to be ignored by his supporters. Other investigators had no more difficulty in showing that the 'system' could be used to produce any message at will. A really masterly study came from the Rev. A. Nicholson, an English clergyman, the incumbent of St Albans (Bacon's home). In 1888 he published a brochure called *No Cipher in Shakespeare*. Taking the very pages (74–6) of the Histories in which Donnelly found the first inklings of his system, Dr Nicholson employed the same principles. Taking each of two 'roots' in turn he obtained the following messages: with root 505 'Master Will I am Jack spurre writ the play and was engaged at the Curtain'; and with root 516 'Master Will I am Shak'st spurre writ the play and was engaged at the Curtain'.

We show below Nicholson's detailed working with root 516:

	Word	Page and Column	
$516-167=349-22$ b and h$=327-$ 49 (76.1.)$=278-146=132$ ...	132	76:2	Master
$516-167=349-22$ b and h$=327-$ $163=164-50=114-1$ h$=113$	113	76:2	Will ⎫
$516-167=349-22$ b and h$=327-$ $30=297-50=247-145=102$	102	76:2	I ⎬
$516-167=349-22$ b and h$=327-$ $49=278-248=30-2$ h$=28$	28	76:2	am ⎭
$516-167=349-22$ b and h$=327-$ $30=297-254=43-15$ b and h$=28$	28	75:2	Shak'st.
$516-167=349-22$ b and h$=327-$ 219 (74.2.)$=108-22$ b and h$=$ $86 \quad 193-86=107+1=108+$ 6 b and h$=114$	114	75:1	spurre†
$516-167=349-22$ b and h$=327-$ $50=277-7$ b and h$=270-$ $50=220$	220	76:2	writ*
$516-167=349-22$ b and h$=327-$ $145=182-80=102-32=70$	70	75:1	the§
$516-167=349-22$ b and h$=327-$ $193=134$	134	74:1	Play§

	Word	Page and Column	
$516-167=349-22$ b and h $=327-$			
$30=297-248=49-22$ b $=27$			
$284-27=257+1=258+3$ h			
$=261$	261	74:1	and§
$516-167=349-22$ b and h $=327-$			
$50=277$			
$447-277=170+1=171$ ...	171	75:1	was§
$516-167=349-22$ b and h $=327-$			
$50=277$	277	76:1	engaged§
$516-167=349-22$ b and h $=327-$			
$284=43$	43	74:2	at§
$516-167=349-22$ b and h $=327-$			
$198=129-79=50$	50	73:2	the§
$516-167=349-22$ b and h $=327-$			
$80=247-50=197-30-167$			
$447-167=280+6$ h $=286$	286	75:1	Curtain.

'*Master William Shakespeare writ the Play and was engaged at the Curtain.*' In the fifteen cases deciphered in the formation of this sentence, I have not only taken Mr Donnelly's root-number, but his specially selected modifiers.

† For the two solutions, *Shak'st* and *Spurre*, I am indebted to Mr Donnelly, p. 726.

* This is Mr Donnelly's, p. 719, with the exception that he forgot to subtract the last 50.

§ Ibid. p. 725:723:724.

Nicholson found identical messages with each of Donnelly's five roots; one example would have been enough to demolish the pretensions of the cipher, but because many Baconians tend to be impressed by extensions of the 'what I tell you three times is true' principle, Nicholson offered blow for blow. He showed in fact that by Donnelly's loose methods there were 3,309,000 chances of finding any word needed to compose a given cipher story (any story). 'With so many tickets in the lottery,' Nicholson said mildly, 'any word desired can be drawn from the column. Donnelly may weave at will unlimited romances, out of the thousands of words in these Plays.' He went on to liken Donnelly's roots to keys, pointing out that the 'modifiers' could be repeatedly used, in effect, to file down the keys and make them fit any lock (not just in the plays, that is, but in any book you like).

PLATE I

Ignatius Donnelly.

PLATE II

A page of Donnelly's workings.

If we have some scores of modifiers [Nicholson continued] and may choose any we please, for experimental filings of the key, until a figure is produced which has no fixed relation in any way to the key, this is merely to substitute one number for another. Identity may be lost either by sudden metamorphosis, or by a gradual series of transformations. Sir John Cutler had a pair of black worsted stockings, which his maid darned so often with silk, they became a pair of silk stockings at last.

In fact, Donnelly's system is just a façade. None the less, he had his adherents. To some persons with no cryptological training and no power of logic, the mere fact that Donnelly patiently produced computations which seemed to justify the choice of each word is accepted as proof that he worked scientifically. Mr Comyns Beaumont, for instance, a former editor of one of Lord Northcliffe's papers, wrote in 1944 for *Baconiana* a series of articles called 'Donnelly's Amazing Cryptogram Re-examined'. He did not, of course, scrutinize the validity of the system; he was merely impressed by the recital of 'counts', and accepted the cipher as authentic. He had no time for sceptics; but his argument against them is scarcely compelling: 'It is so easy to be destructive', he said.

One last point. It never ceased to impress Donnelly that the words in the plays were also the words in his cipher messages. If he could arrive at their choice by some neat method his joy was complete. He said at one point that on p. 75 of the Plays he found the word 'shakst' fourteen times in one column and 'spurre' fourteen times in another. In fact 'shak'st' appears only once and 'spurre' four times; but Donnelly was led to them by fourteen different computations. He asks: 'Can any man pretend that this came about by accident? No; for be it observed that *every number* which produces the word 'shak'st' in the above examples, counting from the beginning or end of pages or fragments of pages *is a Cipher number.*' A really distressing instance of his powers of reasoning is where he extracts, by a dozen or more computations, a secret text composed of four words which occur in exactly the same order in the open text he is working on at the time.

Much that I have worked out came from 523 and 505: let us now turn to the other numbers. And here we have a typical sentence:

516− 284=232− 30=202. 248−202=46+							
1=47+22 *b*=	...	...	...	...	69	74:2	The
513−284=229−50=179. 248−179=69+							
1=	...	...	...	...	70	74:2	times
516−284=232−30=202. 248−202=46+							
1=47+24 *b* & *h*=	...	...	...	71	74:2	are
513−284=229−50=179. 248−179=69+							
1=70+2 *b*=	...	...	...	...	72	74:2	wild.

Observe the perfect symmetry of this sentence. Take it in columns:—the figures of the first column are 516—513—516—513; those of the second column are 284—284—284—284; those of the third column are 232—229—232—229; those of the fourth column are 30—50—30—50; those of the fifth column are 202—179—202—179; those of the sixth column, 248—248—248—248; those of the seventh column, 202—179—202—179; and they produce in regular order the 69*th*, 70*th*, 71*st*, *and* 72*nd words*, to-wit: *the times are wild*. And every one of these words is obtained by going *up* the *same column*. And even in the application of the bracket and hyphenated words the reader will perceive, as he goes on, a regular system and sequence.

And here I would call the attention of the reader to the fact that this expression, '*the times are wild*', was used in that age where we to-day would say the times are disturbed or dangerous. We see the expression in this very column:

What news, Lord Bardolfe?...

The times are wild.

His own view of this decipherment is that 'One such cipher sentence as the above is by itself enough to demonstrate the existence of a Cipher in the Shakespeare Plays'. What it demonstrated to one scholarly but severe critic was, as he put it, 'a desperate gullibility which will accept almost anything as proof; a total lack of self-criticism; and a cheerful confidence in one's own ingenuity which will survive all the arguments of others. When men like Donnelly are born', he went on to say, 'they are given a kind of intellectual armour which will protect them from ridicule at the same time as it insulates them from reason. Perhaps it is just as well; to be at once ridiculous and sensitive to ridicule would be far more harrowing.'

CHAPTER IV

THE CIPHER IN THE EPITAPH

THE present inscribed slab below the bust of Shakespeare in the Collegiate Church of the Holy Trinity at Stratford is not the one first put there after Shakespeare's death. The original slab, it seems, crumbled away, and was replaced by pious Stratfordians in the early nineteenth century (about 1830, according to Halliwell-Phillipps). It reproduces the sense and wording of the original, but not the 'uncouth mixture of large and small letters' in which the inscription was said to have been first carved. This phrase was used by Edmond Malone in his edition of the plays, published in 1821. Malone himself was relying on the evidence of an earlier editor, George Steevens. According to the testimony of these two, the doggerel verse on the tomb of the world's greatest poet ran

> Good Frend for Iesus S A K E forbeare
>
> To diGG TE Dust Enclo-Ased H E . Re.
>
> Blese be TE Man $\frac{T}{Y}$ spares TEs Stones
>
> And curst be He $\frac{T}{Y}$ moves my Bones.

It was to be expected that anti-Stratfordians, meditating on the odd features of this inscription, would arrive before long at the assumption that there was a cipher in it. The first decipherer was Hugh Black, who wrote an article in the *North American Review* in October 1887. He knew the mechanics of the biliteral cipher, and presumed it was being employed here. He took the G's of 'digg' as lower-case letters, and $\frac{T}{Y}$ as a single capital; using lower-case letters as *a*-forms and capitals as *b*-forms, he produced this decipherment:

GoodF	rendf	orIes	usSAK	Eforb	eareT	odigg
baaab	*aaaaa*	*aabaa*	*aabbb*	*baaaa*	*aaaab*	*aaaaa*
S	A	E	H	R	B	A

TEDu	stEnc	loAse	dHERe	Blese	beTE	Man^T_Ys
babba	*aabaa*	*aabaa*	*abbba*	*baaaa*	*aabab*	*baaba*
Y	E	E	P	R	F	T
pares	TEsS	tones	Andcu	rstbe	He^T_Ymo	vesmy
aaaaa	*babab*	*aaaaa*	*baaaa*	*aaaaa*	*babaa*	*aaaaa*
A	X	A	R	A	W	A
Bones						
baaaa						
R						

To an ordinary person the resultant message would be enough to prove that there is no cipher being used. The difference between the ordinary person and the Baconian is, shall we say, one of degrees of persistence and ingenuity. Set out your message as follows:

```
SAEHR
BAYE | EP
RFTA | XA
RAWAR
```

The letters above and to the right of the line, in a different order, produce SHAXPEARE. The remaining letters, in a different order, produce FRA BA WRT EAR AY. This sentence (rather like a message spoken with a hot potato in the mouth) means FRANCIS BACON WROTE SHAKESPEARE'S PLAYS.

In the same year (1887) and probably inspired by Black's example, another American, Herbert Janvrin Browne, published a pamphlet called *Is it Shakespeare's Confession? The Cryptogram in his Epitaph*. Browne's case, briefly, is that:

The Epitaph is a most remarkable cryptogram. The patience and ingenuity of its author are admirable....The Epitaph contains the sentence, FRANCIS BACON WROTE SHAKESPEARE'S PLAYS, and the name Shaxpeare....It will be seen that two alphabets are used in the solution. Under A is placed O, the fifteenth letter, and the new alphabet thus initiated. It seems that the reason for this is to be found in the word Bacon. The equivalent for N is B, for A is O, and in the cryptogram the word turns upon itself.

Browne was taken seriously at the time, but his pamphlet was in fact a dead-pan satire on Baconian methods (he confirmed this on a number of occasions). But the satire is so good that it could easily be thought to be in earnest. As it happens, his mock cryptogram is a good deal better, cryptologically, than many seriously proposed ciphers.

The *North American Review*, when planning to publish Black's article, commissioned a commentary on Black's work from Edgar Gordon Clark. He wrote an article, published in the same issue as that of Black, and another in *Cosmopolitan* in May 1888, together with a book recounting the substance of and adding to these articles.

Clark pointed out that in the words ÆE (used twice) and ÆEs, Black had arbitrarily assumed that the missing h was a small letter, not a capital, and was therefore an *a*-form, not a *b*-form. Clark takes them as capitals, thus producing a different plain-text letter in each case; and, though he does not explain this, he also reads the five-letter groups backwards. Hence he gets this decipherment:

BAFAB
AXAKWB
PLOEAR
BHEAS

He then anagrams[1] these letters, as Black had also done, and his message becomes SHAXPERE, BAKO, WE: F.BA BA A. Of this one can only say that if one were going to take the trouble to encipher a message at all, one would choose something rather more pointed.

From Black's own decipherment, further anagrammed, and with the addition of HZQ (got by considering the dashes as capitals) Clark got these messages:

FRA BA WRYT EAR. AA! SHAXPERE
FRA BA WRT EAR. HZQ AYA!—SHAXPERE
A! FRA BAQ WRYT HEAR AZ SHAXPERE

These he renders as:

Francis Bacon wrote here. Aye, Aye. Shakespeare.
Francis Bacon wrote here. His cue. Aye Aye. Shakespeare.
Aye! Francis Bacon wrote here as Shakespeare.

Clark also varied his treatment of the punctuation, and tried starting at various points. This brought further decipherments:

---

[1] See ch. VII for a consideration of anagrams.

for instance, beginning at the stop in He.Re he gets DRSWD-CAIQAB. The reader will be interested to learn that this 'equals' (by anagram) BAQ RAISD DC W, or 'Bacon raised deceased William'; or, Clark waggishly suggested, 'As some will say "Bacon raised Seedy William"'. Taking the points in the whole epitaph as *a*-forms, Clark produces BA WIL NARRA AL SHAQPERE HEAR BY Q (Bacon will narrate all Shakespeare hereby).[1] The grand climax comes when he treats $\frac{T}{Y}$ (used twice) as a whole five-letter group. This produces SAEHABEBNRAL-RIALARP. This is converted to SHAQ PERE ALL NARA HERE A! I OBAY BA: 'Jacques Pierre [Shakespeare] all narrated here: Aye! I obey (his wishes). Bacon'.

Clark's book was called *The Tale of the Shakespeare Epitaph...Translated from the Anglo-Phonetic*. This term dignifies Clark's method of sound-for-word decipherments in an attempt to give it rational status and the appearance of system. In the book he gives more readings, such as 'Shaxpere, Francis Bacon, Ye are at a War', and 'Shaxpere Ate [both hated and ate] Francis Bacon. Why Roarer!' At one point Clark even drops the biliteral cipher, takes letters of the epitaph, reads them backwards from the end, and converts into Anglo-Phonetics. Of Clark's work all we need say is that the decipherments do not pass the linguistic test; that by a variety of methods a number of equally invalid messages can be produced, and there is no reason to assume that any one of them was intended.

Ignatius Donnelly now turned his attention to the epitaph. In 1899 he published *The Cipher in the Plays, and on the Tombstone*. He paid tribute to Black as 'the first man in 271 years who had perceived a relationship between Bacon's cipher and the inscription on the tombstone', but he felt bound to criticize Black's methods and results: 'Shakespeare was never known to write his name SHAXPERE', he points out. (Not a very good argument: Baconians usually allow themselves great latitude in the spelling of names when it suits them. And there was nothing to prevent Shakespeare signing his name that way if he had chosen to. It is spelt in similar forms in documents at the

---

[1] Clark does not explain the Q.

time of his marriage.) Donnelly goes on, much more cogently: 'If Bacon had inserted a claim of authorship, in cipher, on the inscription...he would not have been content to put it forth in such an enigmatical form....[One] would be entitled to find a coherent and complete sentence.' It is obvious, Donnelly goes on, that there is some significance in the use of large and small letters; this is 'evident when we consider what would have been the result if the stonecutter, to show his religious feeling, had placed the name of Jesus in large capitals'. This, Donnelly points out, would have produced five *b*-forms, or *bbbbb*; and there is no such combination in the cipher. Since it did not happen, we are to infer its deliberate avoidance: a curious piece of logic.

Donnelly goes into some further mechanics of the biliteral cipher. He then states that in at least seventeen cases the five-letter group representing the ordinary letters of the alphabet may be read backwards as well as forwards. In other words, *abbab* is O; its reverse, *babba* is Y; *aabba* is G, *abbaa* is N, and so on. It is fairly plain that he is now beginning to hedge; Bacon never mentioned the possibility of these manipulations, but 'this double-back-action quality', says Donnelly, 'is that on which the cipher on the gravestone depends'. He decides also that the four dashes and two full stops used in the inscription are 'the points of departure from which the cipher moves'. He also inserts letters which have been elided, justifying himself by saying that the dash 'is not only a mark of punctuation but of elision as well'. We give below the text, and his assignments: the arrows show which way a group may be read:

GoodF	rendf	orJes	usSAK	Eforb	eareT	odiGG	T(h)EDu
baaab	*aaaaa*	*aabaa*	*aabbb*	*baaaa*	*aaaab*	*aaabb*	*babba*
S	A	E	H	→ R	B	D	← Y
				B ←			O →

This whole grouping may be moved one letter backwards, giving these alternative groups:

Good	Frend	forIe	susSA	KEfor	beare
?baaa	*baaaa*	*aaaba*	*aaabb*	*bbaaa*	*aaaaa*
	→ R	→ C	D	D ←	A
	B ←	I ←			

After this series of most dubious operations, Donnelly then

further manipulates the decipherments. By the most massive piece of anagramming he arrives triumphantly at this statement: 'We have therefore worked out the four lines of the inscription in these words: FRANCIS BACON WROTE THE GREENE, MARLOWE AND SHAKESPEARE PLAYS.'

He nowhere mentions the anagramming of the decipherments. Nor does he point out that since the inscription has 110 letters, by strict application of the biliteral cipher the plain text should be of twenty-two letters; his has fifty-two. The discrepancy is accounted for by his using the same five-letter group several times, by inverting the order of the open-text letters in order to get the five-letter group he needs, by inserting a letter or letters for a dash (but only when it suits him), and by leaving out some letters of the open text altogether. Though he had stated that the dashes and stops were signals of the direction to be followed, he does not always follow his own rule (which was only invented to suit his convenience anyway).

The transcription below, picked out from his rambling text, shows how Donnelly used letters more than once; letters which he did not use are left blank:

```
Good Frend for Iesus SAKE forbeare
      od Fre      or Ies                    are
To Goo
Tod Go                                        Re
To diGG T(h)E Dust Enclo-Ased HE.Re
        T(h)E Du       lo-Ased HE.Re
        (h)E Dus       lo-Ased HE.Re
                       lo-Ased HE.Re
                       lo-Ased HE.Re
                  Enclo           ReHEd
                        Ased H
Blese be ƉE        s ƉEs Stones
    ese               ƉEs St
Blese                       tones
   les             s ƉEs S
An curst be He T/Y moves my bo
        e T/Y mo
          Y move
      T(haT)m
      (haT)mo
```

Now what system, what methodical and precise application of a genuine key is visible here? Could any other person, given the key as Bacon defined it, undertake to go through the same series of moves and yet not recognize at the end that he had been just plain cheating? Is it not clear that Donnelly started out with a message to find, and found it by deliberately undermining the inflexibility of the key? By these methods he could have found any other messages his invention directed.

A generation after Donnelly a British writer, G. B. Rosher, wrote an article in *Baconiana* (January 1913) about the tombstone inscription. He had begun as a partial sceptic; at any rate he had no faith in Donnelly's decipherment. 'Not a single word of it', he said, 'is deducible from the cipher writing.' He goes back to Black's rendering; adds the letter W, says twelve letters are left, that there are twelve letters in 'Francis Bacon', points out that FRA BA is already there, and states that the other letters must be CIS CON. He justifies the conclusion by saying that 'the copyist had grown weary and careless with the end of the inscription'. Hence ten letters were wrongly carved. The last part of Rosher's argument is mere assumption; it cannot be proved or disproved; it is merely improbable. The first part of his argument rests on Black's own assumptions and alleged decipherment. If one does not accept Black, one need not trouble with Rosher.

In the Folger Shakespeare Library there are some papers by C. Alexander Montgomery of New York, who took out copyright for them in 1927. Montgomery believed Bacon to be the son of a politic marriage between Elizabeth and Walsingham. Montgomery wittily calls the Stratford inscription 'The Monumental Jest'. By anagramming letters and altering the order of words he produces two quatrains, which we are content merely to quote as examples of gadzookery:

Dig Honest Man Dost Ye Forbeare
I SHAKESPEARE but encloased here
Gravest Mystery Below these stones
Gist codes are not my dead bones.

F. B.

Dig Honest Man dost THEE forbeare
I SHAKE-SPEARE England's Tvdor Heire
Graved belovv these mystic Stones
The mystery codes yet gab of bones

F. B.

The late Fletcher Pratt wrote a book called *Secret and Urgent* (1939) which stated that 'Colonel George Fabyan of the American Army', who was 'an able cryptographer', deciphered the inscription by what is called the triliteral cipher, interpreted by the Frederici system. Frederici was a German, who, according to Pratt, devised a system using three alphabets in 1685. The decipherment of the inscription runs:

Goo	dFr	end	for	Ies	usS	AKe	for	bea	reT	odi
aba	*bba*	*aab*	*aac*	*aca*	*cbc*	*cab*	*abb*	*aac*	*bcc*	*aac*
F	R	B	A	C	O	N	H	A	Z	A

GGT	-ED	ust	Enc	loA	sed	HER	eBl	ese	beT	-EM
bba	*acc*	*bbc*	*cbc*	*cab*	*acb*	*aca*	*cca*	*aba*	*abb*	*bba*
R	D	S	O	N	E	C	I	P	H	R

Tsp	are	sT-	EsS	ton	esA	ndc	urs	tbe	HeY	Tmo
cca	*cab*	*aac*	*caa*	*bbc*	*bcc*	*cca*	*bab*	*abb*	*cca*	*cab*
I	N	A	M	S	W	I	T	H	I	N

Ves	myB	one	s
bac	*caa*	*bba*	
W	M	R	

The message is: 'Fr. Bacon hazards one ciph'r in a MS. within. WMR [Wm. Rawley?]'. Note that *aba* gives both F and P, and that *bcc* gives both Z and W, though W can also be represented by *bac*. Note the inconsistent treatment of the symbol $\frac{T}{Y}$, which is treated once as a single letter, once as two letters, YT. Note also that something odd has happened to the plain text at 'Blese be TE M $\frac{T}{Y}$ spares'; two letters of MAN have been omitted. These things shake one's faith in the validity of the method.

Pratt says that Fabyan got the idea from Mrs Elizabeth Wells Gallup, who was the most serious exponent of the biliteral cipher; further, says Pratt, Fabyan extended the idea to the triliteral cipher, and found messages in the First Folio, in Ben Jonson and in other books, but 'his labors in the War Department kept him from developing the theory'. This is nonsense. We deal with Fabyan and Mrs Gallup in chs. xiii–xiv; here it is enough to say that Fabyan, whom we knew, was no cryptographer at all, nor was he ever an officer in any army. The work on the tombstone cipher was by Mrs Gallup; even so it does not bear scrutiny.

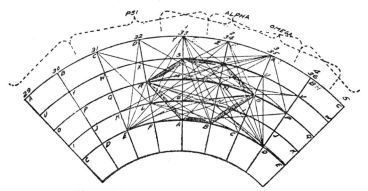

Fig. 4. The 'jewel' from Shakespeare's epitaph.

An American woman, Natalie Rice Clark, produced a book called *Bacon's Dial in Shakespeare* in 1922. Her method (for lack of a better term) is described in ch. vi; briefly it consists of superimposing a compass dial on a clock-face, and relating letters in the text to each other by means of this combination—though the relationship between the text and the 'instrument' is very obscure. However, she finds through her keys the first letter of a sequence; from this starting-point she builds up a criss-cross or web of lines joining other letters. On her dial, if nowhere else, they make a pleasing pattern which she calls a maze-picture. For the tombstone inscription these are her findings:

The Epitaph at Shakespeare's grave shows some traces of a Dial linking....The letters in the Epitaph also construct the Bacon Jewel. It is not wholly improbable that the phrase 'spares TEs Stones' may mean also 'T-Y-Es *pairs* the stones', meaning that the lines on the dial are a basis for 'pairing' the stones or jewels in play and Epitaph. The letters may be so set on the dial that the prominent GG's take their place as Gates, and the S A K E is the chief portion of a set of keys.

She then draws the 'jewel' (Fig. 4). What is one to gather from all this, except that it is possible to set out the individual letters in this way and to join them by innumerable lines? What is the point, and where is the message?

The most recent attempt to find significance in the inscription was by an apparent Stratfordian, Ib Melchior, who wanted only to prove that there was a message there. In an article in the issue of 9 August 1954 of *Life* magazine, illustrated with a number of fine photographs of the castle at Elsinore, he asserted that the manuscript of *Hamlet* is buried somewhere in the castle. His evidence was 'a decipherment' of the inscription.

His method was based on the separation of the letters of the text into groups, according as they were successively capital or small letters. By writing down the number of letters each group contained he got this arrangement:

Good Frend for Iesus SAKE forbeare

I 3 I 7 I 4 4 8

To diGG TE Dust Enclo Ased HE.Re

I 3 6 3 I 4 I 3 3 I

T

Blese be TE Man Y spares TEs Stones

I 6 4 2 2 6 3 I I 5

T

And curst be He Y moves my Bones

I 9 I I 2 7 I 4

Melchior goes on: 'Of the 36 units in my cryptogram the number I was represented 14 times. In English the letter E is by far the leading letter on the frequency scale, so I assigned the number I to the letter E....' By continuing this chain of reasoning he reaches the message: 'ELESENNRE LAEDE WEDGE EERE AAMLEET EDEEASEN.' This is 'Old English with nulls', and means 'Elsinore laid wedge first Hamlet edition'. But in reaching this 'message' (and one cannot seriously accept its linguistic validity), Melchior has in any case introduced certain silent changes in his key. For he reached a difficult point in the second and third lines, and so decided that the word THE was a 'change symbol'. So for the nine units or numbers between these 'symbols' he assigns different alphabetic values. Melchior does not himself record his numerical cryptogram and set down the plain-text values below it, unit by unit. If a check is made, one sees where he changed tactics. His message has thirty-eight letters of which many are null or non-significant; yet his cryptogram had thirty-six numerals of which two were 'change-symbols'. There ought thus to have been thirty-four letters in the message. Here now is the cryptogram and Melchior's first trial decipherment:

13171448136 (3141331164) 226311519112714
ELESENNRELA (LEDELLEEMN) AAMLEETEDEEASEN

The ten numbers and letters in brackets made no sense to Melchior—though to us they seem no less valid than the rest. Going back to the open text, Melchior drops the two THE's in capitals; he also *changes* the numeral assignment for HE.Re from 3.1 to 2.1.1. He nowhere mentions this. But with these two alterations and certain re-numberings which he feels to be permitted by the change symbols, Melchior finally reaches this:

131714481 32 (THE) 131 41321
ELESENNRE.LA   EDE.WEDGE
116 (THE) 1 2263115 19112714
EER   E.AAMLEET.EDEEASEN

'Take away the obvious nulls', says Melchior, 'and you read "Elsinore laid wedge first Hamlet edition".' Well, you do so if you are exceedingly good-natured, rather gullible, and know nothing of cryptography. When Melchior adhered to his key he produced gibberish; when he assumed 'change-symbols' and modified his key, he produced something little better. Even then he had to inject exceptions to his own rules, and at the end discarded a high percentage of nulls to produce something which was not good English—indeed, it was like Clark's Anglo-Phonetics.

To change the alphabet on a given signal is perfectly normal practice in cipher messages. None the less Melchior was only acting on a convenient assumption here; it suited him at the time. The other circumstances which we have noted all invalidate his solution. In any case a short message of this kind, using two alphabets, cannot be solved with absolute certainty. One would require external corroboration of the validity of the decipherment, such as the finding of other messages which could be deciphered by the same method and which made better sense. Basically, Melchior's is in the same category as other unacceptable solutions: by his methods other equally valid messages could have been found.

All the cipher messages produced so far in the examination of the gravestone inscription are invalid. And so, for all anyone knows, is the basic assumption underlying them. How do we know that the 'uncouth mixture' of small letters and capitals existed at all or has been exactly transcribed?

The earliest transcription of the lettering appeared in the reissue in 1801 of the Johnson-Steevens *Commentaries on Shakespeare's Works*. A footnote signed 'Steevens' sets the quatrain forth in capitals and lower-case letters, and draws attention to the 'uncouth mixture'. A possible origin of the note may have been an engraving which appeared in *Picturesque Views of the upper, or Warwickshire, Avon*, by Samuel Ireland, which came out in 1795. But in 1748 the Master of the Stratford Grammar School had noted that the inscription was 'All in Great Letters'—essentially as it is today. In Dugdale's *Antiquities of Warwickshire* of 1656, and in letters of 1673, 1693 and 1694 (the first three now in the Folger Shakespeare Library and the last in the Bodleian), there are eyewitness accounts of the stone. None of these observers remarked upon anything unusual about it.

Hence all this cryptographical endeavour rests on second- or even third-hand evidence, which is directly contradicted by one earlier authority and not authenticated elsewhere. It is a slender basis for an elaborate theory. But even if the inscription were as it was described by Steevens, the attempts to find a cipher in it have proved to be self-refuting.

CHAPTER V

DR OWEN AND HIS WORD CIPHER

INSPIRED, perhaps, by Donnelly's example, the next crypto-graphic proof of authorship was even more elaborate, and made more sweeping claims. This work was called *Sir Francis Bacon's Cipher Story*; the author, Orville Ward Owen, was a Detroit physician. He was born on 1 January 1854, and died on 31 March 1924: a short biography can be found in *American Baconiana*.[1] The *Story* was planned to occupy six volumes, and the first five were published (during the years 1893-5) by the Howard Publishing Co., of Detroit and New York. The sixth volume was written, and still exists in manuscript.

The deciphered message set out in these volumes is supposed, as the title implies, to have been written by Francis Bacon (the natural son of Queen Elizabeth and Robert Dudley, Earl of Leicester), and to contain the inside story of life in Elizabethan England. But at the very beginning of the first volume, Owen's readers find themselves in for a surprise. The first forty-three pages are occupied with the deciphered text of 'Sir Francis Bacon's Letter to the Decipherer'; this is in dialogue, one speaker being Bacon and the other the man who eventually succeeds in deciphering the text. All this, if eccentric, would seem quite legitimate, but for one strange anomaly: the dialogue itself contains instructions for penetrating the cipher. In other words, now that the cryptanalyst has broken down the cipher, Bacon is telling him what to do in order to break down the cipher. This is like picking the lock of a safe, only to find inside it the key to the lock you have already picked.

Owen, at any rate, does not seem to have seen the absurdity. Even apart from this, the message is a disappointment. Here are a few samples of the instructions it gives:

> Therefore, let your own discretion be your tutor
> And suit the action to the word, and the word to the action,
> With this special observance, that you match

[1] I, 3, pp. 6-18.

Conjugates, parallels and relatives by placing
Instances which are related to one another
By themselves, and all the concordances
Which have a correspondence and analogy
With each other should be commingled with the connaturals.
And when you have collected a sufficient quantity
Of absolutely similar matter, by skillful handling
The proper collocation of things may be
Made out and disentangled....

Match the syllogisms duly and orderly,
And put together systematically and minutely
The chain or coupling, links of the argument.
That is to say, the connaturals, concurrences,
Correspondents, concatenations, collocations, analogies,
Similitudes, relatives, parallels, conjugates and sequences
Of everything relating to the combination, composition,
Renovation, arrangement, and unity revolving
In succession, part by part, throughout the whole,
Ascending and descending, leaving no tract behind,
And sifting it as faithful secretaries and clerks
In the courts of kings, set to work, with diligence and
Judgment, and sort into different boxes, connaturals
Concerning matters of state, and when he has
Attentively sorted it, from the beginning to the end,
And united and collected the dispersed and distributed
Matter, which is mingled up and down in combination,
It will be easy to make a translation of it.

To deduce from these enormous breathless cadences any straightforward procedure for decipherment is almost itself an exercise in cryptanalysis, and one from which any cryptologist might be expected to turn with a shudder. In fact even Bacon shows a sense of uneasiness with his own instructions; at one place in the dialogue he puts into the mouth of the 'decipherer' the question 'But may they not say it is chance doth this?' Reassuringly, Bacon answers him:

We thought of that; and if any man conceive
That it is done without any system or common
Centre, let him proceed to form a history,
And neglect the guides. He cannot go through with it
To its completion....

PLATE III

Dr Owen's 'Wheel'.

But this reassurance comes out with more bravado than cogency. We are about to show that that is just what Owen did.

When this 'Letter' is put to the test as a cryptological system, it makes a poor showing (especially if it is set beside Bacon's account of his biliteral cipher, discussed in a previous chapter and found to be perfectly valid). It is, as far as we can see, quite impossible to condense the 'rules' into a clear description of (1) a general system; (2) a set of specific keys; and (3) a set of unambiguous rules for applying the keys. However, Dr Owen got along with the system somehow; and while he was away from home his assistants seem to have done equally well—they produced the fifth volume of the *Story* on their own.

A brief examination is enough to show that the 'cipher story' is constructed by lifting words, lines and passages of various lengths from the works of a number of Elizabethan authors; these are put together to make a more or less coherent text which, naturally enough, follows the lines Owen wanted it to follow. Fig. 5 shows a page of his 'decipherments', and one page is quite enough to give the general idea; the rest of the 1000-odd printed pages (and doubtless the 200-odd manuscript pages of vol. VI as well) are of the same sort.

Owen's method encouraged him to be liberal with his sources; if he failed to find a passage he wanted in one book, it was a simple matter to consult another. As a result, the list of contributors to the story is impressive; besides Bacon's own writings, Owen draws upon the works attributed to Shakespeare, Marlowe, Robert Greene, George Peele, Edmund Spenser and Robert Burton (*The Anatomy of Melancholy* only). The most courageous of all Owen's references, perhaps, were those taken from the English translation of Bacon's *Feliciam Memoriam Elizabethae*. This book originally appeared in Latin; the translation Owen used was prepared by Dr Rawley, Bacon's literary secretary and executor, in 1648—twenty-two years after Bacon's death.

Owen was committed, by the story he wove, to maintaining that Bacon wrote all these source-books (even the posthumous translation): he was not only Shakespeare, Marlowe, Greene, and so on; he was also, in a real sense, a ghost writer for

Dr Rawley. Moreover, Bacon must have gone to the length of writing this substantial part of Elizabethan literature mainly because he wanted to conceal the story which Owen later laid

This paragon

over whose zenith		Marlowe,
Clothed in windy air and eagles' wings		"Tamburlaine the Great."
Joined to her feathered breast fame hovereth,		
Sounding of her golden trump,		
That to the adverse poles of that straight line		
Which measureth the glorious frame of heaven,		
Her name is spread—		
This mighty Queen Elizabeth		
Shall your eyes behold!		
This beautiful tyrant, fiend, angelical,		Shakespeare,
Ravenous, dove-feathered raven,		"Romeo and Juliet."
Wolfish ravening lamb,		
Despisèd substance of divinest brow,		
Just opposite to what she justly seemest,		
A dim saint and honourable lady-villain,		
A whitely wanton with a velvet brow,		Shakespeare,
Aye, and by heaven, one that will do the deed		"Love's Labor's
Though Argus were her Eunuch and her guard!		Lost."
O serpent's heart hid with a flowering face!		Shakespeare,
O God! did dragon ever keep so fair a cave?		"Romeo and Juliet."

Fig. 5. A page of Owen's 'decipherments'.

bare. In the words of Dr Mann, one of Owen's best friends (and consequently one of his severest critics), 'we are asked to believe that such peerless creations as *Hamlet*, *The Tempest*, and *Romeo and Juliet* were not prime productions of the transcendent genius who wrote them, but were *subsidiary* devices which Bacon designed for the purpose of concealing the cipher therein'.

Because Owen's sources were so numerous, the task of extracting the story must have been considerable; fortunately, it was to some extent lightened by an ingenious machine known as the 'wheel'. This was constructed by Owen and his assistants, and a photograph of it is shown in Plate III. The machine consists of two spools, rather like over-sized cinema reels, pivoted to spin freely; stretched between them, and wound round them, are 1000 feet of canvas. Glued to this canvas the 1000 or so pages of the selected texts in turn come into view as the spools rotate, the whole contraption providing an extended anthology of Elizabethan writings.

This device might be heralded as the first example of automation in the service of literature; all the more remarkable in that it was invented some three hundred years ago. And, one might add, all the more noble of Owen that he generously gives Bacon the credit for the wheel's invention, when it would be so easy to claim it for himself. He does this on p. 3 of the first volume of his *Story*. In the 'Letter to the Decipherer' Bacon's inquisitor asks:

> ...The first question is, therefore,
> What simple plain rule is there to teach me
> The way to shift? [that is, from 'clew' to 'clew']

The reply is in the style we come to expect from Bacon; but buried in a mass of anecdote the following key lines emerge:

> Take your knife and cut all our books asunder,
> And set the leaves on a great firm wheel
> Which rolls and rolls, and turning the
> Fickle rolling wheel, throw your eyes upon FORTUNE....

The faithful Owen does his best to follow these instructions, and FORTUNE is henceforth one of his four 'key' or 'guide' words. The others, which he derives by various means, are HONOUR, NATURE and REPUTATION; but he uses as 'connaturals, concurrences, correspondents and collocations' any words which are remotely related to these. The fixed rules and keys which he professes to follow amount to this: first find one of your key words (or one of its various derivatives); then look for a suitable text somewhere near the place where it occurs; and if you find one which fits into the story as you want it to be, there you are—another triumph of decipherment.

With the generous allowance of 'keys' Owen gives himself, it is not surprising that the story he unfolds is so long (though it might be reasonable to expect it to be less tedious). In the First Folio alone, the word 'fortune' and its derivatives—'unfortunate', 'misfortune' and so on—occur about 500 times; 'nature' and its derivatives also about 500; 'repute' and its derivatives 60 or more; while 'honour' and the words related to it put up the highest score of all—they can be found in more than 1100 different places. Simple arithmetic gives the result that on the 454 leaves (i.e. 908 pages) of the First Folio, there are more than 2100 key words: an average of between two and three per page. Taking all the various sources together, the number of keywords is vast; but this has not prevented some assiduous scholar from counting them, and finding the total to be about 10,650. Owen had plenty to choose from.

With these figures, what is surprising is that he does his job so badly. It would seem plausible that there should be a keyword very near, if not actually within, any text that he cared to choose; but again Dr Mann puts a telling argument against him. He finds that 'in one instance the keyword is 47 lines away from the quotation taken, and in a large number of instances it is not even to be found on the same page'. When a rule becomes so flexible that there is nothing which counts as breaking it, it can no longer be said to be a rule at all. Dr Owen's 'rules' fall into this category.

There is, however, a still more crippling defect in Owen's applications of his 'system'. Ignoring, for the moment, the unjustifiable freedom of choice allowed the decipherer, what can be said of the accuracy of the text itself? When Owen quotes a passage, does he always quote it fairly? This question is difficult to answer, because Owen, unlike Donnelly, makes no attempt to blind his readers with science. Nowhere in the course of his story does he give the exact source of a quotation; nor does he indicate the keyword or 'connatural', 'concurrence', 'correspondent' or 'collocation' which led him to choose it. Perhaps that is one reason why so many people have taken Owen's cipher story on trust—challenging it would be such hard work.

Once more Dr Mann comes to the rescue. He proves conclusively that Owen and his assistants had no qualms about tampering with the texts whenever it suited their book (whichever volume they happened to be working on). If a quotation did not do quite the job it was meant to do, a word judiciously altered here and there worked wonders. For example, the lines from *The Merchant of Venice*:

> Yea, mock the lion when he roars for prey
> To win the lady

appear in a new reading on p. 7 of Owen's first volume:

> Yea, mock the lion when he roars for prey
> To win the cipher

And this is only one case among hundreds. As Mann says, 'it is doubtful if a single page is made up of extracts quoted fairly'.

Faced with this kind of performance, the charitable can only maintain that Owen was a visionary; the less charitable will conclude that he was a mountebank. There is something to be said for being charitable; or at any rate we must maintain that if Owen was a fraud, he was a remarkably determined and consistent one. This is amply shown by his quest for Shakespeare manuscripts. The story is not directly concerned with cryptanalysis, but it throws some interesting light upon his character.[1]

During the course of his work on the *Story*, Owen began to be troubled with visitations of Bacon's spirit. As time went on Owen became increasingly convinced that Bacon had buried some more tangible evidence of his authorship of Shakespeare's works in a set of iron boxes. Calling another cipher system to his aid, he began to work out the location of the hidden treasure. The texts of Owen's messages were not recorded, and there is no clear description of the system he employed. But we do know, from the writings of Mrs Kate Prescott, that he named the method 'The King's Move Cipher', and that it was an adaptation of his earlier word cipher. Instead of using whole

---

[1] It also throws a sidelight on the work of Mrs Gallup, who in many ways followed Owen's lead. See chs. XIII ff.

words, he now used individual letters: starting from a key word, he chose letters by moving up or down, horizontally or diagonally (as one moves the king in chess). We are also told that one of the earliest sources for his clues was Sir Philip Sidney's *Arcadia*; and this adds yet another name to the list of people who, according to Owen, were really Bacon.

In 1909, as a result of his researches with the new system, Owen apparently concluded that the boxes containing the original manuscripts were buried near Chepstow Castle, which was at that time owned by the Duke of Beaufort. He managed to persuade a number of people, including another physician, William Prescott of Boston, to finance an expedition to the castle, and was soon digging busily for the boxes he was convinced he would find there. Dr and Mrs Prescott were with him, and Mrs Prescott's *Reminiscences* provide some of the details of the story; these are supplemented by the writings of another eyewitness, Fred S. Hammond. Hammond was an engineer, and had been employed by the Duke of Beaufort (a man of foresight) to watch Owen and ensure that he did as little permanent damage as possible.

The earliest search, Hammond tells us, was for a cave which Owen believed to contain the boxes, and to be located among the rock formations near Chepstow. But Owen gave this up in December 1909, explaining that 'the cipher was incomplete and left much to unravel'. The Prescotts went back to Boston at this point; but Owen stayed on and continued to work on the cipher. It soon yielded a convincing explanation for his failure. Mrs Prescott records that 'he found that Bacon feared the cliff might fall away or be cracked by the winter frosts, thus disclosing the hiding place of the manuscripts. For this reason Bacon had removed them.' Soon Owen had 'found a new lead and directions'. He had given up the text of the *Arcadia*, and was now working on *The Tempest*. This seemed more promising, and yielded the information that the lost manuscripts were hidden in a rift in the bed of the River Wye where it ran through the Castle estate. According to Hammond, confirmation (if confirmation were needed) arrived from an unexpected quarter. Owen was anonymously sent an anagrammatic reading of the second line of the poem, 'To the Reader', which is found at the beginning of the First Folio. This poem, facing the Droeshout portrait of Shakespeare, begins:

> This Figure, that thou here seest put,
> It was for gentle Shakespeare cut....

The letters of the second line can be anagrammed to read 'Seek, sir, a true angle at Chepstow.—F'; and this was enough to assure Owen that he was on the right track. He summoned back the Prescotts in the autumn of 1910, and between them they began to prepare for the second assault.

They were financed, this time, by the Chicagoan, George Fabyan, of whom we shall have more to say later. (Hammond wrote that it was the Duke of Beaufort himself who provided the money, but this, we were told, was not the case.) Fabyan told us that the venture was protracted and expensive; in the end he had to send his financial secretary over to put a stop to it. Owen had not discovered the manuscripts, but after sinking eight or ten shafts in the bed of the river he had unearthed part of the foundations of a Roman bridge, and a disused cistern. Mrs Prescott again sums up the story neatly: 'There is little more I can tell of this visit to Chepstow. The work that was undertaken proved fruitless. Our readers may feel that so far the story spells only defeat and failure, but we never lost faith or hope. It is quite possible, I may say probable, that final directions for finding the treasures were not given in the *Arcadia* of 1638....'[1] This much seems good sense, especially as Bacon was already dead in 1638; but the effect is spoiled a little by her adding that the clues 'may be found elsewhere in the ciphers'.

The third attack was launched a few years later, in 1920, by the determined Dr Prescott. Owen furnished the clues but did not go himself; and a Mr Harold Shafter Howard put up the money. The castle had by this time passed into the hands of the Lysaght family, who appear to have been remarkably long-suffering. They allowed Prescott to excavate the cellar, 'thus',

---

[1] The 1638 edition was chosen because its frontispiece contained symbols which (to Owen) indicated Bacon's authorship and royal birth.

as Hammond remarks, 'jeopardizing the walls of the castle'. The diggers claimed to have found the handle of the iron box in which the manuscripts were hidden, but they found no box, and no manuscripts.

Howard must have felt that his money had been well spent in financing this expedition, for in 1924 we find him setting off for Chepstow himself. He engaged the old boatman at the castle to look for some steps 'which the cipher said were there, but which had not been found due to Owen's miscalculation'.[1] The boatman obligingly unearthed a flight of steps on the nearby Hastings Clay estate; but Howard appears to have changed his mind about the location of the treasure. In 1932 he was maintaining that sixty-six boxes of manuscripts were hidden in a grotto in Piercefield Park, and that it would take two years to recover them. Hammond, who had long since become a convert to the cipher method (in fact, his belief took shape during the first expedition, while he was watching Owen at work), disagreed with Howard about this. According to Hammond, the cipher messages showed that the manuscripts were actually hidden in a chamber in the wall of the castle tower. Here, then, is a clear case of two investigators working on the same material, and claiming to employ the same system, who nevertheless reached quite different results; not, on the face of it, a reassuring situation. Hammond, incidentally, explained why Howard never carried out his projected search in Piercefield Park; his theatrical behaviour roused such doubts in the mind of the owner that permission to excavate any further was refused.

That was the end of the wild goose chase started by Owen's work on the king's move cipher. But some further details of the various expeditions are worth giving before we return to our assessment of Owen's cryptology.

One of Owen's converts, during the second set of excavations (in the bed of the River Wye) was Mr Comyns Beaumont, whom we have already mentioned as an admirer of Ignatius Donnelly. Beaumont went to Chepstow as a newspaper editor, to cover the story of the search and to interview Owen. As his

[1] *Baconiana*, vol. XXI, 3rd series, pp. 286–9.

article many years later, in *Baconiana* of April 1944, records, he was impressed by what he found. Dr Owen, he tells us, was 'suave and genial...foiled in his efforts, he was still determined he was right'. Beaumont mentions the king's move cipher, and recalls that one of the estate employees told him 'the...Cypher has BACON as its key, and BACKON as its directive'; his informant claimed to have 'unravelled a pool' of the cipher himself, 'reading up or down in the slantindicular'. Beaumont goes on to lament that the owner of Chepstow Castle at the time he was writing refused to let anyone near it, though he admits that the year 1944 was not a good time for manuscript-hunting.

An earlier article, in *American Baconiana* of March 1924 (the year Owen died) by 'a young scientist, Mr Burrell F. Ruth, of East Lansing, Michigan', gives some recollections of Owen, and concludes:

I was given the true history of the discovery of the cipher in Sidney's *Arcadia*; how Dr Owen left for England on a six weeks' trip and stayed six years; how the English newspapers reviled him and threatened to keep him out of England entirely; how the government secret agents watched him to claim anything that might be found; how hordes of newspaper reporters followed his trail, as bees follow sweets; how after almost six years of search he achieved success at the bottom of the River Wye, where down in a deep caisson sunk by English engineers, a small, gray, stone structure was uncovered beneath a dozen feet of mud. It was marked with inscriptions of Francis Bacon....But when it was opened it was entirely bare.[1]

It is hard not to feel sorry for a man who, even when he had apparently 'achieved success', was sure to find failure lurking just around the corner.

Mr Ruth adds that 'Dr Owen made other inventions, including a machine to defy gravity. He offered it to the U.S. Government, but it was not considered, possibly because it was

[1] One is reminded of the recent exploits of Mr Calvin Hoffman, who, believing that Marlowe wrote the Plays and that his manuscripts were buried in the tomb of Sir Thomas Walsingham, persuaded the authorities to open the tomb. When this was done, on 1 May 1956, no manuscripts were found; only the coffin, sand, and some rubble.

classed with perpetual motion devices of ill repute'. Reading this reminded us that Colonel Fabyan (the sponsor of Owen's last expedition to Chepstow) believed that Owen had deciphered the records of experiments in which Bacon proved that Christ performed the miracle of walking upon the water by means of some sort of high-frequency vibration. To confirm these findings Fabyan hired a scientist who was unsuccessful in proving Owen's thesis, but whose investigations led to a number of important advances in acoustics.

We have digressed for long enough; but it will not take much time to examine the validity of Owen's cryptographic methods. Although the details of the king's move cipher are obscure, we have already noticed that in using it Howard and Hammond reached entirely different results from one another and from Owen himself. The reason is plain: the method allows so much room for choice on the part of the 'decipherer' that he can produce any answer he likes. The method, in other words, carries its own refutation with it.

The word cipher is in no better position: it has no fixed general system; the keys are not precise and inflexible, and the 'connaturals, concatenations, analogies', etc. force the decipherer to make decisions concerning ambiguous and uncertain matters; there is wide room for choice, which simply cannot exist in a genuine cipher method; and finally, two or more independent investigators, working on the same material, can arrive at totally different solutions.

Dr Frederic Mann, who investigated the word cipher with great thoroughness, once produced a substantial and coherent message, using Owen's four guide words in the works of Bacon and Shakespeare alone. Moreover, he went one better than Owen in giving the full source of each passage used, and in quoting it without distortion. His 'message' purported to be a 'letter from Francis Bacon, Baron Verulam, Viscount St Albans, Lord High Chancellor of England, to Dr Owen, touching the character of Queen Elizabeth'. It contains a description of the Queen's character and personality which is radically different from that set out in Owen's story, and runs as follows:

LEARNED DOCTOR OWEN: Rare in all ages hath been the reign
Merchant of Venice   *Hen. IV*   Bacon, *Felicities*
of a woman, more rare the felicity of a woman in her reign. Queen

Elizabeth (take heed how thou impawnst her person) both in her
Henry V   Bacon, *Felicities*
natural endowments and her fortune was admirable amongst

women, a pattern to all princes living with her, and all that shall
Henry VIII
succeed. Thou art to blame to rate this lovely lady so. Thou hast
Romeo and Juliet   *Henry IV*
misused the King's press damnably. Thine only gift is in devising
Much Ado
impossible slanders, and by compendious extractions of other men's
Bacon, *Advancement of Learning*
wits and labours to take upon thyself that which I am sure thou dost
Cymbeline
not know.

The Queen is spotless in the eyes of heaven, a virgin, a most
Winter's Tale   Bacon, *Henry VII*
unspotted lily, ay, the most peerless piece of earth I think that e'er
Winter's Tale
the sun shone bright on. Saba was never more covetous of wisdom
Henry VIII
and fair virtue than this pure soul. O for a muse of fire that would
Henry V
ascend the brightest heaven of Invention to give her virtue the true
Bacon, *Felicities*
grace and lustre! A mate of fortune she never took—she lived a
Bacon, *Praise of Elizabeth*
Virgin, and she had no children. Owen, thou dost belie her, and
Hen. IV Othello
thou art a devil. Thou art as rash as fire to say that she was false.
Othello
O, she was heavenly true! How it will grieve thee, Owen, when
Othello   *Hamlet*   *Hen. IV. Winter's*
thou shalt come to clearer knowledge that thou hast thus scandalized
Tale   *Henry IV*
and foully spoken of my sovereign Mistress.
Winter's Tale
There be many follies and absurdities in thy book (fantastic
Bacon, *Interpretation of Nature*
reveries utterly bereft of solidity), which, if an eminent scholar had it
Bacon, *On Libel*
in hand, he would take advantage thereof, and make the author not

only odious but ridiculous and contemptible to the world: but I
Hamlet

forbear to show the line and the predicament wherein thou rangest.
Henry V
Owen, I charge thee fling away ambition. Thou hast shown thyself
Hen. IV. Henry VIII   *Merry Wives*
a wise physician, one that indeed physics his subject. Avoid what is
Winter's Tale   *Hamlet*
to come; for who can see worse days than he, that, yet living, doth
Bacon, Essay on Death
follow the funerals of his own reputation. Fare-thee-well, Owen.
Hamlet   *Hen. IV*
These few precepts in thy memory keep. While thou livest, tell truth
Hamlet   *Henry IV*
and shame the devil. He doth sin that doth belie the dead.
Henry IV
Thus, not doubting of thine honourable interpretation and usage
Bacon, Letter to Cecil
of that I have written, I commend thee to the Divine preservation.

FRANCIS BACON.

There are, of course, some Baconians who will remain un-
convinced by all this. Until a few years ago we were still in
touch with a group of people who were doggedly pursuing
'decipherments' based on the word cipher. (One good lady
maintained that Owen, far from using too many guides, connaturals, concurrences, correspondents, and so forth, had
restricted himself unnecessarily; she was inclined to add the
further words ART, TIME and TRUTH to the original list of
four.) For all we know, there are people busily at work right
now, secure in their conviction that one day their search will be
rewarded. With them we can argue no further, for argument
is not to the point.

CHAPTER VI

A MISCELLANY

ALTHOUGH we would like to investigate all the major systems of cryptology that have been used in attempting to prove that Shakespeare was really someone else, it is hardly possible to discuss every system that has ever been put forward: there are far too many. The main ones stand out from the rest, for one reason or another; some because of their large following, some because of the diligence of those who employ them, others for the spectacular results they yield, or for their curiosity value, and a few because they seem to deserve serious consideration. We consider such systems in detail, since they constitute the main stream of Baconian research in cryptology; but the stream has so many minor tributaries that it would be tedious and unprofitable to give a complete description of every one.

The various systems, moreover, are so diverse that there is no neat way of classifying them; any classification is bound to leave out a good many individual cases. The best that can be done is to select, from the mass of heterogeneous and unclassifiable methods, a representative few. In this chapter we discuss, briefly and in turn, five systems; they are chosen to give an idea of the large variety of ciphers that have, from time to time, been extracted from Shakespeare's works.

We shall begin with Mrs Natalie Rice Clark, since her method has already been mentioned in connection with Shakespeare's gravestone. Mrs Clark, the wife of a professor of Greek at Miami University, published her first book at Cincinnati in 1922: it was entitled *Bacon's Dial in Shakespeare: A Compass-Clock Cipher*. Mrs Clark had begun, apparently, by looking for 'cipher clues in Bacon's works'; and she found one in the *ABECEDARIUM Naturae* (Alphabet of Nature), in which Bacon discussed and 'made an inquisition into' certain natural phenomena. For brevity, he had used Greek letters to represent his various classifications: earth, air, fire, water, celestial bodies,

meteors, and so on. His use of the word 'alphabet' in his title
was clearly metaphorical, but Mrs Clark took it literally: she
drew a clock face, and divided it into twelve sections, each
representing one of Bacon's subjects of inquiry, with its
attendant Greek symbol. Having found further 'hints in
Bacon's History of the Winds' where, she claims, 'Lord Bacon

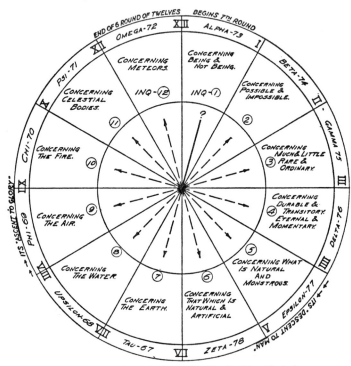

Fig. 6. The Clock Dial, drawn by Natalie Rice Clark from
Bacon's *Alphabet of Nature*.

gave the full list of compass points...thus "boxing the
compass" for future decipherers', she superimposed the face of
a compass on her clock diagram. The resulting figure, which
became in her hands an elaborate spider's web of concentric
circles and radii, formed the 'compass-clock dial' she used in
her researches (see Fig. 6). Her foreword sets out her aims:
she intends 'to show that a cipher designed by Francis Bacon,
and based on the union of a clock and compass in dial form,

exists in the First Folio'. Mrs Clark adds that the cipher 'is used as a literary framework for the plays, and is closely associated with some of the finest passages and allusions'. Having discovered some 170 overt references to compass points and several more to time (the clock), Mrs Clark feels confident she is on the right track: the dial corresponds to a primer; it 'questions', and it 'answers', or 'tallies'. It 'strengthens the force' of cipher messages in the text by showing 'their placements as they tally on the Dial chart'. If this seems obscure, Mrs Clark does little to help her readers in the pages that follow. She works through the plays, putting words and phrases on her dial, listing questions and announcing 'tallies'. But nothing seems to come out of all this except certain vague generalizations of her own; for example: 'Here in *King John* is Bacon tallying his own Absey [ABC] questions with the Dial itself. He does this in the scene at the Inn....' No messages, as such, begin to emerge until she introduces her 'maze pictures', and even then they are a rare event. She describes the procedure with a depressing lack of clarity: 'Capitals in the text often tally on the dial with...an indicating word, and the results of drawing lines between the letters, in the order of their use in the text, and as they are found duplicated on the Dial chart, results in Maze designs, or pictures.'

Her artistry is applied to a wide variety of texts, and takes a number of different shapes: a broken bowstring, a 'plain fish', a 'jewel blazon' and the like. She finds a profitable source in the dedicatory poem to the First Folio, for although 'the capitals in this verse are few', such as there are 'form a curtained room or stage, and in the rear the pointed shadow of a grave'. From her dial she derives the letters of the words 'exit' and 're-enter'; and the name 'F. Bacon' can be seen 'enclosed within the little, but sufficient space'. Having also discerned the initials W.S., Mrs Clark's triumph is complete: 'Plainly, here it says for all to see, Exit W.S.—Re-enter F. Bacon'. Another maze, of the constellation Dipper, is found in the epilogue to *The Tempest*, where 'all capitals taken and joined by lines' produce the message 'I, W.S., am F. Bacon'. These two short sentences are the only 'deciphered' texts in the whole book, and they barely seem worth the effort. Her second contribution to the subject, *Hamlet on the Dial Stage* (Paris, 1930), is more productive, though her procedure is even less straightforward than before. She now uses the dial to manipulate puppet characters on a miniature stage, 'where the Folio text is conformed to and illustrated by the movements and groups of the puppet characters.... When these name tallies are forced upon the observer's notice, there is no resulting break in the intensity of the scene itself.' The results of her manipulations are a few 'signatures' (F.B., Fr. B., Bacon, and Fran. Bacon), although it becomes increasingly difficult to see how these are derived.

According to Mrs Clark, then, the author of the plays, whom she believes to be Francis Bacon, worked with a compass-clock dial, fitting letters or words in specific places; the pattern was carefully preserved in the printed text; and all this with the sole object of producing two enigmatic sentences, a few scattered signatures, and a variety of 'maze pictures'. The elaborate apparatus seems, for the rest, to be quite unnecessary: selecting words and phrases in the plays and asserting a meaning for them can be done without recourse to compasses and clocks.

Mrs Clark at one point expresses the hope that others will join her in 'further development of the cipher message'; but in spite of her claim that hers is 'a most sane and human and worthy cipher' few disciples have so far come forward. Since her method is incomprehensible to practically everybody else, this is not surprising.

In contrast to Mrs Clark, Mrs Gertrude Horsford Fiske used a well-established and entirely valid method, Bacon's biliteral cipher. Admittedly, she used it on the Second Folio, which appeared in 1632, after both Shakespeare and Bacon had died; but she was able to explain this to her own satisfaction. There were plenty of competent disciples of Francis Bacon, capable of carrying on the work he had begun; it was one of these who inserted the posthumous messages in the Second Folio. Mrs Fiske was a devoted follower of Elizabeth Wells Gallup, whose work we shall be discussing in the final chapters of this book; and Mrs Fiske's decipherments, accomplished by means of biliteral type forms compiled by Mrs Gallup, are to be found in the *Studies in the Biliteral Cipher* (Boston, 1913). Their only drawback is that they are quite incomprehensible; here are a few examples:

—(m)ale desce'da't o' the Henry that founds th' Tudors—had the boor W's claim gainsay'd. Trust me mankind is surpris'd to say 'In shor(t) foe! I cry grace—. Is pre-ominate reaping found any less fully your suits? Justice?' [From 'Actors' Names' and Ben Jonson's Poem.]

—toole and we know MS. the fellow masked and us'd F's seale thereon seen Rex. [From the I.M. Poem.]

I lost favour, ergo, oppone'ts presume, as my ciphers at least do put it, to get such as sudde'ly turn playwright, witty or stale, under, wisht, yea, promist Judases. I to aide one writer—one which never liv'd in F. St A.'s service yet knows the deputie of two Kings doth F's fist most—. [From the Prologue to *Troilus and Cressida*.]

The failure of the 'plain text' to make sense argues against the validity of any message; but on the whole the fault is rare among Baconians. One of the few writers who shares this failing with Mrs Fiske is Joseph Martin Feely; and he has another in common with Mrs Clark, for the system he uses is as hard to understand as the messages he uses it to produce. Feely, a lawyer, made a hobby of deciphering Shakespeare and between 1931 and 1942 he wrote, and printed privately at Rochester, New York, five books setting out his various discoveries. He names his system 'Shakespeare's Maze'; and this is appropriate, for it is labyrinthine and tortuous in the extreme. Anyone who studies his entire published writings may at length discern two principles on which he seems to depend. The first consists in picking out certain of the vowels in a given series of words, and associating groups of these vowels with numbers; thus in

Times thrust through the Doublet, foure through the Hose
  E   U   OU   E OU E OUE OU   E

the vowel compound EOUE corresponds with the number 4. The vowels are the 'outer key' and the numbers the 'inner key'. His second principle is that from the vowels 'which mark the

deciphered passage', the counting 'runs up, or down, the stream of the outer text. The up-run is called an "ebbe"....
The several words marked off by the incidence of the counting of the three values or the inner key...together make up the cipher message.'

Even allowing that Feely's system is valid, and validly applied (we ourselves shall make no pronouncement, since we cannot understand either the method itself or its application), his work cannot be accepted as cryptologically sound. For his 'plain texts' are anything but plain, in spite of his claim that the 'series of words...makes running sense, in the condensed style of a cablegram'. It is difficult to find any sentence, among the thousands of decipherments, which is more than a crude caricature of the English language. The whole text is sprinkled with brackets, double brackets, oblique strokes and asterisks; a few sentences will be enough to convey the 'condensed style' of the messages. Here are some examples from *Shakespeare's Maze Further Deciphered* (1938):

To Highnesse person, // as Lords goe up, by end violent (carriage) best.*] Great we a (King) as much (belov'd).

((Lord:)) 'Though it ((were so)), man, why are departure you you not Life? Your (i.e. you are) a (Bastard) by Those past.'

((Will:)) 'Downe // Now injustice at themselves;] Death] themselves strike, the (i.e. "they" or "the (Queene") Death doing.'

Good, hast me old whose, word—'thy (jealousies) too and (i.e. hand); then thy fooleries did (but shew thee) inconstant.'

((Lord with)) oath: 'You bring ((her)) within.'

Feely himself seems to have been able to make some sense of the hundreds of pages of gibberish his books contain; at one point he interprets the decipherments to produce his own biography of the encipherer. This shadowy figure was apparently 'sprung basely from noble Italian blood'. He was educated in Florence, sang and acted in Italy, and later migrated to England where he became a tutor in Greek, mathematics, music, and languages. He joined the English intelligence service and returned to his native land; and then, his spell of duty done, he went back once more to England and 'rose to great prominence as a playwright and a gentleman, in court circles and in their theatrical appendage'. He was the constant and boon companion of lords and ladies; but this did not prevent his imprisonment, for a short time, for offending the king in his plays. After a number of biographical details of this kind, Feely concludes his story with the words: 'Here ends, for the nonce, the incomplete chronicle of...the manifold lover, the courtier, the actor, the exile, the lovechild.'

But while Feely is not alone in that his system and the results he produces are beyond understanding, his work is in one respect unique: he is the only man to use a cipher with the intent to prove that Shakespeare wrote the plays. He claims at any rate to have established that they were written by someone whose first name was 'Will' and whose last name contained 'Shake'; it may not sound Italian, but it makes a refreshing change.

The next system we shall consider is, on the face of it, far more impressive than Feely's; it was first put forward by an Englishman, Edward D. Johnson, in a booklet published by the Bacon Society in 1947 and entitled *Francis Bacon's Cipher Signatures*. Johnson believed that Bacon had hidden secret texts in Shakespeare's works, not in any haphazard way, but by the deliberate placing of the letters on the printed page. The letters of the hidden text bore definite spatial relationships to one another; in this way the element of chance could be eliminated, since 'it is mathematically impossible that the letters in the text have arranged themselves in a pattern...by accident'.

The best way to explain the method is to show it in action; we have chosen one of Johnson's examples, taken from the poem 'To the Reader', underneath the Droeshout portrait of Shakespeare at the beginning of the First Folio. Johnson begins by writing out the poem on squared paper (Fig. 7). From a study of this, he finds 'the author's signature boldly written across the first page of the Folio in such a way as to preclude any question of accident'. He has discovered letters 'the same distance apart from each other', which he displays in his second diagram (Fig. 8). Working step by step through three more diagrams, he finally arrives at the fourth, which yields the complete message, FR BACON AUTHOR AUTHOR AUTHOR (Fig. 9). It is slightly puzzling to find that the pattern contains only twenty-two letters, while the 'plain text'

	1	2	3	4	5	6	7	8	9	10	11	12	13	14	15	16	17	18	19	20	21	22	23	24	25	26	27	28	29	30	31	32
1	T	H	I	S	F	I	G	U	R	E	T	H	A	T	T	H	O	U	H	E	R	E	S	E	E	S	T	P	U	T		
2	I	T	W	A	S	F	O	R	G	E	N	T	L	E	S	H	A	K	E	S	P	E	A	R	E	C	U	T				
3	W	H	E	R	E	I	N	T	H	E	G	R	A	U	E	R	H	A	D	A	S	T	R	I	F	E						
4	W	I	T	H	N	A	T	U	R	E	T	O	O	U	T	D	O	O	T	H	E	L	I	F	E							
5	O	C	O	U	L	D	H	E	B	U	T	H	A	U	E	D	R	A	W	N	E	H	I	S	W	I	T					
6	A	S	W	E	L	L	I	N	B	R	A	S	S	E	A	S	H	E	H	A	T	H	H	I	T							
7	H	I	S	F	A	C	E	T	H	E	P	R	I	N	T	W	O	U	L	D	T	H	E	N	S	U	R	P	A	S	S	E
8	A	L	L	T	H	A	T	V	V	A	S	E	U	E	R	V	R	I	T	I	N	B	R	A	S	S	E					
9	B	U	T	S	I	N	C	E	H	E	C	A	N	N	O	T	R	E	A	D	E	R	L	O	O	K	E					
10	N	O	T	O	N	H	I	S	P	I	C	T	U	R	E	B	U	T	H	I	S	B	O	O	K	E						

Fig. 7.

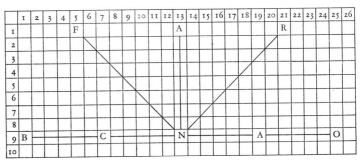

Fig. 8.

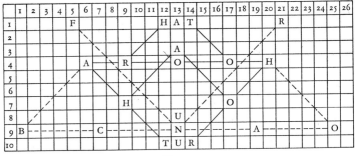

Fig. 9.

has twenty-five; Johnson obviously allows himself a certain amount of liberty in his interpretation of the diagrams. Not only do his rules permit him to use the same letter twice in the resultant message; it is also 'not necessary for the letters...to appear in their correct order, provided that they are the same distance apart from each other in the form of a pattern'. It further seems, from the diagrams reproduced above, that the letters do not really have to be 'the same distance apart', provided the pattern itself is symmetrical.

Granted these small privileges, Johnson extracts a number of other messages from various texts, including MWS IS BACON (which he explains as 'Master William Shakespeare is Bacon') from the Dedication to the Earls of Pembroke and Montgomery, and FR BACON HIDES AUTHOR from the Prologue of *Troilus and Cressida*. His work on the text of *Don Adriana's Letter* has the confident recommendation of Comyns Beaumont that it '*cannot* be refuted'; Johnson shares this confidence in his results, and issues a challenge to sceptics:

If after checking the signatures...the reader is still of the opinion that they are all accidental, the writer would ask him to try a small experiment. Let him take from any book, ancient or modern, 20 consecutive lines of prose or poetry, place the letters in a Table, and then try to see if he can make up any word out of the letters the same distance apart in the text in the form of a chain.

It was hard to resist this courteous request. We decided to use the text of one of Johnson's own examples; and the poem 'To the Reader' divulged the message 'No kidding, Francis Bacon: *I* wrote these plaies!—Shakespeare'. The diagram for our reading is shown in Fig. 10. Our message is nearly twice the length of Johnson's; it is a complete sentence; and it uses each letter of the diagram once and only once. But the disadvantage of this 'method' comes out very clearly here. Since our chosen letters do not have to 'appear in their correct order' (i.e. we can arrange them in any way we please), there may be several alternative 'messages' to choose from: amongst them, one (giving a very different sense to the pattern) runs: 'No kidding! I, Francis Bacon wrote these Shakespeare plaies.' This alone is enough to show that Johnson's method is worthless as a piece of cryptography.

A disciple of Johnson's, writing under the pseudonym of 'Arden', chose *Don Adriana's Letter* for a further series of

	1	2	3	4	5	6	7	8	9	10	11	12	13	14	15	16	17	18	19	20	21	22	23	24	25	26	27	28	29	30	31	32
1	T	H	I	S	F	I	G	U	R	E	T	H	A	T	T	H	O	U	H	E	R	E	S	E	E	S	T	P	U	T		
2	I	T	W	A	S	F	O	R	G	E	N	T	L	E	S	H	A	K	E	S	P	E	A	R	E	C	U	T				
3	W	H	E	R	E	I	N	T	H	E	G	R	A	U	E	R	H	A	D	A	S	T	R	I	F	E						
4	W	I	T	H	N	A	T	U	R	E	T	O	O	U	T	D	O	O	T	H	E	L	I	F	E							
5	O	C	O	U	L	D	H	E	B	U	T	H	A	U	E	D	R	A	W	N	E	H	I	S	W	I	T					
6	A	S	W	E	L	L	I	N	B	R	A	S	S	E	A	S	H	E	H	A	T	H	H	I	T							
7	H	I	S	F	A	C	E	T	H	E	P	R	I	N	T	W	O	U	L	D	T	H	E	N	S	U	R	P	A	S	S	E
8	A	L	L	T	H	A	T	V	V	A	S	E	U	E	R	V	V	R	I	T	I	N	B	R	A	S	S	E				
9	B	U	T	S	I	N	C	E	H	E	C	A	N	N	O	T	R	E	A	D	E	R	L	O	O	K	E					
10	N	O	T	O	N	H	I	S	P	I	C	T	U	R	E	B	U	T	H	I	S	B	O	O	K	E						

	1	2	3	4	5	6	7	8	9	10	11	12	13	14	15	16	17	18	19	20	21	22	23	24	25	26	27	28	29	30	31	32
1			I	S	F																R	E	S									
2	I				S			R	G								A	K			P				E							
3													A																			
4	W				N															E					E							
5		C											A										S									
6		S	E																			H	I									
7						C					P				T				D													
8	A	L				H	T					E		E					I		I			R	A							
9						N									N				D													
10	N	O		O																		B		O	K							

Fig. 10. 'No kidding, Francis Bacon: I wrote these plaies!—Shakespeare.'

	1	2	3	4	5	6	7	8	9	10	11	12	13	14	15	16	17	18	19
2	I	C	I	W	H	I	C	H	T	O	A	N	N	O	T	H	A	N	I
3	O	B	S	C	U	R	E	V	U	L	G	A	R	V	I	D	E	L	I
4	H	E	C	A	M	E	O	N	E	S	E	E	T	W	O	C	O	U	
5	T	H	E	K	I	N	G	W	H	Y	D	I	D	H	E	C	O	M	E
6	E	T	O	O	U	E	R	C	O	M	E	T	O	W	H	O	M	C	A
7	H	A	T	S	A	W	H	E	T	H	E	B	E	G	G	E	R	W	H
8	G	G	E	R	T	H	E	C	O	N	C	L	U	S	I	O	N	I	S
9	K	I	N	G	T	H	E	C	A	P	T	I	U	E	I	S	I	N	R
10	E	R	S	T	H	E	C	A	T	A	S	T	R	O	P	H	E	I	S
11	K	I	N	G	S	N	O	O	N	B	O	T	H	I	N	O	N	E	O
12	F	O	R	S	O	S	T	A	N	D	S	T	H	E	C	O	M	P	A
13	O	W	I	T	N	E	S	S	E	T	H	T	H	Y	L	O	W	L	I
14	I	M	A	Y	S	H	A	L	L	I	E	N	F	O	R	C	E	T	H
15	N	T	R	E	A	T	E	T	H	Y	L	O	U	E	I	W	I	L	L
16	O	R	R	A	G	G	E	S	R	O	A	D	E	S	F	O	R	T	I
17	E	X	P	E	C	T	I	N	G	T	H	Y	R	E	P	L	Y	I	P

Fig. 11. 'Arden's' message: 'See set my one sign C seal
tens signing—Francis Bacon.'

decipherments, which he recorded in *Baconiana* between spring 1951 and winter 1952. He concentrated on an internal section of the text: one of his messages is shown in Fig. 11. In case it is felt that our earlier parody of Johnson was an isolated example, in which we happened to choose a particularly vulnerable passage, we present a variation of 'Arden's' reading too. Taking the same text, and finding a symmetrical pattern (which he failed to do), we produce a message which makes better sense than his, and may even be nearer the truth (Fig. 12).

	1	2	3	4	5	6	7	8	9	10	11	12	13	14	15	16	17	18	19
2	I	C	I	W	H	I	C	H	T	O	A	N	N	O	T	H	A	N	I
3	O	B	S	C	U	R	E	V	U	L	G	A	R	V	I	D	E	L	I
4	H	E	E	C	A	M	E	O	N	E	S	E	E	T	W	O	C	O	U
5	T	H	E	K	I	N	G	W	H	Y	D	I	D	H	E	C	O	M	E
6	E	T	O	O	U	E	R	C	O	M	E	T	O	W	H	O	M	C	A
7	H	A	T	S	A	W	H	E	T	H	E	B	E	G	G	E	R	W	H
8	G	G	E	R	T	H	E	C	O	N	C	L	U	S	I	O	N	I	S
9	K	I	N	G	T	H	E	C	A	P	T	I	U	E	I	S	I	N	R
10	E	R	S	T	H	E	C	A	T	A	S	T	R	O	P	H	E	I	S
11	K	I	N	G	S	N	O	O	N	B	O	T	H	I	N	O	N	E	O
12	F	O	R	S	O	S	T	A	N	D	S	T	H	E	C	O	M	P	A
13	O	W	I	T	N	E	S	S	E	T	H	T	H	Y	L	O	W	L	I
14	I	M	A	Y	S	H	A	L	L	I	E	N	F	O	R	C	E	T	H
15	N	T	R	E	A	T	E	T	H	Y	L	O	U	E	I	W	I	L	L
16	O	R	R	A	G	G	E	S	R	O	A	D	E	S	F	O	R	T	I
17	E	X	P	E	C	T	I	N	G	T	H	Y	R	E	P	L	Y	I	P

Fig. 12. Our message: 'Shakespeare acclaimed true author.'

The main weakness of the system we have just discussed lies in the fact that the decipherer can arrange the letters of his message in any way he pleases. The same is true of the final cipher method we shall investigate in this chapter: it is the invention of William More, whose cryptographic treatise on Shakespeare was published at Birmingham in 1934. We have chosen to consider him because he is the only anti-Stratfordian to rely for his 'proof' on a combination of the substitution and transposition methods in cryptography.

As a kind of appetizer, before he gets down to work in earnest, More gives a brief display of his versatility, singling out a few words and phrases and subjecting them to a variety of treatments. Among his examples he takes the words 'vnum cita', spoken by the Page in Act v, sc. i of *Love's Labour's Lost*. More begins by recalling the cryptic legend, found in an English parish church, which ran:

PRSVRYPRFCTMNVRKPTHSPRCPTSTN

and which was finally interpreted by inserting the vowel E in suitable places, to read:

PERSEVERE, YE PERFECT MEN, EVER KEEP THESE PRECEPTS TEN.

This, he thinks, will help with the elucidation of 'vnum cita' where

we have...a similar kind of Cipher but much shorter, and with two vowels left in '*vnum*' for our guidance, viz., '*v*' and '*u*'; which letters were of course interchangeable at the time *Love's Labour's Lost* was written. All that we need do when solving this Cipher is to supply two missing letters, each of which is the vowel 'o'. We thus have: UNUoMo CITA. Hence: UN UoMO CITA. This may be read either as 'A man name', or, in its transposed form, 'Name a man'. Apart from the meaning of these words, the important point that we have to consider is this: The words are in *Italian*! Now, why should they be?...Possibly the object is to suggest that the *answer* to this request is in Italian. At all events, let us keep well in mind the existence of that language.

This sudden excursion into a new tongue is only one of More's difficulties; another is that his various decipherments are fragmentary and obscure. But their full import will emerge, he promises, when the whole work is completed and the bits and pieces can be assembled in their correct order; the reader, 'in his consideration of the decipherments he has met or will meet with during this part of the inquiry...should not expect to find a complete meaning'.

More shows himself to have a fairly sound grasp of the principles of cryptology, and he discusses the conditions for validity and the criteria for judging cipher methods at some length in the subsequent pages. But in the end he oversteps the boundaries:

Most Ciphers can be placed in one of two categories; they are either Substitutional or Transpositional. In a Substitutional Cipher the original letters are changed into other letters, which thus act as substitutes. Any given letter can be represented by any other letter; but the change must be made in accordance with some method, or system, so that when the recipient of the Cipher applies this method, in its reversed order, he is able to unfold the secret meaning.

The slipperiness lies in the 'Transpositional Cipher', which turns out to consist in nothing more than rearranging the letters of one text to produce another, without any system whatever. The decipherer has absolute freedom of choice in his rearrangement, since there is in this case nothing which corresponds to applying the 'method in its reversed order'—there is no method to apply. But More continues undeterred:

So far, we have dealt with 'pure' Substitutional and Transpositional Ciphers. It is possible, however, to combine these two classes, with the object of making a Cipher more difficult to solve. For an example of the combined class of Ciphers we shall take the word ARMY into its Transpositional Cipher, MARY, and apply the Substitutional system to it by changing its letters one place to the right....Hence we have: NBSZ. It will be observed that the word ARMY in the combined Substitutional and Transpositional Cipher, NBSZ, is more difficult to find than either of the two 'pure' classes... that is to say, it would be so to anyone who was not acquainted with the derivation....

More admits that his substitution-transposition cipher 'is not one that is greatly used at the present time'; but to give it an air of respectability he attributes it to 'the celebrated German scholar Johannes Trithemius...who is justly considered the founder of Cryptography as it is now understood'. It is quite untrue that Trithemius ever employed such a 'system'; nor is it the case, as More asserts, that 'it was in vogue during the sixteenth and seventeenth centuries'. No cryptographer at any time has used, or is ever likely to use, a method which introduces such a glaring source of ambiguity; it is valueless, because of the freedom of choice allowed to the decipherer in picking suitable 'transpositions'.

More, though, finds a use for it in the same scene of *Love's Labour's Lost* as that in which the phrase 'vnum cita' occurs; he now investigates the statement by the Pedant (Holofernes), which appears in the First Folio as 'Bome boon for boon prescian, a little scratcht, 'twil serve.' Concentrating on the words 'Bome boon for boon prescian,' he remarks:

These words constitute a Cipher designed in accordance with one of the systems invented by Trithemius, and it is therefore based on his alphabet. The decipherment is carried out as follows: All the letters that occupy 'odd' positions (1, 3, 5, 7, etc.) must be changed into letters that stand 11 places to the right in the Trithemius alphabet. Here we would mention that whenever the Key-number for this kind of Cipher is 11 there is the following advantage from a decipherer's point of view. It is quite immaterial whether the count is made to the right or to the left, for the results are identical. This identity is owing to the simple fact that 11 is half of 22, the number of letters in the Trithemius alphabet. The Key can therefore be either '11r' or '11l', but we shall use the former. We thus have:

```
11r   11r   11r   11r   11r   11r   11r   11r   11r   11r   11r   11r
  B  O  M  E  B  O  O  N  F  O  R  B  O  O  N  P  R  E  S  C  I  A  N
```

The substitutes for these 'odd' positions letters are to be found in the following alphabet.

```
A B C D E F G H I K L M N O P Q R S T V X Z
```

To avoid the trouble of counting for each letter, we can move all the letters in this alphabet 11 places to the right, and arrange them under the original alphabet, thus:

```
A B C D E F G H I K L M N O P Q R S T V X Z
M N O P Q R S T V X Z A B C D E F G H I K L
```

We are here able to take all the 'odd' letters of the Cipher, i.e. B, M, B, O, F, R, O, N, R, S, I, N, and obtain their substitutes from the lower alphabet. The Cipher now stands thus:

```
 - O - E - O - N - O - B - O - P - E - C - A -
N - A - N - C - R - F - C - B - F - G - V - B
N O A E N O C N R O F B C O B P F E G C V A B
```

The Substitutional decipherment is completed, and we next proceed to the Transpositional.

```
N O A E N O C N R O F B C O B P F E G C V A B
- - - E - - - - - - - - - - - - - G - - - -   E.G.,
N O - - - - - - - - - - C O - - - - - - A B   BACONO
- - - - - - - - R O - - - - - P - - - - - -   PRO
- - A - N O C - - - - - - B - - - - - - - -   BACON.
- - - - - - - N - - F B - - - - - - C V - -   F.B.C.NU
- - - - - - - - - - - - - - - F E - - - - -   FE.
```

Hence, e.g., BACONO pro BACON. F.B.c.nu.fe.

More has to do a little interpreting of the letters 'F.B.c.nu.fe.' before reaching his complete decipherment; and the end-product reads 'e.g. BACONO Pro BACON / F. Baconus fecit'. He explains that the solution by the substitution-transposition cipher is 'a little scratcht', as the second half of the *Love's Labour's Lost* quotation implies; he has repaired the minor blemishes.

We have already claimed that the method is invalid; to drive our point home, we show that More's solution is not unique. Granting his substitutional step, in which half the letters are converted by moving them eleven places to the right, we start with the same sequence NOAEN... and use it to produce a quite different result:

```
N O A E N O C N R O F B C O B P F E G C V A B
N O A - - - C - - - - B - - - - - - - - - - -   BACON
- - - - - - - - - - - - - - - - - G - - A B     BAG
- - - E N O - - - - - - - - - P - - - - - -     OPEN
- - - - - - - - R O - - C - - - - E - - V - -   COVER
- - - - - - - - - - - F - - O - - F - - - - -   OFF
- - - - - - - N - - - - - - B - - - - C - - -   BCN
```

BACON BAG OPEN. COVER OFF. BACON

'A little scratcht' here means, as in Moore's example, that there is a small defect—the 'A' and 'O' of the signature 'BACON' are lacking.

In exposing the failings of Johnson's and More's 'systems', we have already strayed into the territory of anagrams. These are a common feature of Baconian cryptography; it is time now to give them some more general attention.

CHAPTER VII

ACROSTICS AND ANAGRAMS

A NUMBER of anti-Stratfordians rely on proofs of author-ship based on anagrams or acrostics, or more usually on a combination of both. Acrostic devices have the ad-vantage that, unlike ciphers which depend on accidents of page-numbering or particular kinds of type, they leave no doubt that the author of the open text must also have been responsible for any hidden message—once it is established that one exists. For even if a claim to authorship were found in the First Folio, using Bacon's biliteral cipher, this in itself would not be conclusive. The message could have been inserted by the printer himself, playing an elaborate hoax on posterity. But in the case of acrostics, any message found must have been inserted by the man who wrote the open text; and to change or insert any hidden message would be impossible without changing the open text itself. If, therefore, any genuine messages of this kind exist, they must be taken as conclusive. We shall go on to investigate a number of related claims, to see whether they are genuine or not; but first it will be as well to give some account of anagrams and acrostics in general.

We shall begin with anagrams, since we have already men-tioned them briefly in ch. II in connection with the discoveries of Huygens and Galileo. The word 'anagram' comes from the Greek ἀναγραμματίзειν, meaning 'to transpose letters'. 'Ana-gram' is a noun, but it is also commonly used as a verb in the place of the longer 'anagrammatize'. To anagram means to change some word or phrase into some other word or phrase by changing the order of its letters (e.g. live, veil, evil and vile are all anagrams of one another). In order to be 'perfect' an anagram should not only involve a rearrangement of letters without additions or deletions: the resulting word or words should in some way comment upon the original. The following are examples.[1]

[1] Found in Prof. Roger W. Holmes' *The Rhyme of Reason* (New York, 1939).

Radical reform	Rare mad frolic
Presbyterian	Best in prayer
The midnight ride of Paul Revere	Rider gave hint of peril due
Washington crossing the Delaware	He saw the ragged Continentals row, *or* A hard howling tossing water scene

Anagramming has always been popular; in the sixteenth and seventeenth centuries all the best people did it; nowadays newspapers run anagrammatic competitions and people play anagrammatic parlour games such as 'Lexicon' or 'Scrabble'. Most of our readers will be familiar with anagrams in some form, and will know that the number of possible rearrangements of any given word or phrase is often surprisingly high; and though Dryden exaggerated when he suggested that by anagramming one could 'torture one poor word ten thousand ways', it remains true that there is an element of indeterminacy in forming anagrams, and one of which Baconians are quick to take advantage. The method itself, as has been noted before, involves unkeyed transposition and therefore is very flexible; it is only a matter of juggling with the letters to form a new sequence. There need be no system in the rearrangement, and no fixed rules.

The longest English words so far discovered to be anagrams of each other are INTERROGATIVES and TERGIVERSATION; the longest anagram on record is in Spanish, and consists of the name and full titles of the Marques de Astorga, anagrammatized into eight lines of about 140 letters, in a book entitled *Francisco de la Torre y Sebil, Luzes de la Aurora dias del Sol.*[1]

We should mention, for the sake of completeness, a special type of anagram known as the 'palindrome'. Here the letters form the same word or phrase when read backwards (e.g. Madam, Hannah, Rotator). There are some well-known examples of palindromic sentences in 'Madam, I'm Adam', 'Was it a cat I saw?', and the judgment on Napoleon, 'Able

[1] Those who want to read more on the subject should refer to H. B. Wheatley's monograph *Of Anagrams* (London, 1862); there is also some interesting material in I. D'Israeli's *Curiosities of Literature*, vol. II (London, 1834) and in William S. Walsh's *Handy-Book of Literary Curiosities* (Philadelphia, 1893).

was I ere I saw Elba'. A less familiar medieval palindrome is 'Lewd I did live, evil did I dwel'; but the most impressive of all is in Latin, and consists of two palindromic sentences concerning St Martin, Bishop of Tours. St Martin, according to legend, was walking to Rome to consult the Pope, when he was met by the Devil. Transforming the Devil into a mule, St Martin had a less exhausting journey; but while he goaded the animal forward by repeatedly making a cross on its back, the mule is said to have protested: 'Signa te, signa; temere me tangis et angis. Roma tibi subito motibus ibit amor' (Cross, cross yourself; you annoy and vex me needlessly. Through my exertions, Rome, your desire, will soon be near.). D'Israeli comments: 'The reader has only to take the pains of reading the lines backwards, and he will find himself just where he was after all his fatigue.' The inventor of the palindrome is said to have been Sotades, a Greek poet of the third century B.C., who became such a bore that the reigning Ptolemy had him thrown into the sea.

The acrostic has an equally long history.[1] The word comes from the Greek ἄκρος meaning 'extreme' and στίχος meaning 'row', or line of verse. It refers to a composition, usually in verse, in which the initial, final or other chosen letters of the lines have been arranged to make a word or series of words. In its simplest form the acrostic spells out a word letter by letter, taking the initial letters of consecutive lines of the open text. The Greeks of the Alexandrine period were particularly fond of composing acrostic verses.

'Acronymy' or the composing of names from the initial letters of longer official titles, is a comparatively modern phenomenon. The word 'Cabal', though in earlier use, came to be associated with a particular ministry under Charles II, because it happened to be an acronym of the initial letters of the names of the leaders: *C*lifford, *A*shley, *B*uckingham,

---

[1] Acrostics are simple examples of concealment ciphers; they are a special kind of transposition cipher, but unlike anagrams they do have a controlling element which is sometimes rigorous enough to be called a key. Their presence is unmistakable when, for example, the initial letters of an appreciable number of consecutive lines of text (with no omissions or exceptions) spell out a word, phrase or sentence.

*A*rlington and *L*auderdale; recent examples are UNESCO (for *U*nited *N*ations *E*ducational, *S*cientific and *C*ultural *O*rganization) and CARE (*C*o-operative for *A*merican *R*emittances *E*verywhere).

The earliest known acrostician was the Latin poet Ennius, who died in 169 B.C.; Cicero tells us that he wrote a poem in which the initial letters of the lines form the words *Q. Ennius fecit*. Acrostics have been used at various times since, and sometimes to convey the most surprising messages. The first printed example is to be found in the *Hypnerotomachia Poliphili* (The Strife of Love in a Dream), published by Aldus in Venice in 1499. The authorship was anonymous, but the initial letters of the first words of each section, taken in order, spell out the message 'Poliam frater Franciscus Columna peramavit' (Brother Francis Colonna passionately loves Polia); the monk, unable to declare his unspiritual affections, was driven to write a book around them. Professor Balthasar van der Pol has called our attention to a more recent example in a serious mathematical treatise, *Invariantentheorie*, by Ronald Weitzenböck (Gröningen, 1923). The author seems to have been a violent, if secretive Francophobe: the initial letters of the initial words of successive sentences in his Foreword, with breaks for paragraphs, spell *Neder mit den Franzosen!* (Down with the French!).

Besides messages of love and hate, acrostics have been used to convey prophecies; in the *De Divinatione*, Cicero remarks that the Sybils always put their prophecies in this form. In one example attributed to the Erythrean Sibyl the initial letters form the words (in Greek) 'Jesus Christ, the Son of God, the Saviour'. The initial letters of this Greek formula had traditionally been indicated by acronymy by the word ΙΧΘΥΣ, a fish, and the fish had thus come to have an emblematic significance among early Christians. This example of an acrostic within an acrostic is excelled by Boccaccio in his marathon effort in *Amorosa Visione* (1521); the poem is dedicated to Maria d'Aquino, a young married woman, the natural daughter of King Robert of Italy, and the whole work of fifty cantos forms an acrostic on a grand scale. The first letters of the first lines of successive verses make a 1501-letter acrostic, which is itself in the form of two *sonétti* and a *madrigale*. The first of these acrostic sonnets carries within it a secondary acrostic, for the initial letters of its first, third, fifth, seventh and ninth lines spell MARIA. Altogether a most worthy tribute.

Not everyone, of course, regards the forming of acrostics as worth the effort. Addison found it difficult to decide whether the inventor of the anagram or of the acrostic was the greater blockhead, and Samuel Butler acidly remarked that the acrostician 'used to lay the outside of his verses even, like a bricklayer, by a line of rhyme and acrostic, and fill the middle with rubbish'. Walsh, in his *Handy-Book of Literary Curiosities*, comments that the business of composing acrostics 'was carried to its most ridiculous and wasteful excess by the Elizabethan poets'. Certainly, they were very popular at the time. To take a case in point, Sir John Davies, in a burst of patriotic zeal, composed a series of twenty-six poems, entitled *Hymns to Astraea*, each of which is an acrostic on the words *Elizabetha Regina*; but none of them shows much more than a stern mechanical determination. A more readable example, perhaps, is the poem written in memory of Walsingham; we set this out below, so that the reader can see for himself that the first letters of each line, taken in order, disclose the name 'Sir Francis Walsingham'.

> Shall Honour, Fame, and Titles of Renowne,
> In Clods of Clay be thus inclosed still?
> Rather will I, though wiser Wits may frowne,
> For to inlarge his Fame extend my Skill.
> Right, gentle Reader, be it knowne to thee,
> A famous Knight doth here interred lye,
> Noble by Birth, renowned for Policie,
> Confounding Foes, which wrought our Jeopardy.
> In Forraine Countries their Intents he knew,
> Such was his zeal to do his Country good,
> When Dangers would by Enemies ensue,
> As well as they themselves, he understood.
> Launch forth ye Muses into Streams of Praise,
> Sing, and sound forth Praise-worthy Harmony;
> In *England* Death cut off his dismall Dayes,
> Not wronged by Death, but by false Trechery.

Grudge not at this imperfect Epitaph;
Herein I have exprest my simple Skill,
As the First-fruits proceeding from a Graffe:
Make then a better whosoever will.
    Disce quid es, quid eris;
    Memor esto quod morieris.   E.W.

This example is a straightforward case of the simple acrostic, using the initial letters of each line. However, there may be several variations on the basic theme. The simple telestic, for example, takes the final letter of the last word in each line; the progressive simple acrostic takes the first letter of the first line, the second letter of the second line, the third of the third, and so on; the progressive simple telestic likewise takes the last letter in the first line, the last but one in the second line, the last but two in the third line, and so on. As an example of the progressive acrostic, we take a poem by Edgar Allan Poe, which spells out the name of Frances Sargent Osgood:

For her this rhyme is penned, whose luminous eyes,
    Brightly expressive as the twins of Leda,
Shall find her own sweet name, that nestling lies
    Upon the page, enwrapped from every reader.
Search narrowly the lines!—they hold a treasure
    Divine—a talisman—an amulet
That must be worn at heart. Search well the measure—
    The words—the syllables! Do not forget
The trivialest point, or you may lose your labor!
    And yet there is in this no Gordian knot
Which one might not undo without a sabre,
    If one could merely comprehend the plot.
Enwritten upon the leaf where now are peering
    Eyes scintillating soul, there lie *perdus*
Three eloquent words oft uttered in the hearing
    Of poets, by poets—as the name is a poet's, too.
Its letters, although naturally lying
    Like the knight Pinto—Mendez Ferdinando—
Still form a synonym for Truth.—Cease trying!
    You will not read the riddle, though you do the best you
      can do.

Mrs Osgood, not to be outdone, retaliated by writing a poem not to Poe, but to another of her admirers, Rufus W.

Griswold; in this she linked his name with hers in a double progressive acrostic, her name beginning on the first letter and his on the last of the first line, and both names progressing through the lines.

> *F*or one, whose being is to mine a sta*r*
> *T*rembling I weave in lines of love and f*u*n
> Wh*a*t Fame before has echoed near and *f*ar
> A so*n*net if you like—I'll give yo*u* one
> To be *c*ross-questioned ere its truth is *s*olv'd
> Here v*e*iled and hidden in a rhyming *w*reath
> A name i*s* turned with mine in cunnin*g* sheath
> And unle*s*s by some marvel ra*r*e evolv'd
> Foreve*r* f*o*lded from all *i*dler eyes
> Silent and *s*ecret still it trea*s*ured lies
> Whilst mine *g*oes winding on*w*ard, as a rill
> Thro' a deep wo*o*d in unseen *j*oyance dances
> Calling in mel*o*dy's bewi*l*dering thrill
> Whilst through *d*im leaves its partner *d*reams and glances.

When one looks more closely at this, it appears that while spelling her own name with punctilious care, the poetess was less considerate in her treatment of her admirer; the tenth letter from the end in the tenth line is in fact an 'a', and the fourteenth from the end in the fourteenth line an 'e', so that the name actually obtained if the rules are followed is 'Griawole'. Although one is inclined to forgive her these two slips, her composition is a useful reminder of a fundamental point.

There may be any number of varieties of acrostic, but each has one property in common. The mistakes in Mrs Osgood's poem remind us that it is possible to err; but from the very fact that mistakes can be made, and rules broken, it follows that rules do exist. In every acrostic, the rules for selecting the letters of the secret text are invariable, and the selection follows a fixed pattern; moreover, the selected letters are chosen in a particular order, and the rules for setting them out in the form of a text are rigid and inflexible. It is never a matter of taking, say, the first letter of the first line, the seventh and tenth of the second line, and the fourth of the third line; nor is it a matter of rearranging these letters until we find an anagram of them which makes sense.

This must be true of any acrostic whose existence is not to be open to doubt. Suppose, for instance, that the initial letters of the poem to Walsingham, quoted earlier, had occurred in the order L R S N M G S W N A I H S A R F I C A I, or A A A C F G H I I I L M N N R R-S S S W. Would it then have been certain that the name ' Sir Francis Walsingham' had been deliberately inserted as an acrostic? Hardly. This is an important point for, as we shall see, a number of proofs of authorship begin by citing authentic acrostics and then go on to descend the slippery slope of anagrammatic invention. To take a valid cryptographic system and adulterate it to the point where it becomes utterly invalid is not to prove anything in the text; it is only to suggest ingenuity or perverse determination in the investigator.

Having set out the general conditions which genuine acrostics must satisfy, there are two special points we must make before getting to work on the Baconians' claims. We have already remarked that acrostics were popular in Eliza-bethan literature; it should also be stressed that spelling in those days was erratic. Sir John Salusbury, who was as devoted to acrostics as he was to a lady called Dorothy Halsall, enfolded her name in poem after poem.[1] One of them runs:

> *T*ormented heart in thral*l*, *Y*ea thrall to loue,
> *R*especting wil*l*, *H*eart-breaking gaine doth grow,
> *E*ver DOLOBELI*A*, *T*ime so will proue,
> *B*inding distres*s*e, *O* gem wilt thou allowe,
> *T*his fortune my wil*l* Repose-lesse of ease,
> *V*nlesse thou LED*A*, *O*uer-spread my heart,
> *C*utting all my rut*h*, dayne *D*isdaine to cease,
> *I* yield to fate, and welcome endles *S*mart.

This, with occasional irregularities, conceals the name CVTBERT (Dorothy's husband) reading the initial letters up-wards from the seventh line, and the two parts of the name DOROTHY HALSALL as the letters on either side of the break in the middle of each line; the initials I. S. (for Iohn Salusbury) appear as the first letter of the first word and the first letter of the last word in the final line.

But in another and longer poem he uses a series of acrostics

See Bryn Mawr College Monographs, vol. XIV (1913).

to spell out five names; here the ubiquitous Dorothy appears as DOROTHI HALSALL, Salusbury as IOHN SALESBVRYE, and the rest of the *dramatis personae* as FRANSIS WILOWBI, ELIZABETH WOLFRESTONE and ROBERT PARRYE. In all, Salusbury uses six different versions of his own name in various acrostic signatures; spells the name Francis as Fransis wherever it suits him; regards I and IE as interchangeable with Y; and replaces J's with I's or I's with J's according to whim. This disregard for absolute consistency provides an argument for anti-Stratfordians, in that they are often able to cite genuine examples of the various spellings, abbreviations and forms of title to which they resort.

The second point in their favour is that acrostics have unquestionably been used to establish claims to authorship. A striking example is found in an anonymous Latin work published in 1616. The consecutive initial letters of each of the fifty-three sections into which the book is divided spell, without a single deviation, the sentence 'Franciscus Godwinvvs Landavensis Episcopus hos conscripsit', that is, 'Francis Godwin, Bishop of Llandaff, wrote these lines'. In another case, a Spanish treatise on the history of New Mexico, published in Cadiz in 1812, the author was ostensibly a Count of Torene, Don Pedro Baptista Pino; but his ghost writer was not to be denied all credit for his work. The first letters of successive sentences, beginning on p. 43, with paragraphs for breaks between words, reveal the name Juan Lopez Cancelada; a surreptitious but none the less certain manifestation of the ghostly hand which held the pen.

These are only two of a number of instances which could be cited; but what makes it true that they, and the others, are genuine cases of cryptography is that the validity of the deciphered text and the inflexibility of the systems employed are obvious. In other words, they satisfy the criteria laid down in ch. II. In each case, there is no room to doubt that they were put there by the deliberate intent of the author; the length of the hidden text, and the absolutely rigid order in which the letters appear, combine to make it enormously improbable that they just happened to be there by accident.

Enough has been said to clear the ground for our subsequent investigations. We should not be surprised if it is claimed that anagrams or acrostics appear in Shakespeare's works, for they abounded in the literature of the time; nor should we be surprised if these devices concern the authorship of the works, for they have often been used to this end. We should even be tolerant of variable and erratic spelling, for this was to some extent a common Elizabethan practice. The only thing we need insist on is that the systems used should satisfy the conditions for validity to which we have drawn attention. With this single demand, we turn to the anagram- and acrostic-hunters themselves.

CHAPTER VIII

THE LONG WORD AND OTHER ANAGRAMS

THE Northumberland Manuscript provides Baconians with one of their most useful pieces of evidence. This collection of papers, discovered in Northumberland House, London, in 1867, is a set of scribbled notes believed to have been written by John Davies, a copyist who may at some time before 1592 have been employed by Francis Bacon. The first page of the manuscript contains, among a number of other disconnected words and phrases, the names of Shakespeare and Bacon; and on the same page the word 'honorificabilitudini' also appears. This is a contracted form of the famous 'long word', found in Act v, sc. 1 of *Love's Labour's Lost*, when the Clown remarks: 'I marvell thy M. hath not eaten thee for a word, for thou art not so long by the head as honorificabilitudinitati-bus: Thou art easier swallowed then a flapdragon.' The same word is also found in the collected papers of Francis Bacon in the British Museum, in the form of a diagram:

ho
hono
honori
honorifi
honorifica
honorificabi
honorificabili
honorificabilitu
honorificabilitudi
honorificabilitudini
honorificabilitudinita
honorificabilitudinitati
honorificabilitudinitatibus

These facts, taken together, are of course hardly conclusive That a scrivener linked the names (both pretty well known to Londoners) of Bacon and Shakespeare on a page of rough notes,

PLATE IV

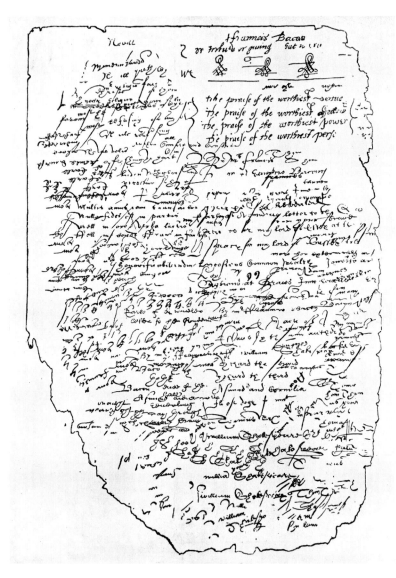

Northumberland Manuscript, f. 1.

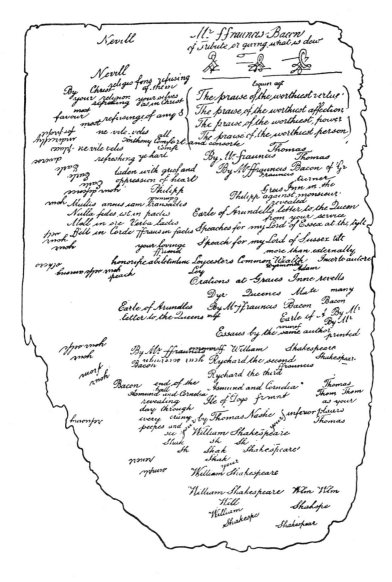

Fig. 13.   Modern script facsimile of Northumberland Manuscript, f. 1.

and also wrote out a long and unusual word found in the writings of both of them, by itself provides only a tenuous thread of reasoning to uphold a weighty conclusion. Those whose aim it was to identify the two authors seem to have realized this, for at the turn of the last century there appeared a whole succession of monographs designed to strengthen the case by arguments derived from the long word.

The first in the field was an American. In an article in *The Conservator* (Philadelphia, 1897), entitled 'Are the Shakespeare Plays signed by Francis Bacon?', Dr Isaac Hull Platt answered his own question with an uncompromising affirmative. His reasons for doing so were based on anagrams he had constructed from the long word in its various forms, and from 'acrostics' in the plays. Here are two examples of his acrostic method, taken from the text of *Hamlet*:

> I*f* you have h*i*therto *con*ce*a*led this sight let *it* be te*n*able in your silence still.
> FIRCONAITNAB (an anagram of FR. BACONI NATI)
> The *fu*ne*r*all *b*a*k*t me*a*ts did *c*oldley fur*n*ish forth the marriage tables.
> FNRBAATCONIO (an anagram of FR. BACONI NATI)

Platt's manipulations with the abbreviated form of the word in the Northumberland Manuscript, honorificabilitudini, convinced him that it was a cryptic way of writing the words 'initio hi ludi Fr. Bacono'; which, he explained, is Latin for 'These plays, in the inception, Francis Bacon's'. But he was not entirely satisfied with his efforts: 'The sentence is incomplete in that it has no verb; moreover, it fails to make a very definite statement. These would appear to be the reasons for its rejection and the selection of the longer form.' Platt accordingly went on to consider the version of the word as it appears in *Love's Labour's Lost*. He divided this into two parts, writing the first backwards:

(1) BACIFIRONOH

(2) ILITUDINITATIBUS

He derived from the first the 'signature' FR BACONO and from the second the words LUDI TUITI NATI. With the letters left over, he formed a third section:

(3) HIIIBS

which he anagrammed into HI SIBI. Finally, rearranging the words into a more convenient form, he extracted his 'message':

HI LUDI, TUITI SIBI, FR. BACONO NATI

which he translated as 'These plays, produced by Francis Bacon, guarded for themselves'.

This complex performance was intended to suggest that there was some kind of system in the steps towards Platt's conclusion: that the word had been deliberately constructed to conceal the sentence he derived. But—apart from the objection that there is (1) no good reason to write the first section of the word backwards if one is going to anagram it anyway; (2) no clear indication why the redundant letters should be made to form a third section to take care of the letters left after Platt had wrested some sense out of the first two; and (3) no attempt to justify his rearranging the words themselves, once the letters have been rearranged—there is a more serious flaw in the argument. Platt's message, when translated, does not seem to make very good sense (what is it for a play to 'guard for itself'?); and further (as W. H. Smith was quick to point out in the *Quarterly Review* of July 1898) the Latin is not Latin at all, nor any other language, living or dead; if Bacon could write the *Novum Organum* he could hardly be credited with such solecisms.

Platt was stung by his critics into defending himself at length, in *Bacon's Cryptograms in Shake-speare, and other Studies* (1905). He agreed with those who ridiculed him that the Latin in his various anagrams was 'somewhat unusual'; but he claimed to have the support of eminent Latinists in England, Ireland and Canada for his claim that it was nevertheless 'correct Latin'.

Following Platt's trail, the German writer Edwin Bormann (a prolific author of Baconian literature) produced in Leipzig in 1902 his *Der Shakespeare-Dichter: Wer War's?*, in which he gave a historical account of the long word as a prelude to an orgy of anagramming. His products included half a dozen phrases in a

Latin even odder than Platt's and an additional body of material derived by putting the word in a circle and reading it clockwise and counter-clockwise. He managed to invest Bacon with a rather heavy sense of fun; one of his anagrams reads 'O subitat in id utili: Baconus ironicus' (Oh, he keeps concealing something of advantage in it: that ironical Bacon).

Other variations of differing degrees of ingenuity by other writers have appeared from time to time. Some anagrams are in English; for example, one version (*Baconiana*, April 1902) runs 'But thus I told Franiiiiii Bacon'. The last word but one, it is explained, is Fran followed by iiiiii, or 6 in Roman numerals: adopting the French pronunciation, Fran-6 yields Francis, and *voilà*! The same source produces the anagram 'Fair uision Bacon built it, hid it', but the author, who signs himself 'E.L.', says he prefers the first alternative. Another enthusiast, Neal H. Ewing, in *The Catholic World* in November 1906, wrote the long word backwards, omitted two of the I's and the final O and H, and produced 'Subitat nid utili Bacfron'; by 'reversed tmesis' Bacfron yields Fr. Bacon: this, Ewing claims, is a stricter anagram than Platt's. Another reading depends on even more drastic deletion: omitting 'such fiery numbers as the prompting eyes' (in plainer words, all the letters 'i'), we have 'honorfcablt'; this, without the initial and final pairs of letters, is an anagram of Fr. Bacon. (There must be easier ways of leaving one's name for posterity.) Bacon's is not the only name to be found, either; one of the more outlandish messages runs 'Ubi Italicus ibi Danti honor fit' (Where there is an Italian, there honour is paid to Dante).

One of the later, but not least impressive, anagrammatists was Sir Edwin Durning-Lawrence. The title he chose for his book (published in 1910) is indicative of his conviction: avoiding the interrogative form, it proclaimed *Bacon is Shakespeare*. Sir Edwin devoted a fair proportion of his space to the long word, and what he called 'its correct anagrammatic equivalent'. This spondaic hexameter, 'Hi lu-di F Ba-co-nis na-ti tui-ti/or-bi', he translated as 'These plays, F. Bacon's offspring, are preserved for the world'. Sir Edwin was willing to admit that 'from a word containing so large a number of letters as twenty-seven, it is evident we can obtain very numerous words and phrases'. But words and phrases were not to the point: he assured his readers that 'it surpasses the wit of man to construct any sentence other than the revealed sentence'.

Sir Edwin went on to add numerical proof to anagrammatic skill. His ingenuity was impressive: finding that in the First Folio the word, twenty-seven letters long, fell on the 27th line of p. 136, and observing that it was the 151st word on the page, and had a numerological value of 287 (a highly significant 'magic number' as we shall soon see), he proceeded to explain the importance of these facts. His conclusion was that the word was skilfully and deliberately contrived to appear where it did in the First Folio; its position was pregnant with significance.

What can be said of these and the many other attempts to find messages in the long word, in order to strengthen the force of the inferences drawn by Baconians from the Northumberland Manuscript? In the first place, the coincidence in Bacon's, Shakespeare's and the scribe's use of the same word is not so striking as it appears. There is some evidence that it was a popular nonsense-word of the period; it is at any rate clear that it was not invented by Bacon. The first printed occurrence is to be found in a *Catholicon*, by Giovanni da Genova; this book, a Latin grammar-cum-dictionary, was published in Mainz in 1460. (Another form, honorificabilitudinibus, appears in *Table de l'ancien philosophe Cebes, natif de Thebes*, 1529.) It could scarcely be claimed that a writer some hundred years before either Bacon or Shakespeare was born invented the word specifically to conceal messages such as 'These plays, F. Bacon's offspring, are preserved for the world'.

Quite apart from the word's origin, the prolific and diverse labour of the anagrammatists, rather than strengthening their case, is itself a sufficient rebuttal. If the long word had been deliberately planted as a text to conceal a cipher message, it would have to have been chosen to yield one plain, unambiguous message. As it is, as many different 'solutions' emerge as there are different 'solvers'. Anyone can make of the word whatever he manages to make; but whatever he makes of it, someone else is sure to produce an alternative. The effort is damned from the start, for the process is without any fixed rules, without any unique solution, and without any cryptological validity.

There are other Shakespearean words in plenty which have been odd enough to catch the attention of the anagram-hunters. One or two of these hunters have strayed from the track from time to time: for instance, Ben Haworth-Booth in *Baconiana* of April 1905 announced his discovery of a variant of the long word in *Don Quixote*, and this variant, sorbonico-ficabilitvdinistally, yielded for him the message 'O in italics it is by old Fr. Bacon L.V.I.' (the meaning of the last three letters remains obscure). *Don Quixote* is a new and unexpected addition to the list of Bacon's works; for the most part, however, the anagrammatists have kept their eyes on Shakespeare. Another popular source in *Love's Labour's Lost* is the phrase 'Bome boon for boon prescian'.[1] Platt discerned in it the message 'Pro bono orbis F. Bacon e nemo'; and finding in the next words that 'a little scratcht, 'twill serve' he put a 'little scratch' over the e, to make it 'é', or 'est'; his message thus became, in translation, 'For the good of all, F. Bacon is nameless'. The Baconians who followed his example, and produced alternative renderings, took themselves to be adding to the weight of evidence for Bacon's authorship; they were in fact destroying their case with every new version that appeared.

Bacon's will might naturally be thought a promising text for exploration; and indeed, anti-Stratfordians have worked on a certain passage of it (which differs in different editions of the complete works; this is Tenison's version):

For my Name and Memory, I leave it to Foreign Nations and to mine own Country-men, after some Time be passed over.

John Moody Emerson produced an ingenious 'plain text' (*Two Anagrams*, 1912):

---

[1] From an exchange between Sir Nathaniel and Holofernes. Modern editors usually render the garbled passage thus:

Sir N: Laus deo, bone intelligo.

Hol.: 'Bone'? 'Bone' for 'bene'? Priscian a little scratcht; 'twill serve.

Priscian was a standard grammar. The sense of the sentence is that precise usage is a little damaged, but the phrase will do. The confusion arose, presumably, because the compositor found the allusive jokes and the latinity hard to understand.

It be not mine desire, for Time to destroye my Name and Memory. Francis Verulam, Montaigne, Swan of Avon—one poet.

Another likely text is the poem 'To the Reader' at the beginning of the First Folio; the Baconians were quick to investigate it. In 1895 Dr Wilhelm Preyer of Wiesbaden picked out all the words in the poem which began with capital letters, and rearranged them to give this spastic message:

> Not This Figure, Shakespeare, But
> It His Booke O Reader Print
> Werein All Nature I As Grauer Picture   B.

Inspired by his efforts, an Englishwoman, Mrs Pott, set to work to produce plainer confirmation of Bacon's authorship. In the same poem she claimed to find repeated three times the message 'Francis Bacon, Viscount St Alban, Shakespeare, writ these plaies, not the rogue Will Shakspurre'.

From time to time other Elizabethan authors were singled out for anagrammatic treatment: for instance in 1931 Henry Seymour, writing in *Baconiana*, announced the discovery of a manuscript of John Barclay's *Argenis*, in Bacon's handwriting: and significantly enough, 'John Barclay' is an anagram of 'Hilary Bacon'; Hilary, 'by legal abbreviation' becomes 'Hail y'r', or 'H'y (i.e. Holy) liar'; and this finally gives us the message 'Holier Bacon'.

But the most remarkable efforts of all are to be found in *Neglected Anagrams of the Bacon Period*, by Ben Haworth-Booth, published in Yorkshire in 1914. Haworth-Booth begins with Du Bartas' *Divine Weekes and Workes* (1633) which, he says, 'has long been believed to be the product of Francis Bacon's hidden labours; and the similarity of much of its contents to the plays of Shakespeare led me to believe with many others that they owed their origin to the same master pen'. Not content with unconfirmed belief, he goes on to give positive proof. The first verse in the book ends with the words 'voy sire saluste', which he notes as an anagram for 'Joshua Sylvester'. But if this seems to miss the target, later efforts are nearer the mark:

'Acceptam refero' becomes 'mee a fat porccer'; 'Ivstus vivet fide R.Y' becomes 'I fry in stevved svet'; 'Deus providebit' becomes 'Svet I provided. B.' and 'Vivitur ingenio caetura mortis erunt' is an anagram of 'I am writing a secret in true O'. (Haworth-Booth explains that 'it is common to use the "O" to signify "cypher" and we know that Ben Jonson so used it'.)

The next books on his list are the 1605 edition of *The London Prodigal* (which has Shakespeare's name on the title-page) and Edmund Spenser's *Colin Clout* of 1595. Both these books bear the motto 'Venere veritas viressit T.C.', and this anagrams into 'A writer in secret 'mong fried reast': as Haworth-Booth points out, 'reastie bacon' is a phrase still used in the north of England. Another motto appears in the *Catalogue of Honour* (1610), *Novum Testamentum* (1629), *Prophetæ* (1629) and 'many other' works: it runs 'Labore et Constantia', which is a disguised form of 'I eat not salter. Bacon'. In the 1623 Folio 'Maister William Shakespeare' becomes 'I maske as a writer I spelle Ham'; from the *New Atlantis* 'Veritas filia temporis' becomes 'It is true I am foil spear'; and so on. Finally the sheer weight of evidence overwhelms the anagrammatist:

> Can it be honestly contended that the examples given are purely matters of luck or fortune?...Matters of chance? Can it be an easy thing to form...sentences purely by means of a lucky chance of all the requisite letters happening to be there?...I have no intention of entering into any controversy on the subject of Baconian authorship. I leave that for those who love controversy; my object is to point out that much information is to be gained by the study of anagram.

A comprehensive collection of genuine anagrams, *Biblia Anagrammatica*, was compiled by Walter H. Begley, an English clergyman, in 1903. It is an object-lesson in the weakness of anagrammatic methods. Begley devotes a whole section (thirty-four pages) to citing a few of the thousands of anagrammatic verses based on the Angelical Salutation, 'Ave Maria, gratia plena; Dominus tecum'. Writing these verses was a popular exercise of the pious in the seventeenth century. Each line consisted of a rearrangement of the thirty-one letters of the Angelical Salutation: some are in the form of dialogues, others are short biographies of kings, saints, bishops, or worthies; some are in Italian, some are straightforward poems in Latin or English. The anagrammatists who composed these verses often did so under extremely adverse conditions; one of the most prolific of them was blind. Their productivity was sometimes impressive: many composed over a thousand specimens, and one, Lucas de Vriese, was responsible for 3100. Here is one of the examples Begley reproduces; it is, besides being a faultless anagrammatic verse, a perfect acrostic on the Angelical Salutation:

> Amacula ter munda, ita per omnia viges.
> Viges, enormi mulcta Adami pura enata.
> Enata Malis pura vige, ac merito Munda.
>
> Munda Mater emicas, o pura Geniti Aula.
> Aula Dei micat, nota summe pura, Regina.
> Regina, o Tu pura macula, et Dia Immensa.
> Immensa, o Tu diva integre pura ac alma.
> Alma ter unice pura Summa io Dei Gnata.
>
> Gnata Dei, pura es communi a Mali reatu.
> Reatu magno pura, micat sine lue Adami.
> Adami sine omni macula pura, rege tuta.
> Tuta o pergas alma ac nimie munda jure.
> Iure mero Genita munda a culpis, Amata.
> Amata veni Summa Regina, delicto pura.
>
> Pura et ter divina o gemmas, Amica luna.
> Luna pura (mira dico) Agni Stemmate Eva.
> Eva, i matris culpa e gremio munda nata.
> Nata maledicti pura, o vere Summi Agna.
> Agna Cœli summa, et Avi ter pura damni.
>
> Damni tu pura Regia es, et a macula omni.
> Omni reatu, ac Avi plagis e matre munda.
> Munda tu pia merito maculæ es ignara.
> Ignara culpæ mera, o Summi Tu Dei Nata.
> Nata Pura Medica, et gloria Summa veni.
> Veni multa munda, Pia et a gremio Sacra.
> Sacra nimie munda, alme pura vige tota.
>
> Tota piaculis munda mera, germina Eva.
> Eva o simul prima et munda genita, Cara.
> Cara, imo Summi Nata, et digne pura, vale.
> Vale, o mendi pura Mater, ac Vitis Magna.
> Magna, o sic pura ad literam, vive. Amen.

LUCAS DE VRIESE, *Metamorphosis Mariana* (1711).

But having shown in his *Biblia Anagrammatica* the quite fantastic variety of anagrams that can be derived from one series of letters, Begley could nevertheless go on to ignore the implications. Anagrammatic methods are too flexible to prove any claim to authorship, since the chances of accidental occurrence must inevitably be very high indeed; but Begley assiduously set to work finding 'significant' anagrams in Shakespeare's texts. In 1903, the year in which *Biblia Anagrammatica* appeared, Begley also published anonymously—the title-page merely admits that the author is 'A Cambridge Graduate' —another book, *Is it Shakespeare?*, which leaves no doubt of his Baconian sympathies. Among the anagrams collected there, he quotes one from the last two lines of the Epilogue to *The Tempest*, claiming that he does not know who discovered it. The lines are

> As you from crimes would pardon'd be
> Let your indulgence set me free.

and the anagram, which Begley says is 'remarkable', runs

> Tempest of Francis Bacon, Lord Verulam
> Do ye ne'er divulge me ye words.

The snag, which he fails to notice, is that the anagram has three a's, while the text has only two.

As possible alternatives, we would like to suggest two readings of our own, using the letters Begley used, including his extra 'a'. One version suggests a different source of authorship:

> R[eade]r: Believe it or not, my rude
> Play was coded for fun. God save me.   CLEMENS

and another upholds Shakespeare's rights in two forthright lines of verse:

> I wrote every line myself. Pursue no code
> E. told me Bacon's a G.D. fraud.

Examples of Baconian anagrammatic 'proofs' could be continued *ad nauseam*; but we have already given some account of the objections that invalidate them. In the absence of a key, any lengthy sequence of letters with the normal proportions of high, medium, and low-frequency vowels and consonants may be anagrammed in a large number of ways. Hence there may be as many 'solutions' as the solver's ingenuity can produce and each will be as valid as any other, but none will carry any objective conviction. There is always room for doubt unless the man who composed the anagram recreates his own message from it; for only he knows for certain what message he intended to conceal. (We gave examples of this kind of anagram in connection with Huygens and Galileo in ch. II.) There is no place for more than one valid solution in cryptology; a method which allows many bears its own refutation with it.

There are cases in which an author's pen-name is a pseudonym developed by anagramming the letters of his real name. The most famous example is that of *Voltaire*, which was derived from his family name *Arouet*, plus the two letters *L.J.* (le jeune, 'the younger'). A present-day example is *Ceram* (C.W.), a reversal of the letters in the writer's real name, Marec. But we have not encountered a single valid or authenticated case in which the writer of a book or play has established his authorship by the anagrammatic method, keyed or unkeyed, within the text of his book or play.

CHAPTER IX

THE STRING CIPHER OF WILLIAM STONE BOOTH

WILLIAM STONE BOOTH was one of the few Baconians who, in looking for hidden 'signatures' in Shakespeare's works, avoided the pitfalls of the anagram. In his first book, *Some Acrostic Signatures of Francis Bacon*,[1] he claimed he had found the letters of his acrostic messages in correct order, without any anagramming; on the face of it a far superior procedure. He describes his method in detail; here are some of the relevant extracts:

Let me illustrate what I mean by a hidden acrostic. Instead of making the acrostic so that it can be read down the initials of the first words of all the lines of a verse...let it be made so that...the interior letters of the acrostic run as they will through the verse. For instance, if you wish to write 'Francis Bacon' into a piece of verse, you see to it that the initial letter of the first word of the first line is an F; and the corresponding letter at the bottom of the page is an N. Then...make sure that if after F you take the next initial R, and if after R you take the next initial A and so on, the last letter of the name will fall on the N which you have placed at the end of your acrostic.

And later he adds:

The device is simply that of a hidden acrostic, the end letters of which are visible and prominent in their position, but the inner letters of which are hidden and follow one another in their proper sequence from one visible end to the other visible end of the acrostic.... The reader will observe that it does not matter how many letters may fall between the letters of a name, so long as they are not allowed to interfere with the spelling of the name itself, from point to point....

That is to say, Booth permits himself to use the initial letters of words anywhere, not just at the beginnings or ends of lines. Nor does his system demand that he should take one initial

[1] Published in 1909 by the Houghton Mifflin Company.

letter from one word in each successive line of a series; some-times many letters of a 'signature' come from the same line, and sometimes many lines are skipped altogether. All he has to do is find a page beginning with the letter F, follow along the lines until he finds an initial letter R, then an A, and so on, until the signature is complete. Provided it ends with the last initial letter of the last line, it is a 'genuine hidden acrostic'. Could anything be less plausible?

But Booth does not leave the matter there. His attempts to persuade his readers that there is something in it, that it is not so footling as it looks, are examples of that method of arguing which begins by stressing the objections and ends by turning them into positive advantages:

Unless all the acrostic signatures in this book are accidents, we must regard them as the means by which Francis Bacon, his brother, or his confidential servants placed an identifying mark upon works for which their author wished not to appear responsible before the world at large....This supposition I use as a working hypothesis.

There is something disarming in this candid admission; but a few pages earlier he had put up the barriers against coinci-dence:

It must not be forgotten that, although acrostics can be produced by intention and by exact methods which I shall exhibit, the same acrostics *may* be the result of chance. It will remain for the reader to determine how often the same rare accidents may be expected to recur with a remarkably definite frequency in the same book, and in corresponding places in that book. It is as if a log of wood were found in the way of an express train two miles out of Boston. This might be regarded as an accident. But a similar log found in a corresponding place two miles out of every important station between Boston and New York would, by many observers, be regarded as evidence of intention.

Argument by analogy is liable to one fundamental defect: the analogy may be false. The signatures Booth finds are not in corresponding places throughout any book, nor are they always the same signature. The comparison with 'a similar log in a corresponding place' is put in to win friends and influence people, but it is not a valid comparison. If we were to find ten miles outside one station a cow grazing beside the track, three miles outside another a signal box, and so on, what could we say? Yet this is the better analogy with Booth's discoveries, which completely lack the precision, system and order he claims for them. Here is another part of his own description:

> In this method of Bacon's the letters...between the first and the last of which is placed an acrostic, need bear no relation to one another. Chance may govern their position. Evidence that design has been exercised is seen in the fact that by placing your pencil on the first letter...you can predict the position of the final letter of the acrostic.

Booth goes on to elaborate what he calls 'the features of this scheme or trick'. His long explanations are designed to show that the whole procedure is somehow scientific; and to add to the excitement he postulates that the lines should be read in a zig-zag: if the first line is followed from left to right, the next must be read from right to left, and so on, 'running alternately with and against the *sense* of the text or composition, and absolutely independent of its meaning'. This is the genesis of his usage of the term 'string cipher', for as Booth explains:

> Here we have the letters of a string. Suppose that each letter is the initial letter of a word; then in order to keep them in a string all that was necessary was to fall back on the zigzag method of writing used by the early Greeks....The Chinese today write in the same way but up and down; and Cicero, in a metonymical sense, uses the word *Exarare*, meaning to write on a tablet, i.e. to plough back and forth over the field.

Now it is true that the ancient Greeks used a form of writing called 'boustrophedon', which ran from left to right on one line and from right to left on the next. But Chinese writing does not zigzag from top to bottom and bottom to top as Booth implies; it always runs downwards on the page. Nor does *exarare* specifically imply 'back and forth' writing; in its figurative sense it means simply 'to mark on tablets with the stylus, write, note, set down'. However, in Booth's system we must zigzag to find our acrostics, and 'the letters are shown as if they were strung on a string, and keyed from different points'.

It is an old device to use an established and respectable name to sell new goods, though in most trades there is a law against it. There is no such law in cryptography. The original 'string cipher' was described by August II, duke of Braunschweig-Lüneburg, who, writing in Latin under the pseudonym of 'The Man in the Moon', explained it in a book called *Cryptomenytices et Cryptographiæ* (Lüneburg, 1623). Bishop Wilkins was sufficiently impressed with the idea to describe it for a more general public in *The Secret and Swift Messenger* (1641). His description refers to a 'way of secret Information, by divers Knots tied upon a string, according to certain Distances, by which a Man may as distinctly, and yet as *Secretly*, express his meaning, as by any other way of Discourse. For who would mistrust any private News or Treachery to lye hid in a Thread, wherein there was nothing to be discerned, but sundry confused Knots, or other like Marks?' The method involves the use of a flat, rectangular piece of wood, whose surface is divided into columns, each column standing for one letter of the alphabet according to some prearranged system. The sides of the piece of wood are notched, and the string is wound between the notches, beginning at the top, so that knots in the string appear in the various columns of the ruled surface. The position of each knot thus indicates a letter, and the message can be read off along the string. Fig. 14 (overleaf) shows the example given by Wilkins himself; and as you can see, 'the Marks on it do express the Secret Meaning: *Beware of this Bearer, who is sent as a Spy over you*'.

But this is a very different thing from Booth's version. No wonder another Baconian, Walter Conrad Arensberg, complained that Booth 'designated inaccurately' in calling his method the 'string cipher'. In the authentic string cipher there is no ambiguity; each line is a standard length, each column is clearly defined, and each time the string is wound round it indicates letters unambiguously. The same, unfortunately, does not hold for Booth's case; he has no knots or marks, and 'chance may govern' the position of the intermediate letters. In the original cipher the distances between letters are fixed (for instance, in the Wilkins example, we have the repeated letters BE and ARE in BEWARE OF THE BEARER; on the string the knots which indicate the B and the E in the first occurrence must be the same distance apart as those which mark the second B and E; the same is true of the two sets of knots marking the

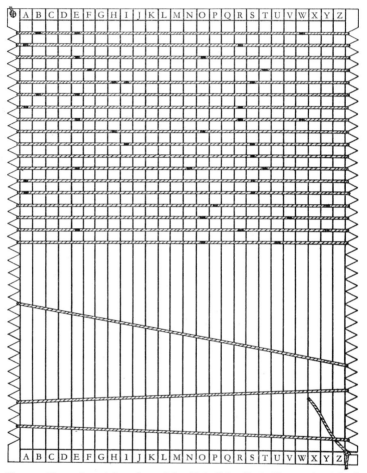

Fig. 14. The string cipher, from John Holt Schooling's 'Secrets in cipher', *Pall Mall Magazine*, vol. VIII (London, 1896), p. 247.

A, R and E in BEWARE and BEARER). There are no such consistencies among Booth's 'signatures'. In the genuine case each turn of the string marks one and only one passage across the board; Booth simply 'ploughs back and forth over the field' as he chooses. It is worth noticing, too, that the message in Wilkins' example is read off straightforwardly from left to right; the string, winding round the board, is always followed in the same direction. Booth, in contrast, makes a great point of alternating the direction of reading for successive lines.

Having explained his method at some length, Booth goes on to give a series of 'specimens' of cryptic writing. These are a skilful blend of the valid and the bogus; the unwary reader is led gently from an authentic method to an 'extension' of it which is completely worthless as a piece of cryptography. The first two illustrations he gives are examples of simple vertical acrostics; in one the initial letters of successive lines spell out 'Sir Francis Walsingham' (an acrostic we have come across before), and in the other they spell the name 'Francoys Martheos Viillons' (François Villon). Among the remainder there are several other genuine examples, including two composed by Booth (using the initial letter of every thirteenth and every seventh word respectively). But the fact that Booth is capable of composing cipher messages according to some valid method is nothing to the point; it has long been known that it is possible to make genuine acrostics.

The rest of the specimens provided by Booth himself are more significant; they illustrate the principles of the string cipher. His third example, Specimen C, is a text written for the purpose; he tells us 'I wrote the composition freely, and afterward threw in the cipher.... The acrostic cipher here is FRANCIS BACON INVENIT....It took me about ten minutes to insert [it] after I had written the text.' As a matter of fact, the passage can also be shown to contain the acrostic FRIEDMAN INVENIT, reading in the same direction as Booth's acrostic; but we claim no special privilege, since anyone whose name begins with F and ends with N (or begins with N and ends with F), and contains no unusual letters such as Q, X, or Z, is likely to find his signature without much difficulty.

In Specimen L, Booth shows how he was able, with a change of one word on the fourth line and four words on the last three lines, to insert the 'signature' FRANCISCO BACONO in one of his own sonnets written in 1899. He remarks that he has done this 'to show how easily an acrostic may be inserted'. Apparently neither this example nor the one in which he 'threw in the cipher' in 'about ten minutes' gave him pause for thought. If it is easy to insert as well as to find a signature in almost any piece of writing you care to select, how far can the method be trusted?

Specimens D and H are the only remaining ones devised by Booth, out of the twenty-four instances he gives in all. Specimen D he believes to be particularly important. He maintains that, since scholars have generally regarded *The Tempest* as the last of the Shakespeare plays, the Epilogue may be considered as the playwright's last word to his audience, 'and the place where he would be very likely to sign his name in cipher'. The first word of the Epilogue is 'Now' and the last word is 'free'; this satisfies his home-made rules, and we expect him to find, reading backwards, the name F R A N C I S B A C O N. In his Specimen D, however, it does not work out quite as we expect:

→ Now my *C*harmes are all *o*re-throwne,	CO	NO
And what *s*trength I have's mine *o*wne. ←	S	O
→ Which is most faint: now 'tis true		
I must be heere *c*onfinde by you, ←	IC	C¹
→ Or sent to Naples, Let me not		
Since I haue my Dukedome got. ←		
→ And pardon'd the deceiuer, dwell		
In this bare Island, by your Spell, ←		
→ But release me from my bands		
With the helpe of your good hands: ←		
→ Gentle breath of yours, my Sailes		
Must fill, or else my project failes, ←		
→ Which was to please: *N*ow I want	N	
Spirits to enforce: Art to inchant, ←		
→ *A*nd my ending is despaire,	A	
Vnlesse I be *r*elieu'd by praier ←	R	
→ Which pierces so, that it assaults		
Mercy it selfe, and frees *a*ll faults. ←		A
→ As you from crimes would pardon'd *b*e,		B
Let your Indulgence set me *f*ree. ←	F	

¹ Booth fails to explain why he uses both the I and the C in the second traverse (for F R A N C I S C O) and only the C (for B A C O N O) in the first.

To get the two short names from a whole twenty lines of text, he has to go upwards twice; beginning with the F of 'free' and ending on the O of 'ore-throwne' he finds FRANCISCO; beginning with the B of 'be' (the last word of the last line but one) and ending again on 'ore-throwne' he finds BACONO. It now ceases to be clear why the page has to begin with an N; but at least he adheres to the condition of using only the initial letters of words and 'stringing out' the signature in alternate directions through the successive lines.

It rather spoils the effect, however, if one notices that, starting from the same B as Booth does, one can find in a single 'string' the signature BEN JONSON, using only initial letters, going in opposite directions on alternate lines, and ending with the N at the beginning of the first line. If one uses a variant of the method, which Booth himself sometimes employs, choosing the final instead of initial letters of words, it is possible to produce, among others, the names EDMUND SPENSER, FRANCIS DRAKE, SIR EDWARD DYER, WILLIAM STANLEY, and CHRISTOPHER MARLOWE.

When he has sated the reader with specimens, Booth proceeds to the second part of the book. Here he lists over two hundred signatures of Bacon, in one form or another, from a variety of sources. He draws freely on Shakespeare, but also on certain 'doubtful' plays, such as *Pericles*, and on 'plays which have appeared anonymously, or over the name of Christopher Marlowe'. Most of the examples are run-of-the-mill 'string ciphers', but a few deserve special comment.

Signature 202, from the first page of *Hamlet*, tends to confuse the issue by exhibiting two names, not one: it pairs WILLIAM SHAKESPEARE with FRANCIS BACON. Signature 216 is more single-minded; from the last page of *Cymbeline* we are shown only the name WILLIAM SHAKESPEARE. Signature 232 changes the subject abruptly, and without warning; it is an acrostic based on two lines facing the title-page of *Nova Solyma*, a work sometimes attributed to Milton. Booth seems to support this attribution, since his acrostic spells Milton's name. So does another acrostic on the title-page of the same book; and the succeeding examples spell out the name of a certain actress from poems in Italian by Milton. After this digression, however, we return to Bacon, and find his name hidden equally superfluously in various works known to have been written by him. Booth does not try to explain why Bacon should conceal acrostic signatures in the text when his name was there, for all to see, on the title-page.[1]

In the case of signature 250, Booth demonstrates that his conception of the truth is as elastic as the method he employs. The text is Bacon's *Essayes*, and Booth 'began to read from the capital F of the word "FINIS" at the end of the book and *read back* through *all the capitals used in the book*; spelling out FRANCISCO BACONO'. This, he tells us, is 'a signature written in the simple method of which we have an analogous example by the monk Francesco Colonna'. If this is not a deliberate mis-statement, it is a remarkable piece of self-deception. The Colonna acrostic is based on the consecutive initial letters of successive sections of the *Hypnerotomachia Poliphili*; every initial letter is used, in the correct order, from start to finish, and there are no initials left over. In contrast, there are 310 capital letters in the *Essayes*, of which Booth selects, according to no system whatever, the fifteen necessary to make up the name 'Francisco Bacono', read backwards.

When circumstances demand it, Booth is not above breaking even the few simple rules he has laid down for himself. There are a number of instances in which he does not confine his use to initial letters of words; and signature 35 is a case in point. It is taken from the Threnos to *The Phoenix and Turtle*; Booth remarks that the signature is FRANCISCO BACONO, and that the two parts of the name come together on the O of '"Twas not', in the middle line of the poem (see opposite).

Booth has a habit of showing his signatures diagrammatically in what he calls 'figures'. These are usually strikingly simple arrangements of the key letters, in circles, squares, crossed diagonals, or single lines. They seldom bear any relation to the actual placing of the letters in the text (compare the graceful curve in the margin opposite with the actual erratic zigzag

[1] Booth's failure in this regard does not stand alone—others have exhibited the same weakness.

		THRENOS
Figure		
B		Beautie, Truth and Raritie
	A	Grace in *a*ll simplicitie
	C	Here enclosed, in *c*inders lie.
	O	Death is n*o*w the *Phoenix* next
		And the Turtle's loyall brest
		To eternitie doth rest.
	N	Leaving *n*o posteritie
Twas nOt		Twas n*o*t their infirmitie
	ISC	It wa*s* married *C*hastitie.
	C	Truth may seeme, but *c*annot be
	N	Beautie bragge, but tis *n*ot she
	A	Truth *a*nd Beautie buried be.
R		To this vrne let those *r*epaire,
		That are either true or faire,
F		*F*or these dead Birds, sigh a prayer.

formed by the letters italicized in the text). Usually the
facsimiles of the relevant pages are shown without any
markings at all, and any reader who wants to check his
'readings' has to go to a considerable amount of trouble. In
the example given above, once the operative letters are made to
stand out, it is clear that the O common to the two names is not
an initial letter; nor are the first O of 'Bacono' and the S of
'Francisco'. He ignores entire lines when they fail to produce
the letters he wants; and he makes a special rule for this specimen alone. If one looks for the name Francisco in the reverse
order of the letters, starting with the last O of 'Bacono', the
signature ends on the F of 'faire' in the last line but one. So
Booth ordains that in this case we must proceed in opposite
directions for the two parts of the name; 'Francisco' must be
read from the bottom upwards, and 'Bacono' from the top
down.

Booth's 'string cipher' is so flexible that it might more
justly be compared with a rubber band. There are 'signatures'
to be found in plenty on any given page; the procedure very
rarely yields a unique result; and it has no cryptological
validity whatsoever. The only surprising thing is that with all

the freedom Booth commands, he manages to find a mere 251 signatures; not all of them are Bacon's at that.

A year after publishing *Some Acrostic Signatures of Francis Bacon*, Booth again directed his attention towards the *Hypnerotomachia Poliphili*, a work which seems to have had a peculiar fascination for him. And once more he was concerned to undermine the valid and straightforward system it contains, in order to suit his own ends. The details of the acrostic have already been given in ch. VII, but we shall summarize them again here. The book is written in sections, each of which is clearly marked by a heading consisting of several lines of capitals. Each section begins with a large ornamental woodcut containing the initial letter (see Fig. 15). These initials, consequently, stand out clearly from the rest of the text; and they spell consecutively the message 'Poliam frater Franciscus Columna peramavit'. There are no redundant initials, and no anagramming or reversing is necessary.

But Booth, who calls his book *The Hidden Signatures of Francesco Colonna and Francis Bacon: A Comparison of their Methods*, must make light of all this:

As the chapters or sections of Colonna's folio are not numbered, and as they do not begin on pages by themselves, but wherever the previous section ends, the sequence of the first initials of the chapters is not noticeable as it would be if each chapter began on a clean page. Their arrangement is further obscured from the view of the casual reader by the use of three very different designs of woodcut, and by the fact that one of the designs is made in two sizes. The folio also contains many other beautiful woodcuts of all sorts and sizes, so that the initials themselves are not obtruded on the view.

Anyone who looks at the original text can very easily see what a distorted picture this gives. Booth, as if stricken by conscience, proceeds to qualify his own argument by remarking that 'the hidden signature seems to have been known as early as 1512', that is, only thirteen years after the work first appeared. (This is all the more surprising because, in his earlier book, he has already asserted that the message was not found until 'long after publication'.)

produceffe,quali fono quefti nel diuo fronte affixi, di quefto cælico fig,
mento præfulgidi &amorofi,Et percio per tanti iurgii obfeffo el trifto co
re & da tanta difcrepante controuerfia de appetifcentia fuftiniua, Quale
fi tra effi una fronde del aftante lauro del tumulo del R e de Bibria in me-
dio collocata fuffe,Ne unque la rixa ceffare,fi non reiecta, Et cufi penfita
ua non ceffabondo tanto litigio,fi non da effo core tanto piacere de coftei
(non factibile) fuffe ablato.Et per tale ragione non fe potea firmaméte có
uenire el uoluptico & inexplebile defio de luno ne de laltro,Quale homo
da fame exarcebato & tra multiplici & uarii eduli fremente, de tutti cupi-
do di niuno integramente rimane di lardente appetito contento, Ma de
Bulimia infecto.

LA BELLISSIMA NYMPHA AD POLIPHILO PER-
VENTA, CVM VNA FACOLA NELLA SINISTRA MA
NV GERVLA, ET CVM LA SOLVTA PRESOLO, LOIN
VITA CVM ESSA ANDARE, ET QVIVI POLIPHI-
LO INCOMINCIA PIV DA DOLCE AMORE
DELLA ELEGANTE DAMIGEL
LA CONCALEFACTO, GLI
SENTIMENTI INFLAM
MARSENE.

ESPECTANDO PRAESENTIALMENTE EL
reale & intelligibile obiecto duna præftantiffima repræ,
fentatione de tanta uenuftiffima præfentia & diuo afpe-
cto,& de uno copiofo aceruo & uniuerfale aggregatione
de inuifa bellecia & inhumana formofitate, Exiguo &
exile per quefto & impare reputaua tutte anteuidute iex-
timabile delitie,& opulentie & elate magnificentie, ad tanto ualore quan
to e coftei.O fœlice dunque colui che tale & tanto thefore di amore quie
to poffiderae.Ma non folamente poffeffore fœlice,ueramente beatiffimo
dico colui che ad tutti fui defii & imperio humile fuccumbendo dallei fa
ra per qualunche modo poffeduto & obtento, O altiffimo Ioue,Ecco lo
ipreffo ueftigio della tua diuina imagine,relicto in qfta nobiliffima crea,
tura,Onde fi Zeufis effa fola hauelfe hauuto ad cótemplatione, laudatiffi
ma fopra tutte le Agrigétine puelle & dello orbiffimo mondo di fúma &
abfoluta pfectione,cógruamente per fingulare exéplario harebbe oppor
tuniffimo electo.Laquale formofa & cælicola Nympha,hora ad me fefte

Fig. 15. A page from Colonna's *Hypnerotomachia Poliphili* showing an initial letter.

Booth then produces a demonstration designed to clarify how 'the typographical trick by which Francis Bacon put his name to the first folio of *Mr. William Shakespeare's Comedies, Histories and Tragedies* has several points in common with that which was used by Francesco Colonna'. This argument relies on a groundwork of exaggeration and tactful omission. He, of course, uses the 'string method' to find his Baconian signature. He is fortunate in finding a B as the first initial of the first spoken word, 'Boatswain', in the *Comedies, Histories and Tragedies* and an F, in 'Frownes', in the last word of the first line in the final play. Going forwards from the B, and backwards from the F, he picks out the letters BACONICSICNARF and BACONOC-SICNARF which form, he tells us, the 'Italianate' signatures 'Francisci Baconi' and 'Francisco Bacono'. Since the B is the first letter of the first play, he is able to say, with perfect truth, that both the Bacon and Colonna signatures begin 'with the first letter of the first section of the body of the folio', and that both ignore 'the prefatory matter, which consequently serves as a blind; intentionally or not'. Booth's signature is derived from initial letters of words which appear in the first lines of the plays, so there is something in his contention that both signatures possess this in common; and if one is prepared to accept the peculiar order of letters in his version of a 'signature', it could even be said that both Bacon and Colonna 'used the first spoken line of each section (chapter or play) taken in its proper sequence throughout his folio'. Apart, however, from the doubts over the phrase 'its proper sequence', it should be mentioned (as Booth never does) that while the beginning of *every* section plays its part in Colonna's message, Booth has to do a good deal of skipping in the First Folio to find Bacon's. The second letter of his 'signature' is not found in the second play: it is the A used as the indefinite article which is the ninth word of the third play. He has then to skip ten more plays to find the third letter, the C, occurring as the initial of the fourth word of the fourteenth play. There is another point of difference which is so obvious that even Booth has to admit it, although he minimizes it as much as possible: 'the only difference', he tells us, between the methods of the two acrostic-makers lies in the use of the initials of the words of the first lines of the successive sections. In Colonna's folio, *only* the first initials are used. In Shakespeare's folio the letters of Bacon's name follow in their proper order, B, A, etc., extending between two fixed points, with nulls or non-significant letters interspersed between them without interfering with the spelling of the name between the fixed points.

In his diagram of the Colonna acrostic, Booth carefully includes all the words of the first lines of each section. By this device he apparently hopes to persuade the reader that there are also 'nulls or non-significant letters' in the genuine message. But, since the initials of only the first *word* in each section of Colonna's book are relevant, quoting the whole of the first *line* in each case is so much dust in the eyes. It is simply done to lend plausibility to Booth's own method, which relies heavily on intervening 'nulls'. There are altogether 264 words among the Shakespearean first lines he combs for his 'signature'; 250 of these have to be ignored, and he selects the necessary fourteen as he pleases, according to no definite scheme whatever.

There is a pleasant note of unintentional irony in Booth's remark that 'he who suspects Francis Bacon to be the author behind the name of William Shakespeare, and also suspects that the poet signed and concealed his own name in his folio, can easily prove the correctness of his suspicion by the simple method of spelling...between the two given points'. And there is even a certain naïve charm in the remark that 'the obvious advantage of each method lies in the fact that any man can read the signature of Francesco Colonna at sight, while the signature of Francis Bacon must be spelled to be discovered'. But there is downright dishonesty in his contention that 'in a mechanical sense the trick of Francis Bacon is as precise, and as definite as that of Francesco Colonna, *and as inevitable*'. There is no precision, and no inevitability about Booth's 'discovery'; only the determination to find the letters he needs for a 'signature', in some form, of the name he is looking for. Anyone with similar preconceptions has a good chance of finding any name he cares to choose among the wealth of initial letters at his disposal; and his results will be just as invalid.

In his later works Booth appears to have grown tired of the 'string cipher'. In 1920 he published *Marginal Acrostics, and other Alphabetical Devices, a Catalogue*; and in 1925 another book along the same lines which dismissed this, together with *Some Acrostic Signatures of Francis Bacon*, as 'a collection of laboratory notes, a record for the examination of students'. The title of the final, definitive work which replaced them was taken from *The Rape of Lucrece*; it went by the impressive name *Subtle Shining Secrecies, Writ in the Margents of Bookes*. Booth's new method he called 'devices'; and by means of it he found (and listed in the Introduction) the names F. Bacon, A. Bacon, Fra Bacon, Fran Bacon, Bacoun, Beacon, Becon, Baco, Baconus, and (more surprisingly) Tommy Aitken, Anifbal, Johann, Gillam (or Gilliam), R. Allot, Beauvais, Davis, Hilda, and Satan.

Booth begins his chapter on 'Technique' by describing and giving legitimate examples of the acrostic, the acrotelestic, the telestic, the mesostic (which uses the final or initial letters of words at the caesura of lines of verse) and 'the gallows, or to give it the French name the *potence*...often used by Shakespeare, and as will be seen, sometimes in connection with some use of the verb *to hang*; the *gallows* acrostic device is so called because of its shape'.

Booth's own attempts to find examples of these devices in Shakespeare's works do not meet with unqualified success; most of the words he finds are very short, and of a kind that could appear purely by chance on any page of any text whatever; there are no sequences forming the words of a connected sentence, and no names of any substantial length can be produced without anagramming. The 250 or so instances he gives require a good deal of sales-talk to justify the claim that they were placed there by design; for instance, when he finds, in twelve successive lines in *Timon of Athens*, the letters PACONDRALATPUR, Booth explains:

> The acrostic play here is with the name on the gallows PACON, or BACON.... The next acrostic is the word LARD, a substance made out of Swine, or Bacons. Following the word LARD is the Latin word RUPTA, meaning *violated*, which would appear to bear a slant on the open meaning of the text.

Among the rest, there are several straightforward three- and four-letter words such as HOT, COLD, TOAD, BLAB, TEL (explained as a short form of *Telos*, meaning 'the end'), YAWL, WHAT, and so forth; some five- and six-letter words (most of which are claimed to be Greek or Latin) such as TACUIT, FUMAT, VYVAT, SAPINS, NODAT, FANOS, TACIM (which Booth reverses into MICAT) and others; and one six-letter acrostic on an English word, BROWSE. This is the prize discovery, in Gloucester's speech to the Peers in *II Henry VI*, Act I, sc. I; and Booth says the poet has made it as 'a textual opportunity' for the reader. He is plainly delighted with his find, and allows himself a passage of lyrical commentary:

Let us browse back and forth and up and down the letters of the text, nose out the odoriferous flowers of fancy, nip off the tops, taste the syllables, and we soon see the poet's name Fran. Bea. Coun, or equivocally Fran. Bacon. This equivoque is again made across the page as it is marked with a line. Shall our Fame be cancelled, blotting our Names for Bookes of Memory, Shall these labours and these honours die?

The various 'signatures' Booth cites make a generous use of anagramming, abbreviation, and Latinization: Fr. an. Sic (Francis); OCBA (Baco), B.a. coun.F. (F. Bacoun), BACHVn, FRAHOBAC (Fra. Bacho), fr.b.e.A.Con (Fr. Beacon), b.a.r.F (Fra B), and similar 'equivocations' abound. The letters and syllables are not always taken from the beginnings of lines, and each 'signature' is so short that it can only plausibly be explained as the outcome of chance. Examples as good as Booth's, or better, can be found in almost any volume of collected poetry. For instance, Matthew Arnold's *Merope* reveals, in six consecutive lines, a double Baconian signature, reading in opposite directions, with a minimum of anagramming:

*C*laims ever hostile else, and set thy son—
*N*o more an exile fed on empty hopes,
*A*nd to an unsubstantial title heir,
*B*ut prince adopted by the will of power,
*A*nd future king—before this people's eyes.
*Con*sider him! consider not old hates!

Booth, for all his searching, found only one or two examples as impressive as this. But we are not putting forward the claim that Bacon concealed his 'signature' in the poems of Matthew Arnold; rather, it should be plain that the character of the English language is such that there is a good chance that the name BACON will appear quite fortuitously. Certainly, B is a common enough initial letter and 'Con' a common enough prefix for Bacon to have scattered his name liberally on every page, without abbreviation, Latinization or anagramming, had his heart been in the job. Booth's poor showing makes it plain that it was not: and his last volume is as devoid of validity as the earlier ones it was designed to better.

Nevertheless, he has had a surprisingly large following; which is the main reason why we have given him so much space. Not only was he able to find a long-established publisher for his books; suitable journals and the correspondence columns of newspapers are also peppered with the discoveries of his disciples. The reviewer in *Baconiana* of April 1909 eulogized his first volume, and believed that there could be 'no...doubt as to the existence of these signatures'; and a Harvard University professor who began by scoffing was reported to have confessed that he was 'shaken' when confronted with thirty proofs or more. This authoritative sanction of Booth's work, combined with the ease of finding 'signatures' by his 'string acrostic method' was enough to lay the cornerstone of a tradition.

Not all the inheritors of this tradition are equally important, but we will mention a few who stand out from the rest. The most enthusiastic convert was Frank A. Kendall, author of *William Shakespeare and His Three Friends, Ben, Anthonie and Francis*. He seems to have subscribed wholeheartedly to the theory that there is safety in numbers, for on one page alone he succeeded in finding the string acrostic signature '*Antonius Baconus et Ben Jonsonus et Franciscus Baconus Scripserunt* [or *Invenerunt*]' fifty-four times. On the same page the signature 'Shakespeare' appeared seven times, earning the Bard of Avon a small share of the credit. Kendall, with some modesty, admitted, 'I am not credulous enough to believe that *all* the acrostics indicated...are intentional... but does it seem to the

reader that they are *all* accidental?' Kendall concluded that
'the first and last pages of the quartos...and many of the title-
pages are rich in acrostics, often repeated in the same passage
and often grouped so that the same combinations occur in
related passages'.

An Englishman named Cornwall concurred with Owen in
the theory of Bacon's royal birth; and in *Francis the First* (1936)
he used an even looser form of Booth's 'string cipher' to
reveal, twice in the same poem, the message 'I am a sonne to
Elizabeth and Ro: Dudley, lo: Leicester. F.B.' (The 'Ro' and
'lo' sound rather like the chorus to a sea-chantey, but in fact
they are intended to be abbreviated forms of 'Robert' and
'lord'.) The text concealing this startling piece of history is the
dedicatory poem to the anonymous edition of *The Shepherd's
Calendar* (1579). Booth had already used his system on the same
poem to get a radically different and less spectacular result: he
merely found the names 'Francis Bacon', 'Bacon', and
'Bacono', each repeated twice in full.

There have been a number of suggestions, based on the
'string method', for improving upon our bibliographical
knowledge. Smith, an American correspondent in the July–
October number of *Baconiana* in 1917, showed himself to be a
keen student of Booth's work, with a shrewd head for figures.
He pointed out that Booth discovered the signature 'Francis of
Verulam' in a Shakespearean sonnet allegedly published in
1603; but since Bacon was not created Baron Verulam until
1619, the true publication date could not have been until post-
1619. By parity of reasoning the dates on the title-pages of the
Quarto editions of *King Lear* (1600, 1608 and 1609) must, he
implied, have been either misprints or deliberate attempts to
mislead.

George Frisbee, of San Francisco, introduced a new variation
on the string acrostic theme; he was not a Bacon man, but his
Edward De Vere, a Great Elizabethan (London, 1931) was based
on Booth's methods. His modified form of the 'string cipher',
using not only the first or last letters of words, but any letters
he needed (as was also true in Cornwall's case), gave him ample
scope; and he made the best of it by examining the works of

Gascoigne, Marlowe, Sir John Harington, Edmund Spenser, Sir Walter Raleigh, Sir Philip Sidney (and his biography by Sir Fulke Greville), Anne de Vere, and Shakespeare's Sonnets. For good measure he added Webster's *Arte of Poesie* to the list (the work is enormously popular among Baconians). He found signatures everywhere; here is one brief example from Gascoigne's *Jocasta*:

Th*e* order of the *d*umme shewes	E D
And Musick*es* before *ev*ery Acte	E VER E
	(E. DE VERE)

In his book Frisbee displayed only two signatures ('Edward de Vere' and 'E de Vere') in Spenser's sonnets, *Amoretti* and *Epithalamion*. Two years and many man-hours later he had worked it up into a more impressive vehicle. He sent us an expanded interpretation containing eight more 'acrostics'; there were two new 'de Vere' signatures, four of 'Mary Sidney', one 'Mary, Countesse of Pembroke', and one 'I love Mary Pembroke'. His accompanying letter did not attempt to conceal his triumph:

Here is a sample from 'Spenser'. That was the pen-name of Edward De Vere, 17th Earl of Oxford. He introduced the acrostics into English literature in 'A Hundreth Sundrie Flowers', 1573. He wrote for many years, under many names, but always wove his own, in acrostic, in his stuff. This Sonnet is the one the great collector, Dr Rosenbach, values at $70,000.00, because, so he says, Spenser inscribed it to a gal named Elizabeth Boyle. I smile.

The book Frisbee mentioned in his letter, *A Hundreth Sundrie Flowers*, was the subject of an earlier study by B. M. Ward. He brought out an edition, with introduction and notes, in 1926, and claimed that while Elizabethan scholars commonly ascribe it to George Gascoigne, there are at least sixteen poems in the anthology which are the work of de Vere. Ward's evidence relies largely on the finding of two signatures 'Edward de Vere', by Booth's 'string cipher' method, in a poem signed *Meritum petere, grave* ('To seek reward is a serious matter'). The theory is that this 'posy' is de Vere's family motto; and since the title-page of the book carries the same device in place of an author's name, de Vere must have been an important contributor. The poem with the curious signature has an equally curious legend in place of the title: 'The absent lover (in ciphers) diciphering his name, doth crave some spedie relief as followeth'. Because of this it has often been the subject of discussion among scholars and laymen.

One of the most plausible theories put forward so far is the work of Prof. Charles T. Prouty. In *A Hundreth Sundrie Flowers* (University of Missouri Studies, 1942) he clarifies the enigma by suggesting that the name 'in ciphers' is Scudamore. The motto of the Scudamore family was a pun on their name, *Scuto Amoris Divini*; the poem parallels this by beginning with the words 'L'Escu d'amor'. Further, Gascoigne in his prefatory letter explicitly says of the poems 'the most part of them were written for other men, but this one was written for Sir John Scudamore'. The phrase 'diciphering his name', according to Prouty, means 'explaining his name'; at any rate it does not seem to imply that the name is hidden where only the string cipher can reveal it.

But in their recent book, *This Star of England* (1955) the Ogburns (who share Ward's belief that de Vere was the real Shakespeare) ignore this thesis and quote Ward's work with approval. They remark that 'this cipher has been recognized by Grosart and others as an excellent one', and tell their readers that 'the Shakespeare Scholar, Dr Greg, makes the following comment (*The Library*, Dec. 1926): "We are expressly told that the name is concealed, and the acrostic found is an excellent one"'. This remark, taken out of context, seems to imply Sir Walter Greg's assent to Ward's theory; but in fact he was against it. His objections, however, seem to us to miss the main point, and he says at one stage that he would be 'reluctant to believe that [the acrostic's presence] could be due to chance'. To show that it very easily could, it is enough to set out Ward's description of the method and see if we can apply the rules to suit our own different purposes.

Fig. 16 (p. 135) reproduces Ward's workings on the sonnet and his acrostic 'figure'. He obviously feels that this performance needs some kind of justification, and he remarks:

But now I can see the reader saying: 'Surely with a string of letters nine times as long as the one just given, you can spell almost any name you like to imagine.' Very true. Therefore the rule is that the correct name must be so 'keyed' into the string as to eliminate all possibility of chance. For a name to 'key' into an acrostic poem it should—

Commence on some prominent letter in the first line;

Finish exactly on a letter in the last line;

Read backwards through the poem, beginning and ending exactly on the same two letters.

I think that the reader will agree with me that if we can find a name to do this, remembering the whole time that you are told that there is a hidden name in the poem, it is highly improbable, if not impossible, that it should be a fluke.

One might begin by objecting, as Fredson T. Bowers did,[1] to Ward's third condition for 'validity', namely that the acrostic should, when read backwards, begin and end on the same two letters as it did when read forwards. Clearly, this rule is tailor-made to fit the name Ward finds; any name beginning with one letter and ending with another is automatically ruled out of the system. But there is a more radical objection to be made, and that is that Ward's rules do not by any means 'eliminate the possibility of chance'; nor is it 'highly improbable' that his discovery of de Vere's name 'should be a fluke'. If anyone were prepared to take the trouble, they could find several alternative signatures. Here is an 'acrostic figure' for one of our own readings:

L'	L'(Escu)
E(scu)	L(ove)
W(hich)	O(f)
I(n)	R(emove)
S(terve)	R(est)
C(older)	A(re)
A(re)	C(ressyde)
R(evived)	S(o)
R(elief)	I
O(r)	W(oes)
L(ong)	E(ase)
L(end)	L(end)

[1] 'Gascoigne and the Oxford Cipher', *Modern Language Notes*, vol. LII, March 1937.

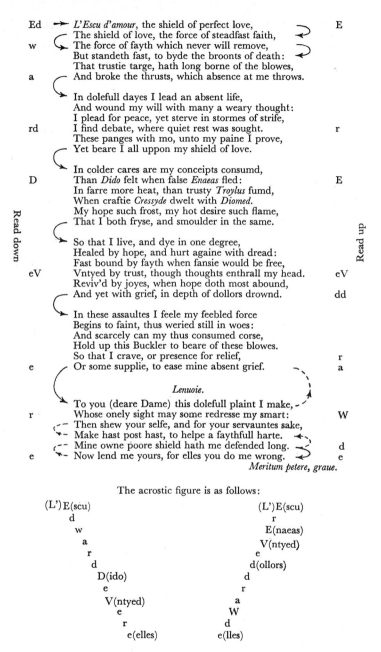

Ed → *L'Escu d'amour*, the shield of perfect love, E
   The shield of love, the force of steadfast faith,
w   The force of fayth which never will remove,
   But standeth fast, to byde the broonts of death:
   That trustie targe, hath long borne of the blowes,
a   And broke the thrusts, which absence at me throws.

   In dolefull dayes I lead an absent life,
   And wound my will with many a weary thought:
   I plead for peace, yet sterve in stormes of strife,
rd   I find debate, where quiet rest was sought. r
   These panges with mo, unto my paine I prove,
   Yet beare I all uppon my shield of love.

   In colder cares are my conceipts consumd,
D   Than *Dido* felt when false *Enaeas* fled: E
   In farre more heat, than trusty *Troylus* fumd,
   When craftie *Cressyde* dwelt with *Diomed*.
   My hope such frost, my hot desire such flame,
   That I both fryse, and smoulder in the same.

   So that I live, and dye in one degree,
   Healed by hope, and hurt againe with dread:
   Fast bound by fayth when fansie would be free,
eV   Vntyed by trust, though thoughts enthrall my head. eV
   Reviv'd by joyes, when hope doth most abound, dd
   And yet with grief, in depth of dollors drownd.

   In these assaultes I feele my feebled force
   Begins to faint, thus weried still in woes:
   And scarcely can my thus consumed corse,
   Hold up this Buckler to beare of these blowes.
   So that I crave, or presence for relief, r
e   Or some supplie, to ease mine absent grief. a

     Lenuoie.

   To you (deare Dame) this dolefull plaint I make,
r   Whose onely sight may some redresse my smart: W
   Then shew your selfe, and for your servauntes sake,
   Make hast post hast, to helpe a faythfull harte.
   Mine owne poore shield hath me defended long. d
e   Now lend me yours, for elles you do me wrong. e
      Meritum petere, graue.

Read down   Read up

The acrostic figure is as follows:

  (L')E(scu)   (L')E(scu)
   d   r
   w   E(naeas)
   a   V(ntyed)
   r   e
   d   d(ollors)
   D(ido)   d
   e   r
   V(ntyed)   a
   e   W
   r   d
   e(lles)   e(lles)

Fig. 16. Ward's use of the string cipher method to find the name Edward de Vere.

This meets all Ward's specifications: we begin on a prominent letter in the first line, finish exactly on a letter in the last line, and then read the name LEWIS CARROLL backwards through the poem, beginning and ending on the same two letters. And, like Ward, we use only the initial letters of words. If we were to allow ourselves Frisbee's modification of the 'string cipher', using any letter anywhere, it would be easy to find in addition Lewis Carroll's real name, Charles Lutwidge Dodgson, and the title *Alice in Wonderland*. But enough is as good as a feast, and this is enough of Booth and his various imitators. None of their improvements and innovations has been able to lend his system any kind of cryptological validity; the foundations are so shaky that it would be hopeless to try.

CHAPTER X

WALTER CONRAD ARENSBERG

SINCE without a specific key to guide the operation there are often so many plausible ways of rearranging a given set of letters, and often no way of telling whether any one arrangement among these was in fact intended as a cryptic message, anagrams introduce an element of flexibility into any cryptographic system that uses them; and flexibility, once introduced, makes it a good deal easier to find any 'message' one wants to find. So it is not surprising that elegant, if implausible, combinations of anagrammatic and acrostic methods are popular among those who seek evidence of a hidden hand in Shakespeare's works.

Of all the acrostic signatures 'revealed' by Baconians, more perhaps were the work of the late Walter Conrad Arensberg than of any other man. Arensberg was a scholar, poet, and student of occultism; he was also a patron of the arts (the Arensberg Collection, which was bequeathed to the Philadelphia Museum of Art, is among the foremost collections of modern painting in the United States). But above all he was an enthusiastic amateur cryptologist. Having studied Italian literature at Harvard, it was natural that he should select Dante as his first victim; he found enough examples of what for him were valid acrostics to fill a large volume, and published it in 1921 under the title *The Cryptography of Dante*. It did not take him long to switch his attack. He had discovered in Dante's writings a system he called the 'compound anagrammatic acrostic' and he now began to apply this to Shakespeare's works. A year later, in 1922, he was able to publish privately at Los Angeles the first part of *The Cryptography of Shakespeare*. The 280 pages of this work were meant to be supplemented by a second volume, but the project was abandoned before it could appear.

The book starts off impressively, with a dismissal of rival Baconian theories, including those of Booth, Owen and

Donnelly. 'In my opinion', Arensberg tells us (and we agree), 'none of the methods to which I have referred has been proved to have been employed by Francis Bacon in the works of William Shakespeare.' In spite of this, his own conviction remains unshaken: 'The conclusive evidence that *William Shakespeare* is the pseudonym of Francis Bacon is incorporated in the original editions of the Shakespeare plays and poems. This evidence consists of cryptograms in which the name of the poet is signed as Francis Bacon.' Or, one might add, as one of the numerous variations acceptable to Arensberg, from 'FF. Baconus' to 'Verulamii'.

He goes on to explain acrostics and anagrams, and it is quite plain that he knows what he is talking about. His account of acrostics is impeccable; and his definition of an anagram, since it is copied verbatim from the *New English Dictionary*, could hardly be bettered. His comment at this point is worth quoting:

> Though the correspondence between...the anagram and the... original spelling is inflexible as to the number and identity of their letters, the correspondence is flexible as to the sequence of the letters, since the sequence rests upon the arbitrary choice of the maker of the anagram. The method employed in the construction of a common anagram is therefore flexible.

All this is true, but one might be forgiven for sensing the thin end of a stout wedge in the reference to 'flexible' methods of construction. As he continues, however, suspicion is allayed; it even begins to seem unworthy. Arensberg explains that the acrostic, the telestic and the acrotelestic, which are the systems he intends to adopt, can be used quite rigidly and inflexibly. The number of letters in the acrostic is made to coincide exactly with the number of text units in which it is concealed. As an example, he takes the memorial poem to Sir Francis Walsingham (quoted in ch. VII) and remarks:

> In the construction of an acrostic on the total number of lines (or other units) of a text, the author of the text establishes an inflexible correspondence between the physical form of the text and the acrostic spelling....The identity of the line initials corresponds to the identity of the letters in the acrostic spelling. And the sequence

in which the various letters appear as the line initials corresponds to the sequence in which the same letters appear in the acrostic spelling....

The original paragraph in Arensberg's book is much longer than the section we have just quoted; he seems particularly anxious to make himself clear, and puts the same point again in different ways. He emphasizes and re-emphasizes the fixed, precise nature of the regular acrostic method, and concludes:

In the event that it is possible to discover in a given text an acrostic spelling which conforms to an inflexible method such as I have described, the evidence that the author of the text intended the spelling may be deduced from the mere possibility of the spelling itself....Any acrostic spelling which may be deciphered in a text in accordance with an inflexible method is its own proof that it was intended by the author of the text.

With the proviso (which Arensberg fails to consider) that the acrostic must be of a reasonable length, this is again perfectly true. Short acrostics could appear by accident, but any text as long as the one he is discussing, 'Sir Francis Walsingham', must indeed have been put there deliberately.

For the first twenty pages of *The Cryptography of Shakespeare* it is possible to agree with almost everything that is said. On p. 21 the disillusionment begins. Arensberg now describes the 'flexible' acrostic method which he will use in his future revelations:

In the construction of an acrostic on less than the total number of the lines of the text, the author makes an arbitrary choice; first, as to the proportion of the number of the letters in the acrostic spelling to the number of the lines in the text; and second, as to the position which the consecutive lines to be used for the acrostic spelling shall occupy within the limits of the total number of lines. By reason of this arbitrary choice, the method which he uses in the construction of the acrostic is flexible....The beginning of the spelling is not necessarily the initial of the first line; the end of the spelling is not necessarily the initial of the last line; and the number of the letters in the spelling is not necessarily any particular proportion of the total number of lines....So far as the form of the text is concerned there is no indication as to the line on which the spelling begins, the line on which the spelling ends, or the number of lines which the spelling includes. And there is consequently no indication as to the identity or the sequence of the initials of the lines which are to be used for the acrostic spelling....The only indication...is simply that a spelling of some sort is discoverable on an indefinite number of consecutive initials.

Even this does not seem too bad so far. There is, admittedly, an element of uncertainty; but if there exists, within a sizeable portion of the text, a firm and inflexible system, this uncertainty may be offset by the impressive length of the acrostic message itself. (Juan Lopez Cancelada, the ghost-writer of the history of New Mexico—see p. 100 above—began to establish his claim as late as p. 43; it is never too late, if the message is long enough.) But we have already moved one step away from the perfect acrostic. Arensberg is prepared to be generous; he concedes that the method alone cannot prove that the message was intended by the author of the text. But if we find hints in the open text itself, if its author, so to speak, digs us in the ribs, the situation is more promising.

The same, apparently, is true of anagrams. Arensberg tells us how to look in the texts for clues to their presence; and this done, he fires off both barrels at once, and embarks on the description of the acrostic anagram:

By reason of the fact that it involves an anagrammatic transposition of the letters at the *extremities* of the acrostic, this peculiar structure is essentially a combination of the anagram and the acrostic; and I shall accordingly call it the acrostic anagram....And the extraordinary and most manifest use that is made of the acrostic anagram in the first Shakespeare Folio is intended, as I shall show, to suggest the analogous anagrammatic acrostic as the method to be used in deciphering the author's signature.

It takes a lot of ink and paper before Arensberg feels that his account carries conviction; but somehow he manages to brew up some kind of analysis of its characteristics before going on to cite examples. This he does in profusion; all the 'signatures' he derives consist of a few letters, which are the result of anagramming simple, if occasionally unorthodox, acrostics which he finds in various Elizabethan works. Among these, it seems on the face of it surprising to find a large number taken from Bacon's own writings, spelling out anagrammatic claims that Bacon wrote them. But if this is rather like shipping oil to Texas, Arensberg is ready with a high-minded explanation:

> In *The Advancement of Learning* and indeed in all his philosophical works, Bacon is concerned with a method of remedying the deficiencies of human knowledge.... The cryptographic method itself, which is based on a regularity in the apparent irregularity of natural phenomena, may be reduced to laws; and the method of reading the cryptograms is accordingly intended as an illustration of the method which must of necessity be employed for the *advancement of learning* in philosophy and science.

It will be illuminating to quote some of the examples used by Arensberg, together with the 'clues' he gives for their presence. What emerges most plainly is the fertility of his imagination and the extent of his inventiveness; he sees allusion in all things.

Troilus and Cressida (ii, ii, 121–3) provides an anagrammatic acrostic where 'the acrostic spelling, as the expression of a concealed truth, corresponds to the allusion to Cassandra as an unbelieved prophetess:

> Nor once deiect the courage of our mindes;
> Because Cassandra's mad, her brain sicke raptures
> Cannot distaste the goodnesse of a quarrel....

Consider in these lines the following acrostic letters:

No
B
Ca

Read: BACON.'

Again, 'another acrostic appears in the following passage from *Hamlet*' (i, ii. 70–3):

> Costly thy habit as thy purse can buy;
> But not exprest in fancie; rich, not gawdie:
> For the apparel oft proclaims the man.
> And they in France of the best ranck anp station....

Consider in these lines the following acrostic letters:

Co
B
F
An

Read: F. BACON.'

Arensberg's explanation of the 'clues' is as ingenious as ever: 'The presence of the acrostic spelling of the author's name in the text may be hinted in the phrase "Proclaims the man". As an acrostic is not the ordinary method of expression, the name may be understood to be "exprest in fancie".' (The last sentence seems more apt than Arensberg meant it to be.)

An interesting variety of method characterizes Arensberg's work. Sometimes he chooses letters from consecutive words rather than consecutive lines; for example (from *The Advancement of Learning*, p. 264):

> Knowledge is of those things which are to *be ac*cepted *of* with great limitation and caution....

> Read: F. BACO.

And sometimes he uses an anagrammed telestic, not an acrostic; for example (from the first three lines of the *Catalogue* in the First Folio):

A CATALOGVE

of the severall Comedies, Histories, and Tra-

gedies contained in this volume.

Consider in these lines the following telestic letters:

```
.......VE
.......ra
.......lume
```

Read: VERULAME.

The varieties of cipher and the writings in which they are concealed soon begin to multiply at an alarming rate, as Arensberg conjures up more and more ways of establishing his claim. First comes the 'anagrammatic acrotelestic', which he defines as 'an anagrammatic acrostic composed of the *initials* of the final words of consecutive units of text in conjunction with an indeterminate number of consecutively adjacent letters to the right of these initials'. Close on its heels follows the 'compound anagrammatic acrostic and acrotelestic', based, he reminds us, 'on modifications of the simple acrostic form':

> The first modification...consists of the composition of a single acrostic spelling by the use of the acrostic letters in consecutive

lines, in conjunction with the acrostic letters of an indeterminate number of words that are consecutively adjacent to the acrostic words of the same lines. This...is essentially a combination of acrostics based on two different kinds of units of text, consecutive lines and consecutive words.... The novelty in the feature now under discussion is the fact that the two units are used simultaneously in the construction of a single acrostic spelling.

He seems quite complacent in the use of the indeterminacy principle; and as if to show how vague the method is and how far removed from the precise, straightforward acrostic with which he began, he works through page after page of explanation and example before reaching this *pièce de résistance*:

The compound anagrammatic acrostic is a method of constructing a spelling in another spelling, or text, by arranging the letters of the acrostic spelling in an anagrammatic sequence as an indefinite number of the acrostic letters of an indefinite number of consecutive words, beginning with either the first word or the last word of an indefinite number of lines.

Possibly because he has by now become so used to mincing words in the texts, Arensberg carries the habit over to his own explanations. Put in plain English, his recipe amounts to this: Take any initial letters you like, as long as you take them from consecutive words at the beginning or the end of any line, or from consecutive lines, or both. Rearrange the letters to form any word or phrase you care to choose, and serve with a flourish.

Most of the remaining pages of the book (apart from a short final section on 'The question of other pseudonyms of Francis Bacon') are taken up with examples of another new confection, which Arensberg terms 'the cross-gartered acrostic'. This allows him to use any number of consecutive letters from the beginning of the first word, or from the beginning of the last word of consecutive lines; but with a brief genuflection to propriety he remembers that there must be some restrictions somewhere. The method is inflexible only to the extent that the beginning and the end of the same line cannot both be used; it must be one or the other. The final 'signature' Arensberg deciphers (and therefore presumably the one he took to be the most impressive) is derived from Jonson's dedicatory poem

'To the Reader' in the First Folio. Using 'the cross-gartered acrostic', and italicizing the nineteen 'significant' letters we have

To the Reader

*T*his *F*igure, that thou here see*s*t put,	T, F
It was for gentle *S*hakespeare *c*ut;	S, C
Wherein the Grauer had *a s*trife	A, S
with Nature, to out-doo the *l*ife:	L
O, could he but haue drav*v*ne his *w*it	W
*A*s well in brasse, as he hath hit	A
His face; the Print would then *su*rpasse	S, U, R
*A*ll, that vvas euer vvrit in brasse.	A
But, *sinc*e he cannot, Reader, looke	B, S, I, N, C
*N*ot on his Picture, but his Booke.	N

B.I.

Read: FRANCISCUS ST ALBANUS.

(The W in the text appears as a U in the signature; but this, to Arensberg, is a small matter.)

Arensberg admits that his system is flexible; a pair of examples is enough to show the force of his admission. Taking the same poem, and using the same method of 'the cross-gartered acrostic', it appears that there are at least two dissenters from Bacon's claim to authorship:

*To t*he Reader	T, O, T
This Figure, that *t*hou *here seest pu*t,	T, H, E, R, E, S, E, E, S, P, U
It was for gentle Shakespeare cut;	I, T
Wherein the Grauer had *a s*trife	A, S
with Nature, to out-doo the *life*:	L, I, F, E
O, could he but *haue dravv*ne *h*is *w*it	H, A, D, R, A, H, W, I
*A*s *well in* brasse, as he hath hit	A, W, E, L, L, I, N
His face; the Print would then *su*rpasse	S, U
*Al*l, that vvas euer vvrit in brasse.	A, L
But, since he cannot, *Reade*r, *looke*	R, E, A, D, E, L, O, O, K, E
*N*ot *on his P*icture, but his Booke.	N, O, H, I, S, P

B.I.

Read: I AND ONLIE I, WILL SHAKESPEARE, WAS THE AUTHOR OF THESE OLD PLAIES.

A more daring claim emerges if we 'decipher' as follows:

To t*he* R*eader*	T, T, R, E, A, D, E, R
This *Figure*, t*hat* t*hou* here seest put,	T, F, I, G, U, R, E, T, T
It was for gentle Shakespeare cut;	I, T
Wherein t*he* G*rau*er had a strife	W, H, E, R, E, I, N, T, G, R
with Nature, to out-doo the *li*fe:	L, I
O, could he but haue dravvne his wit	O
As w*ell* i*n* brasse, as he hath hit	A, S, W, E, I
His face; the Print would then s*urp*asse	S, U, R, P
All, that vvas euer vvrit i*n* b*r*asse.	I, B, R
But, since he cannot, Reader, *looke*	R, L, O, O, K, E
Not on his Picture, but his B*ooke*.	B
B.I.	

Read: GERTRUDE STEIN WRIT THIS GREAT WORK OF LITERA-
TURE—BOB RIPLIE [Ripley].

Both these messages are longer than Arensberg's own, and each is a complete sentence rather than a mere name; they ought at least to be granted as much credence.

This kind of game could be played indefinitely; as far as the simpler 'anagrammatic acrostics' are concerned, you will be able to find the signature 'BACON' on any page of today's newspaper, together with clues to its presence. This is not because Bacon's ghost haunts the editorial offices of the daily press, nor because all journalists are involved in a vast conspiracy to keep his name in the news. The reason is simpler, even though it takes longer to give it.

First of all, let us consider the chances of finding the name BACON, as a simple acrostic of initial letters, in a 1000-page anthology of English poetry, each page printed in two columns of fifty lines each. That is, we allow ourselves 100,000 lines of verse; and as we are looking for a simple acrostic, taking only the first letter of any line, we have 100,000 letters to choose from. In order to make the calculation, we need to know the relative frequencies of the letters B, A, C, O and N as initial letters of lines of English poetry. To be more precise still, it is clearly preferable to deal with the frequencies of initial letters of the lines in the First Folio itself. We have worked out the figures for ourselves, making a count of 20,000 initial letters of the text in both columns of over 170 pages taken at random from the 900 or so pages of the First Folio text, and reducing the frequencies to a basis of 1000 letters (omitting, of course, the names of speakers, stage-directions and so on).[1] Statistically the letter B occurs as an initial letter 53·7 times in a thousand, so in our hypothetical book there will be about 5370 lines beginning with a B. Again, A has a frequency of 117·9 per thousand lines; so, among the 5370 lines beginning with a B, about 11·79 per cent of them, or 633, will be followed by a line beginning with an A. Similarly, about 2·41 per cent of these will be followed by an initial C, so there will be about 15·26 sets of successive lines, on an average, beginning BAC. The frequency of the letter O is 4·25 per cent, so there will probably be ·649 acrostic BACO's; and 3·74 per cent of these will be followed by an N, so that there will probably be ·0244 acrostic BACON's in the book of 100,000 lines.

Arensberg allows himself to anagram his solutions, and this increases his chances considerably. The number of various sequences in which the five letters B, A, C, O, N can be arranged is 5 × 4 × 3 × 2 × 1, or 120. So the chances of finding an anagrammatic acrostic, as opposed to a simple one, are 120 times as great: in our hypothetical book, 120 × ·0244, which is 2·928. In other words, an anagrammatic acrostic of the signature BACON will happen by accident about three times in 100,000 lines of poetry.

Now in *The Cryptography of Shakespeare* Arensberg does not cite a single case of a simple straightforward acrostic BACON in any Shakespeare play. This should not surprise us, for the chances of its occurrence are small; a good deal less than once in the 100,000 opportunities offered in a 1000-page book with 100 lines to the page, as we have just seen. Nor does Arensberg

---

[1] The frequencies are as follows:

A	117·9	F	34·5	K	3·5	P	17·4	U	7·8
B	53·7	G	19·0	L	22·7	Q	1·0	V	4·6
C	24·1	H	61·7	M	45·7	R	9·3	W	105·7
D	21·8	I	104·6	N	37·4	S	60·5	X	·0
E	8·0	J	·7	O	42·5	T	165·7	Y	30·2
								Z	·0

give a single instance from the First Folio of an acrostic based on anagramming the letters A, B, C, N and O. This, too, is hardly surprising, since even this event will occur only about three times in the book used for our model. Arensberg has less than 100,000 lines to choose from, but to compensate he has ingenious ways of increasing his chances. For one thing, he does not restrict himself to initial letters; he can pick out two or three or more letters at the beginning of any line. The initial letters B, A, O all have a reasonably high frequency; but to make matters easier, so have the initial pairs of letters AB, BA, CO, AN and ON; and you will soon discover, if you look at a dictionary, that there are a good many words beginning with the three letters CON. So even if he restricted himself to anagrams of BACON, using only the initial letters (and perhaps one or two of those immediately following) of successive lines, Arensberg could have put up a quite impressive performance.

As it is, of course, he is not committed to finding just the name 'Bacon'; there are 'Baco', 'F. Baco', 'Verulam' and other varieties to choose from. Nor does he limit himself to the anagrammatic acrostic; he has all the various systems, from the anagrammatic telestic to the cross-gartered acrostic, at his disposal. With so many rounds of ammunition and so many targets it is not difficult to score a direct hit, even if you are shooting at random.

Similar objections can be made against Arensberg's earlier work on *The Cryptography of Dante*: the 'signature' DANTE is composed mainly of letters which have a high frequency as initial letters in Italian; the word is a short one, and is again the end-product of anagramming. Had the letters appeared in their proper order in dozens of different places, one would rightly have been impressed. As it is, it becomes plain that here, too, Arensberg was carried by his enthusiasm beyond the bounds of good sense.

Nothing which has been said detracts in any way from the impressiveness of long, straightforward and systematic acrostic messages. The longer the acrostic, the less likely it becomes that it is the result of sheer chance; eventually the point is reached where doubt cannot be sustained. For example, the chance of finding by accident the name 'Sir Francis Walsingham' would be roughly one in 26^{20}; in other words we can only expect it to happen once every 20,000,000,000,000,000,000,000,000,000 times in any group of twenty lines taken at random. (The figure is only approximate, because we have made the assumption that each of the twenty-six letters of the alphabet is equally likely to occur at the beginning of a word; but while this is not so, the result of an accurate calculation would be of the same order of thousands of millions of millions of millions of millions.)

This is a suitable point to introduce a warning against a mistake which is often made in dealing with mathematical probability. Theoretical calculations tell us only what it is reasonable to expect, not what actually occurs; they deal only with what is predictable, not with what is fortuitous. In the real world, as opposed to the world of logic, we know that surprising coincidences often happen. And it does not necessarily follow that because something is theoretically very improbable, it is also very rare. One example is enough to show this: a card-player who picks up a hand containing thirteen cards of one suit considers it a rare one, and of course it is. The probability of its happening is only four in 635,013,559,600; but it is not this which makes it rare. Mathematically, *any* specified combination of thirteen cards is equally hard to predict; the probability, in advance, of being dealt any hand you care to mention is exactly the same. Whenever a card-player picks up a hand, he sees an arrangement which has a mathematical probability of four in 635,013,559,600; this happens every time a hand is dealt.

But while we must not confuse the mathematically improbable with the practically unlikely, the theory of probability is nevertheless a useful guide. There are limits even to coincidence; if the mathematical probability is very small indeed, and we take other factors of the situation into account, it often becomes unreasonable to maintain that what happens is the result of accident. If a man continues to throw seven after seven at dice, and this happens again and again, it would be absurd not to think that the dice were loaded. At the other end of the scale, the theory is even more useful. If we can show that the mathematical probability of a certain result is high, say one in ten, we need not expect that in practice it will be equally frequent and will dutifully happen once in every ten trials; but the fact remains that it is predictably a common phenomenon, and its happening frequently need not impress us.

This is the case with Arensberg's signatures; he gives himself so many chances of finding what he wants that his discoveries are unimpressive. It is relatively easy to find his brand of signature in any book whatever, but this proves nothing about its authorship. Here are two examples:

In the construction of an acrostic on less than the total number of the lines of a text, the author makes an arbitrary choice, first, as to the proportion of the number of letters in the acrostic spelling to the number of lines in the text; and second, as to the position...

Read: F. BACON.

Clue: note the blatant reference to acrostics!

...ends of main divisions, or continuously through passages of considerable length. The evidence as to the author's intention based on the possibility of such a repetition of identical or similar acrostic spellings would be practically incontrovertible....

Read: BACON.

Clue: 'the author's intention' is plain enough.

Both these examples are taken from randomly chosen pages of Arensberg's own book, reproducing the lines exactly as they are printed. However many times they are multiplied (as indeed they can be), it seems implausible that Bacon spent his time writing and supervising the printing of *The Cryptography of Shakespeare*, especially as he was in all probability, at the time it was being written, busy turning in his grave.

Even the more remarkable example of a simple acrostic anagram, using only the initial letters in six consecutive lines, may quite properly fail to convince us:

But on the acrostic or acrotelestic letters of consecutive lines in conjunction with the acrostic letters of a word adjacent to one of the acrostic words involved in the acrostic spelling. In the *f*orm of the anagrammatic acrostic which I am describing the *a*crostic spelling may include the acrostic letters of an indefinite *n*umber of words consecutively to any acrostic or...

Read: F. BACON.

The mathematical probability of finding any anagrammatic acrostic of 'F. Bacon' in a piece of ordinary prose, using the initial letters only, can be shown to be about 187 in 10,000,000; Arensberg's own book is 280 pages long, and has about forty lines to the page, so it offers only about 11,200 opportunities. The predictable chances, therefore, are about one in five of finding such an example in *The Cryptography of Shakespeare*; but this is scarcely enough to rule out coincidence altogether.

In the final paragraph of his book, Arensberg promised to provide, in Part Two, examples of longer acrostic spellings (he was honest enough to add that these, too, would be derived by 'the flexible method'). While he was at work on these longer 'signatures' he came to see us, in order to disclose a series of anagrammatic spellings which would, he believed, finally clinch the matter of the authorship of Shakespeare's plays. Taking the first play in the First Folio, *The Tempest*, and beginning with the first line of Act I, sc. I, he told us he had produced by the method of anagrammatic acrostics, the message 'The author was Francis Bacon' seven consecutive times. He was disappointed at our calm reception of the news, and sceptical of our contention that the method was so flexible that anyone could, with patience, produce equally impressive but quite different results. We met him again the next afternoon, and had by then produced seven consecutive times, using his own methods and his own book as a text, the message 'The author was William F. Friedman'. We began, as he did, at the beginning, starting from the first line of chapter I; and for good measure our message was four letters longer than the one derived by Arensberg from *The Tempest*. We were hesitant of showing him our findings; we found that we need not have been. He rallied splendidly from the shock, and his reply showed that blend of incurable optimism and illogicality which characterized his work: he admitted that we had made good our contention, and added 'But you know, and I know, that I wrote *The Cryptography of Shakespeare* and not you, so I am not particularly disturbed by that. All the same, what you have done does not disprove the presence of the sentence "The author was Francis Bacon" which I found in *The Tempest*'.

As a final comment on the 'system' devised by Arensberg, we quote from one of his disciples, Granville C. Cunningham, writing in *Baconiana*:[1]

> I think that Bacon kept this cipher of his entirely to himself. I have searched in many books on cipher-writing of his period, and immediately subsequent to it, and find no hint of it anywhere. He said nothing about it, but trusted entirely to the keen eyes of future examiners to discover it.

Arensberg, however, although he finally abandoned the 'anagrammatic acrostic system', had by no means given up the search for cryptographic methods. The year after he brought out Part One of *The Cryptography of Shakespeare* he produced a volume with the long-winded title *The Secret Grave of Francis Bacon and His Mother in the Lichfield Chapter House* (San Francisco, 1923). Using a new method, 'The Baconian key cipher', he concluded that Bacon did not die in 1626, as the historians will have it, but at a later date—possibly 1631; his resting-place, as the title implies, was in the Chapter House in Lichfield Cathedral with his mother. A later and longer book, *The Shakespearian Mystery* (Pittsburgh, 1928: privately printed) backs up his contentions with the help of mystic symbols; in it he adds that the secret grave was meant to serve as a shrine for the Rosicrucian Society, and symbolized rebirth. At the end, after a long and virtually incomprehensible discussion, he hints darkly that the Rosicrucians could unlock the secret if only they were willing to do so.

A more elaborate explanation of his 'key cipher' was presented later the same year, 1928, in *The Baconian Keys*; this was meant 'to replace the defective definition' given earlier in *The Secret Grave...* and in the Preface Arensberg tells us:

> Since I was ignorant at the time of the publication of *The Cryptography of Shakespeare, Part One*, not only of the existence of the

---

[1] Vol. xvii, no. 64, 3rd series, June 1922.

Baconian key-cipher, but also of important aspects of the meaning which the various cryptographic methods are employed to express, the form of continuation which I originally planned as *The Cryptography of Shakespeare, Part Two*, is abandoned.

He does not explicitly go back on his earlier methods and theories; he offers no admission that the anagrammatic acrostic system is invalid and the results of applying it worthless. Rather, he goes forward to higher things, to the secret significance of numbers. His first sentence of text explains: 'The numerical key-cipher employed by Bacon and by members of the Rosicrucian Fraternity is a method of representing a text by a number which is represented by another text.' This is about the most comprehensible sentence in the book; the rest is embarrassingly obscure, and deadly dull. He pursues his theme through page after page of calculation and frequent tables of 'counts'. It is reassuring to know that each calculation was checked by two mathematicians hired for the purpose, although Arensberg generously adds that they 'are exonerated by me from any endorsement of my views'. The result of all this mathematics is disappointing, and consists merely in a repetitious list of the names of Shakespeare, Bacon, and Bacon's mother, in various forms and spellings; Arensberg does not wish to claim that all three co-operated in writing the texts, so the significance of their repeated appearance is not entirely clear. It may be that Shakespeare was Bacon's father but, on the other hand, it may not.

Two final contributions, in 1929 and 1930, obscure the issue still more; *Francis Bacon, William Butts and the Pagets of Beaudesert*, and *The Magic Ring of Francis Bacon*. In these, Arensberg enlists some entirely new devices; 'the magic ring' is the general name he gives to his process of extracting messages in turn from the First Folio and *The Advancement of Learning*, and to do this he uses a magic chess board, a cryptographic watch, calendrical symbolism, the cyclical index, three alphabets (one of twenty-four letters, one of twenty-one and one of twenty), the heptadic pattern, ephemeral letters, augmentation, tetradic forms of dates, various mathematical operations, and transformations and substitutions. It is a fantastic catalogue, and its results are in keeping. He finds that Bacon was descended from Edward, Prince of Wales, son of Henry VI, and that he was therefore of royal descent and a pretender to the throne; that he was the illegitimate son of Sir William Butts (the eldest son of the physician to Henry VIII) and Lady Anne Cooke Bacon; that moreover Bacon himself had a son who was adopted by the Pagets of Beaudesert; that the Paget family were to carry on the Rosicrucian Fraternity founded by Bacon, and were to reveal the Shakespearean mystery as soon as it was safe to do so; and that Bacon used Beaudesert as his secret hide-out from 1626 (when he was popularly supposed to have died) until his actual death 'which probably occurred on or about May, 1631'.

The appropriate atmosphere of speculative fantasy can be evoked by a single quotation from *The Magic Ring* (p. 44); the rest is of a kind with it:

In accordance with the use of the letter I, as having the value 9, for the digit 1, 9—either 9 or 1, as signifying either I or A. By analogy with this variability of 9 as 1 the date, as printed in the *Essays*: 1597, may be read as 9597, 1597, 9517, or 1517. If the form 1517 be divided as follows: 15, 1, 7, it may be read: PAG. Thus read, PAG may be understood as an allusion to the name of PAGET, just as PIG, as read from 1597, may be understood as an allusion to the name of Bacon....In addition to the spellings PIG and PAG, the date 1597, in the form of an anagram—5, 9, 17, may be read: EIR (heir). The date 1597...may thus be understood to involve an association of the words PIG (Bacon), PAG (Paget) and EIR (heir)....

It is hardly necessary to add that there is no cryptographic validity at all in methods of the kind Arensberg used. Their complexity, their number and variety, the absence of any indication of the key or keys to be used, the utter lack of precision, and the clear possibility of producing any number of different messages from the same text, combine to make them almost copy-book cases of all that a cipher system should not be.

Arensberg's progressive abandonment of his earlier methods suggests that he himself was somehow dissatisfied; in the unbiased observer it gives rise to profound and justifiable scepticism. Nevertheless, Arensberg remained convinced to the end of his life that there were cryptographic messages for the finding in Shakespeare's texts, even if he himself had failed to unearth them; and after devoting the major part of his life and a small fortune to the cause, he left a large fortune to it when he died. Late in 1954 the Francis Bacon Foundation, endowed by the wills of the late Mr and Mrs Walter C. Arensberg, opened its offices in Pasadena, California. The library has an impressive collection of Elizabethan and Jacobean works, early text-books on cryptography, and Rosicrucian literature; the research there is presumably being conducted along the lines devised by Arensberg himself.

His history illustrates the academic rake's progress by which a promising scholar can become so enamoured of a single theory that he pursues it far beyond the bounds of good sense. His life is in a way reminiscent of that of Gabriele Rossetti, the father of Dante Gabriele, Christina and William Michael. Rossetti too had searched for, and found, acrostics in Dante's *Divine Comedy*; he too had gone on to the conviction that a secret society was at work, communicating in a secret language of their own. It is, indeed, possible that Arensberg, as a student of Italian literature, had come across Rossetti's work and had been influenced by it. At any rate, E. R. Vincent's comments in his *Gabriele Rossetti in England* have a startling appropriateness, and the two men could have shared the same epitaph. Arensberg, like Rossetti,

has left a vast body of writings...in which he has attempted to prove the truth of his unorthodox interpretation of medieval literature. They present a formidable record of unsystematic research in which we see an enthusiast plunging farther and farther from the logic of facts and good sense until truth is lost in the dreadful nightmare of an *idée fixe*. There is no real evolution of the Theory although it grows and expands until it embraces ever wider horizons. The numerous inaccuracies of deduction, mis-statements of historical fact, and self-contradictions...have caused critics to turn away from them in disgust....Conversely they attracted, and continue to attract, a certain type of mind for whom the appeal of esoteric mysticism is stronger than that of reason....It is impossible to read far...without realizing that we have to deal with a work of faith and imagination rather than of reasoning. There is an appearance of reason, for the author is set on proving by logic the truth of what he already believes by intuition. The truth is plain to him and he cannot comprehend why others do not immediately accept it, but as they desire demonstration he has multiplied his proofs. It is the redundancy and confusion of a prophet expounding by a familiar method the truth revealed to his own simple soul in a flash of inspiration....In such work as this...it is idle to look for the calm reasoning of a scholar; we do not find it, and there is little or no advantage in attacking the obvious inconsistencies and absurdities that abound.

CHAPTER XI

THE STRANGE STORY OF
DR CUNNINGHAM AND
MARIA BAUER

WE now come to the case of a pair of anti-Shakespeareans who used anagrams to achieve results far more spectacular than the few disconnected signatures and phrases found by Booth and Arensberg. Quite apart from the strangeness of their system, their case-histories typify something that is common to many of their fellow-enthusiasts, and their behaviour is worth a brief investigation.

Dr Wallace McCook Cunningham was a distinguished economist; this would suggest that the thesis he put forward and the method he developed deserve a fair hearing. He was the author of one short treatise which had nothing to do with economics: it was entitled *The Tragedy of Sir Francis Bacon, Prince of England* (Los Angeles: The Philosophers Press, 1940), and the story it unfolded was a curious one. Dr Cunningham was able by his method to extract whole plays that had apparently been concealed in the text of Shakespeare's works. He claimed to have proof that these were the work, not of Francis Bacon alone, but of a group of Rosicrucians and Freemasons which included Bacon and 'his dear friends Sir Myles Bodley and Sir Toby Matthews', two other Bodleys (Joshua and Thomas), Ben Jonson, Henry Wotton, Sir Walter Raleigh, Thomas More, Francis Drake, Christopher Marlowe, Edmund Spenser, and Lancelot Andrewes (one of the translators of the Authorized Version of the Bible).

This impressive collection of twenty or so 'able writers in prose and poetry' held their meetings at the Mermaid Tavern. According to Cunningham, their combined genius enabled them to use the characters in the Shakespeare plays as masks for living contemporaries; the secret plays concealed in the text were simply a record of current events. Cunningham relates in an appendix to his book that Francis Bacon was as a child given the punning nickname of 'Hamlet', or 'Little Ham'; the name in *Hamlet* corresponds in the 'code' to Francis, Bacon, or Moon-man. In the same hidden play, the King and Queen of Denmark become, 'by code coordination', Queen Elizabeth and Robert Devereux; Horatio is really William Hatton, Marcellus is a disguise for Marlowe, and so on.

The concealed text, considering the assembled talents responsible for it, is sometimes rather a disappointment, but Cunningham is prepared to be frank about this; in one place he remarks that 'while our interest lies in a brief illustration of the one hundred per cent proof always available throughout the play for each character's true name, we have been unable to avoid noting the atrocious quality of the passage'. He is ready with an explanation, however:

Quite aside from its quality, it is entirely unsuitable for inclusion in the true play because Bacon was brilliantly sane in spite of the incest in his own family and the danger to his own life; and of course he did not even feign insanity when with his dear friends Will Hatton and Kit Marlowe.

Prior to reaching this passage the decoder had been informed in code that Myles Bodley had written this scene for Francis Bacon. Then, in two separate, perfectly located code passages, the following code messages were found.

'Bacon and Myles Bodley (Bodlie in the code) leave out these heavy coded vile lines.

'Myles Bodley wrote this vile coded matter in order to win a bet from good rude old Ben Jonson, the Mermaid Tavern Host, for a wonderfull dinner with good wine in the noble Masonry Room. Myles Bodley won with one code word over.'

The noble Masonry room was used also for the monthly dinners of the 'Wild Goose Club'—all Masons and including all of the Shakespeare authors. Bacon, in describing one particular dinner, states: 'At the Mermaid Tavern at a Wild Goose Dinner, my groom Shake uttered such dulcet and melodious tones that even rude Ben Jonson gave approval to his song, and certain Mermaid Members made music madly.' William Shakespeare served as a private waiter at the Wild Goose dinners; and, from the ample evidence already available, he will without doubt take high rank among the singing waiters of all time.

Cunningham referred to the system which enabled him to extract this remarkable information as 'the Masonic Code'. There is some historical evidence that the members of the Masonic Order in its early days did in fact use a cipher system based on geometric figures. The key was

a, j, s	b, k, t	c, l, u
d, m, v	e, n, w	f, o, x
g, p, y	h, q, z	i, r, space

and the letters were represented by dots inside an angle (or square). The first letter of each trio was represented by the angle (or complete square) alone; the second by a single dot inside it; and the third by a pair of dots within the appropriate shape. Thus, ⌐ represents 'a', ⌐ stands for 'j', and ⌐ for 's'. To spell out 'Mason' one would write ⌐. ⌐ ⌐ ⌐ ⌐.

It is difficult to understand why Cunningham should have named his system as he did, for it bears no relation whatever to this method. He explains his own 'Masonic Code' as follows: 'A word in the Masonic Code consists of letters in the manifest or cover text in the form of an anagram (i.e. the letters are in any order) lying on or adjacent to a base line drawn in any direction; and each code word, or each text word used in the code must connect with the word before it and with the word after it by an uninterrupted connection line.' Now quite apart from the fact that Cunningham is working with a cipher system and not a code (and this elementary confusion suggests a certain failure to grasp even the fundamentals of cryptology), and the fact that he at one point attributes the system to Bacon, who never mentioned anything at all comparable, this explanation is somewhat obscure. It looks, on the face of it, as if Cunningham is saying: 'Make up your mind what secret text you want to find, then look for suitable letters in the open text to spell it out; if you can draw straight lines connecting or adjoining these letters, without passing through any letters not used for the secret text, you have proved the validity of your guess. You can of course take the letters from anywhere on the page, because it is nearly always necessary to anagram them.'

In practice, Cunningham does not draw on his working diagrams the 'uninterrupted connection lines' which are supposed to connect each word in the secret text with its successor. Most of the words in his decipherments are lifted directly from the open text, without any anagramming or re-combining; for the rest, he draws in the 'base lines' to connect the various letters he needs, and anagrams these letters to give the necessary results. As a check on the meaning of his 'cover names' (e.g. 'Hamlet' for 'Bacon' and so forth) he insists that they must give '100 per cent proof'; in other words, on each occasion on which the 'cover name' appears, it must be possible to find nearby the corresponding 'true name' enciphered.

Save for these few principles, which emerge during the course of Cunningham's book, he nowhere explicitly sets out the rules to be observed in following his 'system'; there is no indication of the way the decipherer is informed where to begin his base lines, and no regulations are given about the directions in which they are to be drawn. On each occasion, apparently, the decipherer has to guess at the secret text before proceeding to find it. As we have already remarked, in genuine cryptanalysis it is sometimes necessary to do this: to break down an unknown system it is often a great help if one has a suspicion that a given open text conceals a certain message. But once the cryptanalyst is successful, once he has broken down the system, guessing is no longer to the point. If one has found the key to a lock, it is no longer necessary to pick it.

If Cunningham's system is a genuine one, it must be possible to set out the rules so fully that we do not have to keep on guessing. Unfortunately Cunningham does not take the reader into his confidence in this way; it seems that the only conclusion to be drawn is that there are no keys to the system whatever: his so-called 'Masonic Code' is totally without validity. If this condemnation seems a little too rapid, it would be better first to let Cunningham speak for himself and to give him a chance to demonstrate, as he fails to do in his book, the principles on which his decipherments rest.

This seems a vain hope, for Cunningham died in 1945; but in fact we were able to ask him during his lifetime for a personal demonstration of the 'code' and the full details of its manipulation. In 1938 he had submitted the manuscript of his book to Doubleday-Doran; the late Brigadier-General Theodore Roosevelt, Junior, was at the time Vice-President of the firm, and he asked us to report on the system Cunningham had devised. Cunningham was given his expenses for a visit to Washington and we had a series of interviews with him during the week 18–25 October. The diary we kept during that period, together with the fairly voluminous notes and correspondence, give a clear record of what happened.

During the first meeting, Cunningham set to work on a facsimile page of *Julius Caesar* in the First Folio. He explained that the play was a 'cover' for the murder of William Hatton at Windsor Castle; Hatton had persuaded Elizabeth to kill off the entire Masonic group, but they had discovered the plot in time and had taken their revenge. Cunningham then produced the message (see Plate V):

Dear[1] Reader: The Asse Will Shakespeare brought William Hatton down to his grave. The Asse beares sland'rous tales to Hatton. Hatton beares them to the wart-sow (not marked see swet) Elisabeth. She gave our death Sentence and Proscription—Walter Raleigh.

We asked Cunningham why he chose a specific part of the page to begin a base-line; he answered that it was because he noticed certain letters which were part of a name he was looking for. When we asked what rules determined the direction in which a line was to be drawn, his answer was extremely vague. We decided that it would be best to give him a chance to explain the system in writing; he attempted this some time later, after his return to New York, but the system remained incomprehensible.

The next few days were taken up with testing his claim for '100 per cent proof'. Cunningham was positive that no name other than the genuine 'code correspondent' could be found enciphered near each occurrence of a given 'cover' or 'key-name' in the text. He wanted us to give him a chance to demonstrate this principle in action, and we asked him to find either of two names we had chosen, Richmond and Gardiner,

---

[1] This way of beginning a letter or message did not come into common use until after the seventeenth century.

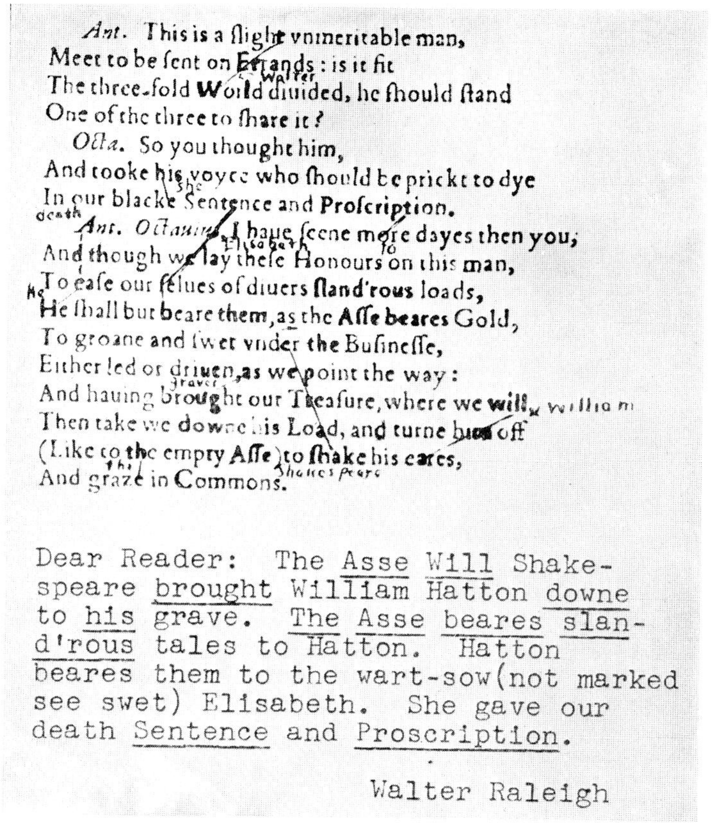

PLATE V

Ant. This is a flight vnmeritable man,
Meet to be fent on Errands : is it fit
The three-fold World diuided, he fhould ftand
One of the three to fhare it?
   Octa. So you thought him,
And tooke his voyce who fhould be prickt to dye
In our blacke Sentence and Profcription.
   Ant. Octauius, I haue feene more dayes then you;
And though we lay thefe Honours on this man,
To eafe our felues of diuers fland'rous loads,
He fhall but beare them, as the Affe beares Gold,
To groane and fwet vnder the Bufineffe,
Either led or driuen, as we point the way :
And hauing brought our Treafure, where we will,
Then take we downe his Load, and turne him off
(Like to the empty Affe) to fhake his eares,
And graze in Commons.

(handwritten annotations: *Walter*, *she*, *death*, *Elisabeth*, *fo*, *He*, *trauell*, *william*, *the*, *Shakespeare*)

Dear Reader: The Asse <u>Will</u> Shakespeare <u>brought</u> William Hatton downe
to <u>his</u> grave. The Asse beares <u>slan-
d'rous</u> tales to Hatton. Hatton
beares them to the wart-sow(not marked
see swet) Elisabeth. She gave our
death <u>Sentence</u> and <u>Proscription</u>.

                   Walter Raleigh

Cunningham's message derived from a facsimile page of *Julius Caesar*
in the First Folio.

PLATE VI

Sc. II.]   *JULIUS CÆSAR*   7

You bear too stubborn and too strange a hand
Over your friend that loves you,   Cassius,
Be not deceived: if I have veiled my look,
I turn the trouble of my countenance
Merely° upon myself. Vexed I am
Of late with passions of some difference,°   40
Conceptions only proper to myself,°
Which give some soil perhaps to my behaviors;
But let not therefore my good friends be grieved —
Among which number, Cassius, be you one —
Nor construe° any further my neglect
Than that poor Brutus with himself at war
Forgets the shows of love to other men.

Dear Reader: Theodore Roosevelt is the true
author of this play but I, Bacon, stole it
from him and have the credit. Friedman can
prove that this is so by this cock-eyed cypher
invented by Doctor C.

Our message derived, by Cunningham's method, from a school
edition of *Julius Caesar*.

against the keyname 'Cassius' in the text of *Julius Caesar*. This keyname appears 274 times; Cunningham announced, after working for two days, that he had only been able to find 'Richmond' or 'Gardiner' enciphered nearby in about 30 per cent of the cases. We began to check his results. On the first page 'Cassius' appeared once, and Cunningham had marked it '0', meaning that neither of our bogus names could be found; we immediately discovered a 'Gardiner' which he admitted to be valid. On another page there were nine occurrences of 'Cassius', and he said he could only account for two or three of them; we produced all nine 'code correspondents' and he agreed that these, too, were valid. We asked him if his beliefs would be shaken if we could produce '100 per cent proof' on a page with a good many keynames; he said they would not.

At this point we suggested that he should go back to New York and await our report, as a longer test would involve unnecessary expense for Doubleday-Doran. Cunningham, however, insisted that a further session would clear up all our difficulties. We asked him to go over his work very carefully in the meantime, making sure he had not overlooked places where a 'Richmond' or 'Gardiner' could be found. Three days later he returned, saying that he 'couldn't find' his working notes; all that we could get from him was a reluctant admission that he had discovered many more occurrences than at first. We got the impression that he had in fact found enough to ruin his case.

He demanded one more test; this was beginning to seem a waste of time, but finally we agreed. We asked him to write a list of the names and equivalents he expected to find in *Macbeth*; selecting three pages at random we then set him to work finding the enciphered names. The next day he returned with his results. The name 'James Hepburn' was not on his original list, but he had since found several occurrences of it; he had changed his list overnight.

After he returned to New York, Cunningham wrote to us; here is an extract from his letter:

In making your written report to Doubleday-Doran I feel that it would be only fair to them and to me to state that no true name observed in work previously done or checked by your orders failed to check 100 per cent with the cover name, and that you found no case in which a test name chosen by you so checked. With my recollections fresh on these points no misunderstanding seems possible. . . .

In spite of this, we remain convinced that Cunningham was never intentionally dishonest with us. He seemed entirely sincere; he was deeply convinced that his theory was valid. This is true of most of the people who search for cryptographic evidence to prove that someone other than Shakespeare was responsible for his plays; the worst that can be said of even the most bizarre of them is that they are in other respects sensible people who, in pursuing the elusive proofs they hope one day to discover, have allowed their good judgment to be undermined.

What can be said of Cunningham's method? It fulfils adequately one of the two conditions for validity; the language of the deciphered text is on the whole acceptable and coherent. This is not surprising, since the bulk of the words are taken verbatim from Shakespeare's text; but most of the anagrammed words make sense too. The system, however, collapses utterly when we consider the second demand: there are no unambiguous keys, and even Cunningham himself was unable to give any account of his rules for applying them. Base lines can begin at any letter and be drawn in any direction; and it is possible to find almost any message one wants to find in almost any text one chooses.

Cunningham laid a good deal of emphasis on the point that the 'code' could only be made to work in the First Folio, since it 'is dependent on the position and alignment of the letters'. No other text would do: the printing layout was deliberately arranged for suitability by the Masonic group, using their own printers for the job; any text not printed specially in this way could, according to Cunningham, produce only a meaningless jumble of letters. But the truth is that the method is so flexible that one can apply it freely in an infinite number of other cases. We were able to show this in our report to Colonel Roosevelt (as he then was). Taking a page from an ordinary school edition of *Julius Caesar*, we produced our own message, a good outspoken one (see Plate VI):

Dear Reader: Theodore Roosevelt is the true author of this play but I, Bacon, stole it from him and have the credit. Friedman can prove that this is so by this cock-eyed cypher invented by Doctor C.

Doubleday-Doran subsequently rejected the book, but Cunningham found a publisher for it in California.

Like other Baconians who were the first to discover a particular 'system', Cunningham attracted a number of kindred spirits, and had his share of imitators: one of these, a Frenchman writing under the pseudonym F. Bonac-Melvrau—a fairly obvious anagram of 'F. Bacon-Verulam'—drew his base-lines to connect anagrammatic 'signatures' of Bacon (but not a coherent text) in books written neither by Bacon nor by Bacon-as-Shakespeare. Cunningham's most notable disciple, however, was a certain Mrs Maria Bauer, who subsequently married the man who published his book, Manly P. Hall, a mystic and lecturer in philosophy who founded the Philosophical Research Society of Los Angeles. Neither Dr Cunningham nor Mrs Bauer explicitly mention one another in their works; it was clearly best in any case that they should maintain a healthy air of independence. Nevertheless, that they were known to each other is made clear by newspaper articles written in Williamsburg, Virginia, in September and October 1938, and by an article in *Baconiana* (April and July 1951); and they both lived in the same town, Glendale, California, at the time of publication of Cunningham's book.

Mrs Bauer's short pamphlet, *Francis Bacon's Great Virginia Vault* (privately published, 1939) tells a more racy story of luxury and incest in high places than Cunningham ever told; for example, she has

definite information as to the actual burying place of 'the Virgin Queen' and 'the gentle Shakespear'....They are buried together under a barn and not in their respective tombs....Over their grave is an inscription on a marble plate stating: 'Here lie the two most famous and yet most infamous people the world has ever produced'....Francis and his group despised the degree of degeneracy they represented.

There are other new revelations, including a hitherto un-published account of the voyages of Francis Drake, 'decoded', she tells us, from Shakespeare's Sonnets. But once having whetted the reader's appetite, she gets down to the serious matter of the 'code':

Francis Bacon and his group greatly desired that the Anagram-matic Code and the information therein should be discovered. They left definite instructions as to the rules of the Code...with a secret inner group of Masons. Many poems and writings produced by the Shakespeare group were never published during their lifetime, but were handed down to this inner Masonic group with definite information as to the time and circumstances of their release. All those writings contained the Anagrammatic Code....For instance in trying the Code on one of Charles Lamb's poems....

It is not difficult to guess the rest of this passage. Mrs Bauer of course finds exactly what she wants to find; with such a method, it would almost be harder to avoid finding it. The code tells her that Bacon and Lancelot Andrewes wrote the poem; it also reveals instructions for its publication, including (with remarkable clairvoyance) a demand that the poet to whom it is bequeathed should add the two lines

Obedient to instructions, lo, I am
A zealous, meek, contributory Lamb.

Another instance of the foresight of the early Masonic group occurs in the passage where Mrs Bauer assures us that:

In the Shakespeare works there is frequent mention of the date June 9, 1938, which marks the beginning of the collapse of the Shakespeare myth. The statements read: 'Soon after June 9, 1938, the Shakespeare myth will die a quick death'; or 'The frail Shake-speare story will fall of its own weight soon after June 9, 1938'.

This is just about the date that Mrs Bauer herself made a discovery which, had it been better received, might have had the whole learned world in an uproar. (More credit to the Baconian group of Masons that they should predict the season so accurately; for how could they have guessed that Mrs Bauer's decipherment would meet with so uncharitable a response?) Working on one of the more 'recent' poems, Mrs Bauer had suddenly come across the mention of a 'Great Virginia Vault'.

As the story unfolded, it became clear that the original Shake-speare manuscripts had been brought to Jamestown, Virginia, in 1635, and hidden in a vault there by a direct descendant of Francis Bacon; his real name was Henry Blount, but on reaching the New World he adopted the name of Nathaniel Bacon. From the vault in Jamestown the manuscripts were moved in 1674 to Williamsburg, and buried under Bruton Parish Church.

Mrs Bauer had been planning to go to New York 'for the purpose of establishing the Code on its own proof and merit'. But a discovery of such moment demanded a change of plan; 'it seemed to me most plausible then to go to Williamsburg', and go she did. The Rockefeller Foundation was at the time restoring the town, but gave her permission to excavate under the tower of the present Bruton Parish Church. She found nothing, and the Restoration officials withdrew their support.

This did not deter her: she was soon at work, armed with a new method, examining the inscriptions on the tombstones in the nearby graveyard. The story of her progress is told, partly in the *Great Virginia Vault*, and partly in a later work, *Foundations Unearthed*. On the very first tombstone she examined, she found the coat of arms of the 'moon-man' (Bacon); and then, noticing misspellings in another inscription, she 'decoded' it to find the exact location of the now-forgotten original parish church. Encouraged by her good fortune, she hired a surveyor and workmen. She records that parts of the old church foundations were actually unearthed when, after two days of digging, the Restoration authorities summarily stopped the excavation. Eventually, frustrated by shortage of funds and lack of sympathy, she went home to write her pamphlets.

Her grievances against the Rockefeller Foundation naturally occupy a good deal of her available space. It seems fair to mention that the Restoration officials disagree with her version of the facts; they altogether deny that she discovered the remains of the old church. It appears that they were also willing to give her a fair hearing. Mrs Bauer remarks: 'Officials of the Restoration suggested that the code be submitted to a code expert selected by them and that in the event of a favourable outcome they would finance me. Though my resources are extremely limited I refused, lacking confidence in their assistance.' She adds that 'two code experts' supported her in her method, but 'the man selected by the Restoration refused to give a report of his findings'.

The 'code' she relied on for all except the tombstone decipherments was identical with that used by Cunningham. Her discourses on its nature are reminiscent of his:

The insertion of the code into the text presents a tremendous labour, and accounts on the basis of necessity for the addition of over 3000 words to the English language by the authors of the Shakespeare works....The spacing and spelling errors represent a sacrifice of the apparent text to the true text in code. The various characters in the plays are by anagrammatic rule converted into contemporary historical characters ('Hamlet' is Francis Bacon, the ghost of the King is the Earl of Leicester, etc.)....There is only one name, that of the character who actually played the historical role, which will follow through 100 per cent.

Mrs Bauer goes on to list the various 'true names' corresponding to the 'cover names' in the text: in *Macbeth*, which is really *The Tragedy of Mary Stuart*, Macbeth is played by James Bothwell, Lady Macbeth by Mary Stuart, and Duncan by Henry Darnley; in *Julius Caesar* the *dramatis personae* include William Hatton as Caesar and Bacon as Brutus. *Hamlet* is *The Story of the Tragedy of Windsor Castle* and tells of the murder of the Earl of Leicester by Queen Elizabeth and her son and lover, the Earl of Essex.

Mrs Bauer is full of confidence in her 'system'; she does not hesitate to make large claims for it:

The Anagrammatic is the only code by which extensive information could be given....In the past codes and cyphers have been found in the Shakespeare works...but this code is the first one which has had a physical proof. This is borne out by discovering, in the code, the existence of the old Bruton Church, and then, *by excavation*, authenticating the code messages.

How far are such claims justified? Our discussion of Cunningham has suggested that the cipher system which he and Mrs Bauer persist in miscalling a 'code' has no validity. Further, the facts cited in support of it are, to say the least highly disputable. Who the so-called experts were who 'passed favourably on the tests submitted', we have no idea; nor do we know the identity of the expert 'selected by the Restoration' who 'refused to give a report on his findings'. But it seems clear to us that Mrs Bauer's efforts with the 'Anagrammatic Code' amount to nothing but a remarkable piece of self-delusion; her messages can only be explained as the products of a powerful imagination.

It now remains to investigate the alternative 'code' which assisted Mrs Bauer in her interpretations of some of the tomb-stones in the Bruton parish burial ground. Unfortunately, being more explicit about the merits of her system than its mechanics, she has left no clear record of it. There is, admit-tedly, a passage in *Foundations Unearthed* which runs:

> Various codes and ciphers were employed to bury the true and intended content beneath the apparent cover-text....To guard against imitation by others in case of possible detection, it was prudent to coordinate known methods in an unknown manner. The 'new invention' peculiar to the work consists in the rearrangement of the letters and words of the apparent text in accordance with the natural abilities of the text constituents....

The author also refers to 'laborious methods of extraction'; but nowhere is there any explanation of what kind of 'natural abilities' the text constituents are gifted with. One is left completely in the dark.

The only further source of information is an article on 'The Buried Secret of Bruton Churchyard' by Albert Stuart Otto (*Baconiana*, April and July 1951). Otto begins by assuring his readers that as a journalist and lecturer his sole interest, initially, was in getting a story. Details from other sources proved curiously difficult to come by, and he was forced in the end to rely on the unsupported evidence of Mrs Bauer (who had by that time remarried to become Mrs Manly P. Hall, the mystic's wife). She told him that it had all begun in Dr Hall's library in 1938: while looking through a book published by Hall, under the forbidding title *An Encyclopedic Outline of Masonic, Hermetic, Cabalistic and Rosicrucian Symbolical Philosophy* (1927), she had noticed an acrostic on Shakespeare. This appeared under the heading 'Emblems, Illustrated by George Wither' in the section devoted to Elizabethan works. Her interest was immediately aroused; she went on to study the rest of the book, and this, in conjunction with her grounding in Cunningham's system, led to the discovery of the secret of the old Bruton Church. She told Otto that the hiding-place there contained, in addition to the Shakespeare manuscripts, the manuscript of the Authorized Version of the Bible, unpublished Baconian writings, Tudor birth records, and esoteric Masonic documents.

Presented with the news of this literary treasure trove, Otto's scepticism vanished; he came to believe wholeheartedly in her story of the discovery of the church foundations. Nevertheless, he admits in his article to some discomfort over her various decipherments. Here is one example of the kind of discrepancies he found: she had extracted from a tombstone the names 'Anne' and 'Graham', because they had suggested the word 'anagram' to her. This, she believed, was linked in some way with one of George Wither's 'emblems' in the *Encyclopedic Outline* she had studied so carefully. Wither's illustration, she argued, had shown a woman holding a spray of grain in her hand; and 'Graham' was another name for grain. But as Otto points out, Wither can hardly be expected to have known this; the word 'Graham' only came into currency 200 years after his death, being taken from the name of an American dietetic reformer of the nineteenth century.

Mrs Bauer confided to Otto that she had ten volumes of such 'decipherments', all in manuscript, and privately circulated. Otto contents himself with the remark that the cipher is very difficult to follow. In fact:

> She claims that strict adherence to the rules of mechanical code and cipher will get one nowhere in this case. Rather, she says, the code is broken by a psychological key. Offhand this would seem to be merely a convenient excuse for taking extreme liberties, for it does appear at times that she alters the rules to obtain letters needed to 'verify' certain data. This she denies, contending that there are very definite rules, but that their application depends on certain psychological insight.

We can say no more; if any reader feels that a comment is necessary, he should return to ch. II and study the fundamental principles of cryptology again.

CHAPTER XII

ODD NUMBERS

THE word 'numerology' is of comparatively recent origin; it began to find its way into dictionaries only about thirty years ago, and is still not listed in some of the more exclusive ones. But the activity the word covers—the assignment of numerical values to letters, and the investment of these numbers with magical powers—dates back to the early Egyptians and the Babylonians. The Talmudic Jews were familiar with it; and during the whole Christian era people have puzzled about the meaning of certain numbers mentioned in the Scriptures (a popular enigma is presented by Rev. xiii. 11 to 18, where the mystical 666 is cited as 'the number of the beast'). More generally, philosophy, astrology, alchemy, and mathematics were all influenced in their early stages by the speculations of the numerologists. Plato's writings suggest that he was interested in the subject; Pythagoras and his followers devoted a good deal of their attention to it;[1] and many other great thinkers were at one time or another ardent believers in the miraculous properties of numbers.

Baconian cryptologists have often shown an interest in Secret Societies, cabals, and occultism; it was perhaps inevitable that they should finally turn to numerology. The search for 'seals', or hidden numerical ciphers, began in the early years of this century and since that time has continued to be enormously popular.

The basic cipher sequences used in Baconian numerology are given by assigning numbers to the 24-letter Elizabethan alphabet in a straightforward way, A being equivalent to 1 and Z to 24, or in reverse, with Z as 1 and A as 24. In other words, the sequences are:

---

[1] Eric Bell, in his book on *Numerology* (Baltimore, 1933), says of Pythagoras that, having made a brilliant discovery of the Law of Musical Intervals, 'he proceeded to indulge in an orgy of mathematical speculations...got numerologically drunk, and died scientifically of intellectual delirium tremens'.

Simple

A B C D E F G H I–J K L M N O P Q R S T U–V W X Y Z

1 2 3 4 5 6 7 8 9 10 11 12 13 14 15 16 17 18 19 20 21 22 23 24

Reversed

Z Y X W V–U T S R Q P O N M L K J–I H G F E D C B A

1 2 3 4 5 6 7 8 9 10 11 12 13 14 15 16 17 18 19 20 21 22 23 24

To find the numerical value of a name, one simply works out the total of the individual values of its letters. Thus, for example,

$$\text{B A C O N}$$
$$2 \quad 1 \quad 3 \quad 14 \quad 13$$

gives 'Bacon' a value of 33 in simple cipher, and

$$\text{S H A K E S P E A R E}$$
$$7 \quad 17 \quad 24 \quad 15 \quad 20 \quad 7 \quad 10 \quad 20 \quad 24 \quad 8 \quad 20$$

gives 'Shakespeare' a value of 172 in reversed cipher.

One of the foremost numerologists was Frank Woodward, at one time President of the Bacon Society of Great Britain. He and his brother, Parker Woodward, were between them responsible for about five dozen books and pamphlets on Bacon's authorship of the Shakespeare plays; and a high proportion of these contained references to numerological discoveries. In his book on *Francis Bacon's Cipher Signatures* (London, 1923) Woodward seizes on the number 33, which we have just seen to be equivalent to 'Bacon', and points out that in the left-hand column of p. 56 of *I Henry IV* in the First Folio, the name Francis is mentioned exactly 33 times. 'Bearing in mind that 33 means BACON', he remarks, 'this repetition of his Christian name is very significant....The name "Francis" is dragged into the dialogue, in a most absurd manner.' (This is the passage in which Prince Henry confuses the serving man Francis by calling his name. Francis replies 'Anon, anon, sir', which is no doubt equally significant.)

In the same volume Woodward introduces a new cipher system, the discovery of which he attributes to another Baconian, William Clifton. In the 1605 edition of *The Advancement of Learning*, Bacon remarks that 'the kinds of cyphars... are many...Wheele-cyphars, Kay-cyphars, Doubles, etc.' And now, according to Woodward, the 'kay cipher' has been brought to light:

A	B	C	D	E	F	G	H	I–J	K	L	M
27	28	29	30	31	32	33	34	35	10	11	12

N	O	P	Q	R	S	T	U–V	W	X	Y	Z
13	14	15	16	17	18	19	20	21	22	23	24

The values of the letters, from K onwards, are the same as those in the simple cipher; and hence the name. Woodward does not explain why A does not have the value 25, following Z as 24, as one might expect. The only reason that has so far been offered is that the value 25 is assigned to '&', and 26 to another letter 'E' (probably the alternative form, *&*, of the ampersand). But in fact there is no need to explain this kind of eccentricity: in legitimate cryptography the man who devises a system can assign any value he likes to any letter he chooses, provided that, once this is done, those who work with the system keep strictly to the rules. And in this particular system the numbering has the advantage of fitting in neatly with Woodward's own preconceptions, so we can hardly expect him to quibble.

There is, unfortunately, an erroneous assumption at the basis of the 'kay cipher': the Baconians concluded that in using the term 'kay cyphars' Bacon had meant that the numbering of the alphabet should begin with the letter K. It is at once obvious to anyone who knows anything about cryptography that Bacon meant nothing of the kind: he was referring to key-ciphers, which are systems using several different alphabets, each being identified by a key-word or key-number. This is suggested by Bacon's spelling of the word 'cyphar', where he uses an 'a' for an 'e' five times in the same passage; it ought to have occurred to Woodward that the 'a' of 'kay' might similarly be understood as an 'e'. The interpretation is confirmed by the enlarged Latin edition of *The Advancement of Learning* in 1623, where in the corresponding passage Bacon uses the expression 'Ciphrae Claves' (*clavis* being the Latin for key).

However, the system became established as one of the tools of the numerologist's trade, and Woodward proceeded to apply it to his texts. A large part of *Francis Bacon's Cipher Signatures* is taken up with the pursuit of the mystic number 287. The 'kay cipher' is a great asset, since the 'seal' 287 stands for FRA ROSICROSSE in this system; hence it can be taken as the secret sign of the Rosicrucian Fraternity. Woodward, like a number of his fellow-Baconians, believed that Bacon was the leader of the Fraternity, and that its members included other eminent Elizabethan writers.

He finds the number almost everywhere he looks. In Ben Jonson's poem 'To the Reader' in the First Folio, he counts the number of letters in each line, including the title and the signature 'B.I.': the total is 287, providing he counts the two W's in the eighth line as four letters (after all, they are really double V's), and treats the W's in the preceding lines as single letters (but then, he claims, they are plainly W's). In the second column of the first page of the First Folio *Tempest* he finds 'exactly 287 words' in roman type (though he is nowhere explicit in his rules for counting: he does not make it clear, for example, whether hyphenated words count as one or two); again, in the first column of the first page of *The Histories* there are the same number of roman words. Woodward is amazed: 'This seemed a most extraordinary coincidence. It seemed impossible to have been by chance, so I next turned to the first page of *The Tragedies*. At first this page seemed a little disappointing, as there were in the first column 318 words of roman type. I was, however, beginning to learn a little of the author's methods....' Woodward's readers soon go on to learn a little of his: the count has so far been of words, not letters, but Woodward is undaunted by this. The number of italic words is not helpful, but the number of their constituent letters is 31; and this subtracted from 318 yields once more the mystic 287.

Here and there Woodward has to make allowances for errors or for variations in the rules; but he has no difficulty in finding the number 287 scattered throughout the First Folio, *The Advancement of Learning*, and other Elizabethan books. He does not restrict himself to mere word counts: 'Another way of directing attention to this number is by having the work written with 287 pages, as is done in the *Pleasant Notes* by Edward Gayton, published in 1644. Robert Burton's *Anatomy of Melancholy*, published in 1621, commences its second part on page 287, and the work finishes opposite page 782, which is merely 287 backwards....' Nor does he limit his reading list to works by Elizabethan authors, for 'the use of this secret number 287 was not confined to Shakespeare or to Bacon, or even to their contemporaries, as it was used for over a hundred years after the death of either of them'. There are exactly 287 words in roman type in the Epistle Dedicatory of Dugdale's *History of Warwickshire* (1656), and in the last two pages of the Dedication in Nicholas Rowe's 1709 edition of Shakespeare's works.

He is even able to invoke this method as an aid to literary scholarship: by studying the seven 'doubtful' plays included for the first time in the 1644 folio edition, and by grading the degrees of success with which he was able to find numerical 'seals', he concludes that Bacon was partly responsible for four of them.

Another of Frank Woodward's books, written jointly with his brother, rejoices in the title *Fratres Roseae Crucis. Secret Shakespeare Seals. Revelations of Rosicrucian Arcana. Discoveries in the Shakespeare plays, sonnets, and works, printed circa 1586–1740, of 'Secreti Sigilli', concealed author's marks and signs.* This work contains the details of the Rosicrucian group of sixty or seventy men, led by Francis Bacon, who controlled the printing of all the books issued in Elizabeth's time and onwards into the eighteenth century. Their authorship was anonymous, and their pseudonyms diverse and frequently changed; their secret numerical signatures gave the only clue to their creativity. The secrets of the order were passed on from generation to generation within the group; and, according to the brothers Woodward, they survive to this day.

It was Frank Woodward who discovered that Bacon's numerical signatures could be divided into periods, according to his status at any given date. He was knighted in 1603, created Baron Verulam in 1618 and Viscount St Albans in 1620; the signatures therefore run:

From 1579 *to* 1603

	'Simple'	'Kay'
Bacon	33	111
F. Bacon	39	143
Fr Bacon	56	160
Francis Bacon	100	282

From 1603 *to* 1618

Francis Bacon Knight	166	426
Fr. Bacon Kt.	85	189
Francis Bacon Kt.	129	311
Sir Francis Bacon Knight ...	210	496

From 1620 *to* 1626

Fr. St Alban	88	192
Francis St Alban	132	314

Woodward shows his theory in action in an article in *Baconiana* of March 1924, on 'Bacon's Cipher Seals in Hamlet'. The grave-digger's song in the quarto edition of *Hamlet* in 1603 contained 91 roman letters and 39 italic letters in nine words: 39 is the seal for 'F. Bacon' and 91 plus 9 is 100, or 'Francis Bacon'. In the 1604 quarto edition the song was altered to contain 84 roman letters and one italic word; this time Woodward does not add the number of roman letters to the *total* number of words, but only to the number of italic words: the sum is 84 plus 1, or 85, which is 'Fr. Bacon Kt.' In 1623 the verse was changed again, since Bacon was by this time a viscount: there are 88 roman letters in the 1623 edition, and this is the seal for 'Fr. St Alban' in simple cipher. Woodward also calls attention to the versions 'Picke-axe' (1603), 'Pickax' (1604) and 'Pichaxe' (1623), which give further evidence of Bacon's social progress.

In their various other books and articles the Woodward brothers put forward a series of numerological finds. In June 1922 in *Baconiana* they turned their attention to the Shakespeare portraits: among these, the Marshall portrait has a printed legend containing one italic letter in the first line and 32 in the second, making 33 (Bacon); the total number of letters is 81, which in simple count yields 'Messias', or 'Leader', or

'Ch. Rosen C.' (in full, Christian Rosy Cross). Similarly, the legend of the portrait in the 1624 edition of the Poems contains 282 letters, signifying 'Francis Bacon' in kay cipher. Parker Woodward, together with Clifton (the discoverer of the kay cipher), had earlier calculated that the inscription on the Bacon statue in St Michael's Church at St Albans has a count of 287 for the combined letters and figures; they pointed out that A.D. 287 was the year in which St Alban became the first Grand Master of Freemasonry.

The Woodwards' most impressive discovery was set out in *Baconiana* in October 1916, and later developed in full in *Sir Francis Bacon, Poet, Philosopher and Statesman* (1920). The Yorkshireman Ben Haworth-Booth had, as a result of his anagramming of the 'long word' in *Don Quixote*, concluded that Bacon was the true author. The Woodward brothers reached the same surprising conclusion independently, and by a different route. Frank had noticed that Gayton's *Pleasant Notes upon 'Don Quixote'* was one of the significant books which contained exactly 287 pages; the brothers began to study the last page, and found that it contained 341 roman and 54 italic words: subtracting one number from the other again produced the number 287, or 'Fra Rosicrosse' in kay cipher. Furthermore, the form 'Quixot' used by Gayton has a count of 100 in simple cipher, which points at once to 'Francis Bacon'.

Frank Woodward's predecessor as President of the Bacon Society was Bertram Theobald, who began his numerological researches in about 1912; after years of assiduous computation he produced his great work, *Francis Bacon Concealed and Revealed* (1930). In this book he announces that there are 'two general rules which I find Bacon observing in his cipher work—one, he omits catchwords at the bottom of the page; and two, he excludes large initial letters'; Theobald adds that 'a favourite Bacon device' is to use the lines in which the initial letters are inset. The example overleaf is from Theobald's work on p. 25 of Bacon's *Essays*. He points out that the first full line of text has a count of 33, signifying 'Bacon'; and the total number of roman letters is 259, which is 'Shakespeare' in kay cipher. The total number of roman letters on the short lines (114) minus the total number of roman words on the short lines (23) is 91, or 'Spenser' in simple count; the same subtraction for the text as a whole is 259−59, i.e. 200, which yields 'Bacon' in reversed count. This one short section of print, therefore, yields three signatures; Theobald interprets it as a declaration that Bacon wrote the works of Spenser as well as those of Shakespeare.

Roman words		OF STUDIES	Roman letters	
	3	Tudies serue for pas-	17	
	3	times for ornaments	17	
	4	& for abilities. Their	17	
	3	chiefe vse for pasti-	17	
	4	me is in priuatenes	16	
	3	and retiring; for or-	16	
23	3	namente is in dis-	14	114
	7	course, and for abilitie is in iudgment	33	
	6	For expert men can execute, but lear-	29	
	8	ned men are fittest to iudge or censure.	32	
	7	To spend too much time in them	24	
36	8	is slouth, to use them too much for or-	27	145
59				259

In all, Theobald lists nearly 500 'seals' taken from a wide variety of sources: there are 170 in about twelve pages of Marlowe alone; others come from lesser Elizabethan works such as *The Scourge of Folly* by John Davies of Hereford, *The Sisters* by James Shirley, and *England's Mourning Garment* by Henry Chettle; and yet others from the works of Bacon, Spenser and Shakespeare, and from the legends to the various Shakespeare portraits. The 'seals' take various forms of Bacon's name and titles, or the favourite 287 of 'Fra Rosicrosse'.

In one of his numerous articles in *Baconiana* Theobald had earlier discoursed on 'Pierre Amboise and Gilbert Wats'. Pierre Amboise was the author of an *Histoire Naturelle*, which shows a marked parallelism with Bacon's *Sylva Sylvarum*, though Theobald claims it as an independent work; Gilbert Wats issued the first English translation of Bacon's *De Augmentis*

Scientiarum in 1640. After a few polite preliminaries, Theobald announces:

And now for a little discovery of my own. It was while pondering over the elusive personality of Pierre Amboise that the idea occurred to test his book [*Histoire Naturelle*] by cipher methods. But an examination did not yield results of sufficient importance to carry much weight. It then struck me that the name Amboise itself might provide a clue; and to my great surprise the remarkable fact was revealed that in both the Simple and the K counts, the equivalent for Pierre Amboise is 'Francis Bacon Kt' [Knight]. But what value is to be placed on this curious fact?...Here comes in the second part of my little discovery. The Dictionary of N.B. [National Biography] distinctly gives his name [Gilbert Wats] as Watts. Why does it appear as Wats on the title page of A.L. [*Advancement of Learning*] 1640? I hazard the opinion that this alteration was intentional; the reason being that 'Gilbert Wats' is 'Francis Bacon Kt', both in Simple cipher; while in K cipher 'Gilbert Wats' is 'Shakespeare'! It would indeed be miraculous if all this were merely coincidence....In any event I think we may conclude here, as with the 'Histoire Naturelle', that if this double Bacon signature on the Wats production of 1640 were deliberately planned, it gives added interest to a work which already bears...the Rosicrucian seal of 287 on four separate pages.

Among his other works, Theobald devoted an entire volume to the Shakespearean Sonnets, and called it *Shakespeare's Sonnets Unmasked*. A profusion of Baconian pseudonyms emerge, including Puttenham, Greene, Peele, Spenser and Marlowe, whose names are combined with Bacon's in the 'seals'. In this volume Theobald counts italic letters as well as roman; and in *Dr Rawley's Epitaph Deciphered* he introduces yet another new variation on the rules, this time counting the Roman numerals as letters.

Since Rawley was Bacon's literary executor it might be expected that his epitaph should produce several forms of Bacon's name. In addition, however, Theobald finds numerous 'seals' of Shakespeare, and even one numerically equivalent to 'Bacon is Shakespeare'. In the same epitaph, turning from numerology to acrostics, he finds 'Queen', 'Robert', 'Parent' and 'Leycester', and several string acrostics on 'Francis Tudor' and 'Shakespeare'. Finally, taking the initial letters of alternate lines, HSCIIT, and moving five letters to the right in the alphabet he gets NAHOOB; moving six to the left he gets BMTCCN; anagramming these together produces 'B'con, M. Bacon h't'; and so the end product of this elaborate and haphazard process is the message 'Bacon, Mr Bacon hid' (h't being an abbreviation for hit, the old form of hid, he explains). The epitaph as a whole, taking all the products of numerology, acrostic and anagram together, persuades Theobald that Bacon was the son of Queen Elizabeth and Robert Leicester as well as the author of Shakespeare's plays.[1]

When he turns his attention to the family mottoes of Bacon and Shakespeare (*Baconiana*, January 1941), he produces as many 'solutions' as ever. He begins by declaring that Shakespeare's father was granted a coat of arms in 1599, that two of Bacon's associates (the Earl of Essex and William Camden) were officials of the College of Heralds at the time, and that therefore Bacon could easily have influenced the choice of a suitable motto. And he did, indeed: for the motto, 'Non Sanz Droict', has a value of 163 in reversed cipher, and this is equivalent to 'Francis Bacon is Shakespeare'. Combining the two mottoes of Bacon and Shakespeare yields a rich reward of over two dozen 'seals', including Francis Tudor, Queen Elizabeth, Robert Leicester, and Prince of Wales.

Another indefatigable computer was J. Denham Parsons, who, recalling that 'the age of Shakespeare was the age of cryptography', turned his arithmetical prowess to good advantage. Between 1918 and 1935 he published the fruits of his labours in a number of volumes produced at his own expense, as well as writing articles in *Baconiana* and letters in the correspondence columns of *The Times Literary Supplement* and *Notes and Queries*. His discoveries include eighteen 'proofs' of Bacon's authorship in *Venus and Adonis*, seven in *Lucrece*, and forty-eight in the First Folio: while working through this, he discovered that the word 'Bacon' occurs only twice in the text, each time with a capital B; both occurrences fall on p. 53, a number which represents the word 'Poet' in simple cipher. He

---

[1] Compare Owen's and Mrs Gallup's theories of Bacon's parentage (pp. 63 above and 191 ff. below).

also studied the Sonnets, in which he found a large number of proofs: the very first word, 'To', yields one, for its numerical value in simple count is thirty-three, standing for 'Bacon'. He found numerical seals in the inscription on Shakespeare's Monument in Stratford-on-Avon Church, and in a large number of other sources.

For some of his examples Parsons worked with a chess-board pattern; in an article in *Baconiana*, June 1923, he describes how he set out the letters of the dedication page to *Venus and Adonis* in this way. The white squares had a total value of 103 (Shakespeare), and the black squares 177 (William Shakespeare); this in itself hardly proved what he wanted, but he was able eventually to produce the name 'Francis Bacon' after a long series of computations. The same process, when applied to the 'I.M.' poem of the 1623 Folio, gave 100 (Francis Bacon) and 177 (William Shakespeare). This he calls a 'double Bacon-Shakespeare equivalent coincidence'; he adds that an eminent mathematician he consulted had gauged the odds against a chance occurrence of this event as 'multitudinously over-whelming'.

The same article contains the results of a marathon calcula-tion in *The Tempest* and other pages in the 1623 Folio:

Total numerical value of letters
in the epilogue and facing page of *The Tempest*	9900
in 'Names of Actors'	5335
in Digges and I.M. Poems	13092
	28327

The reverse of this grand total is 72,382, which can be written as $55 \times 1311 + 277$. Now 277 is $100 + 177$, i.e. 'Francis Bacon' and 'William Shakespeare'; and what is more, if we set out the name Francis Bacon with its equivalent numbers

F	R	A	N	C	I	S		B	A	C	O	N
6	17	1	13	3	9	18		2	1	3	14	13

and add the *digits* together and not the numbers (i.e. treating 'R' as '1+7', 'N' as '1+3', 'S' as '1+8' and so on) the total is 55. So the number 55 in the solution represents 'Francis Bacon' too; and this, Parsons remarks, is a 'double-double coincidence'. He gives no explanation for the number 1311; but just to show how easy it is to invest *any* number with significance, given sufficient determination, we now add a result of our own. 1311, we suggest, is important to numerology because its factors are 3, 19 and 23; the total of these is 45, which is 100−55, or in other words 'William Shakespeare' minus 'Francis Bacon' (the equivalence with 55 being obtained as before by adding the digits).

In 1933 Parsons issued a protest against another Baconian who used a similar method to his own, but reached the very different answer that Sir William Stanley was the true author of the plays. Parsons, bristling, flatly denied that the names 'William Stanley', or 'William Stanley, Earl of Derby' would fit the text properly: they would not, he remarked somewhat obscurely, provide 'a brace of possible signals in line with each other'.

Two years later Parsons repudiated all the work that had gone before; he had by this time discovered a new 'short' or 'cross-count' alphabet, with A to I as 1 to 9, K to S as 1 to 9, and T to Z as 1 to 6. All his earlier interpretations must, he says, be ignored: he believed himself to be on the track of a new theory. Nothing very conclusive emerged, but the true author was 'somehow capable of being associated by letter numerical value with the numbers 153 and 100'. Returning to the ordinary simple cipher, he remarked that there are exactly 666 letters above Shakespeare's signature in *Venus and Adonis*, with a total numerical value of 7644; these two numbers added together give 8310, which can be written as 277 × 30. And 277 is 177 plus 100, or 'William Shakespeare' and 'Francis Bacon'. The numerical value of the title, *Venus and Adonis*, is 153, or 'just 100 more than the key POET, 53'. And this suggested to Parsons that Bacon may only have been an associate author of the plays. He never developed the theory further, and this was his last contribution to the authorship problem.

The lesser disciples of the numerological method are legion. Tanner, an English Baconian, in 1910 announced that the dedicatory poem 'To the Reader' in the First Folio was an elaborate table of numbers (the year 1623 being chosen for publication to underline the significance of the numbers 1, 6, 2, 3 in the table), and pointed out that the long word 'honorificabilitudinitatibus' has a value of 287 in simple cipher, and is accordingly the 'seal' of 'Fra. Rosicrosse'. A German, Baron von Blumberg, pointed out that Romeo equals 62 in simple cipher and 26 in 'short count', and that F and B stand for 6 and 2 respectively; R. L. Hennig discovered five Rosicrucian 'signatures' in each of three books, *Pilgrim's Progress*, *Robinson Crusoe* and *Gulliver's Travels*; more recently Edward Johnson (*Baconiana*, 1947) showed that the last word in *The Tempest*, 'free', was equivalent to 33 (Bacon) in simple cipher and 67 (Francis) in reversed count—'a neater cryptic signature can hardly be imagined'. These are only a few of the enormous number of examples that could be quoted.

The Americans, though not the first in the field, soon made up for lost time, and numerological articles are to be found in plenty in *American Baconiana*. Among them, Dr W. H. Prescott (who financed one of Owen's manuscript-hunting expeditions) shows how Bacon signed *The Story of the Learned Pig* with the name 'Transmigratus', which is 171 in simple cipher ('Francis' in kay cipher has, of course, the same value); George M. Battey Jr. exhibits the numerical relationships between 'Francis Bacon' (100), 'Daniel Defoe' (77), 'William Shakespeare' (177) and 'Robinson Crusoe' (177); and H. A. W. Speckman turns his attention to 'The Odd Cryptogram on Spenser's Tomb', adding a flourish to the ordinary numerological treatment, and producing Bacon's name again and again by what he calls the 'orchematical' method.

Spenser is also the chosen victim of W. G. Royal-Dawson, 'Edwin S. Drood', and others; but the numerologists have spread their nets wider than this. Among the odd fish they have caught are the sixteenth-century Italian cryptographer Ioan Baptiste Porta, numerous seventeenth-century authors, and Elizabethan writers in shoals. Pierre Henrion, writing in *Baconiana* in July 1950, finds Bacon's 'signatures' on the portrait page of Gustavus Selenus' *Cryptomenytices et Cryptographiæ* (1623), which suggests to him that 'Selenus' was really Bacon; the editorial in the following issue, though not disputing the signatures, points out that the real subject of the portrait was Trithemius, Abbot of Spanheim, whose *Steganographiae* (1499) was incorporated in the same volume.

It is, however, the Authorized Version of the Bible which offers some of the best opportunities for numerical experiment. Prof. D. S. Margoliouth of Oxford, in the *Saturday Review* of September 1924, supported the idea that there are ciphers in the Bible, remarking that 666, 'the number of the beast' in Rev. xiii. 18, 'probably depends on the numerical value of the letters'. An interesting cipher (not mentioned in Margoliouth's article) concerns the word 'Sheshakh' in Jeremiah, which is interpreted as a cryptic symbol for 'Babylon'.[1] Writing the Hebrew alphabet (which has no vowels) with the second half of the letters under the first, in reverse order, we have the solution at once:

Jer. xxv. 26:...and the king of Sheshakh shall drink after them.

Jer. li. 41: How is Sheshakh taken!...how is Babylon become an astonishment among the nations!

11	10	9	8	7	6	5	4	3	2	1
Kh	I	T	Ch	Z	V	H	D	G	B	A
כ	י	ט	ח	ז	ו	ה	ד	ג	ב	א
ל	מ	נ	ס	ע	פ	צ	ק	ר	ש	ת
L	M	N	S	O	P	Tz	Q	R	Sh	Th
12	13	14	15	16	17	18	19	20	21	22

Sh(e)Sh(a)Kh = BBL = Babel = Babylon.

The Baconians were not to be denied their share of the fun. Parker Woodward and Clifton had already noticed, in their quest for the mystic signature 287, that in the *Address to the Reader* in the 1611 Bible the 287th word from the beginning pointed to the acrostic:

> *being*...
>
> *are*...
>
> *con*science....

And as early as 1902, a contributor to *The Book-Lover*, signing himself 'S.L.H.' had called attention to the fact that the name 'Shakespear' has four vowels and six consonants, so 'if you write

[1] Modern versions give 'Sheshach', but it is clear that the cipher requires the spelling 'Sheshakh'.

down the figure 4 and follow it by the figure 6, you get 46. Very well, turn to Psalm 46....' There, it is claimed, the 46th word from the beginning is 'shake', and the 46th word from the end 'spear' (this is only true if one omits the final word 'Selah' from the count). It follows that, since Shakespeare wrote the Psalms, and Shakespeare was not the real Shakespeare, the Authorized Version must show the hidden hand of Francis Bacon.

The numerologists set to work, apparently undeterred by the fact that the Great Bible of 1539 showed the same two words in the same positions (although it was published twenty-five years before Shakespeare's birth and twenty-one years before Bacon's). Some of them, including the American Dr Kenneth S. Guthrie, searched for numerical signatures throughout the text, but for the most part they confined their attention to the 46th Psalm itself. Even this small portion of the Authorized Version proved rich in numerological treasures. The Shakespeare 'signature' was completed by W. H. M. Grimshaw in 1919; he wrote the tenth verse backwards, 'earth the in exalted be *will I*, heathen the among exalted be will I: God *am I* that know and still be', and taking the sixth and seventh words from the beginning and the end, produced WILL-I and I-AM, or 'William'. Henry Seymour followed this up in *Baconiana*, September 1924, with the announcement that the word 'shake' had appeared in an earlier Tudor Bible as 'shoke', and fifty-five words from the beginning; he argued that the change in the Authorized Version was deliberate, and significant: Shakespeare was forty-six years old when it first appeared, and 46 stands for 'S. Alban' in simple cipher. Bacon, Seymour suggested, had been responsible for this series of coincidences; he had 'imbibed the Pythagorean doctrine that *number* was the active principle of the visible world'. In July 1945 an anonymous contributor to *Baconiana* produced calculations to strengthen Seymour's argument: Shakespeare's birthday is agreed to be 23 April, and his death also occurred on 23 April;[1] 23 and 23 make 46, the number of the Psalm (the fact that the date of Shakespeare's death in 1616 could be predicted in 1611

---

[1] The actual dates shown in the register of Trinity Church, Stratford-on-Avon, are 26 April 1564 (his baptism) and 25 April 1616 (his burial).

is, one assumes, another example of Bacon's clairvoyance); 46, the number of the Psalm, and 46, the position of the word 'Shake', make 92, which is equivalent to 'Bacon' in reversed count. Other results in the same article include the addition of the numbers 46 (words up to 'shake'), 111 (words between 'shake' and 'spear') and 46 (words from 'spear' to the end), to produce 203, which is 100 (Francis Bacon) plus 103 (Shakespeare); and the addition of 46 to 111 to produce 157, which is 'Fra Rosicrosse' in simple cipher.

Other Baconians who, at various times, have added their voices to the discussion, include Sir Edwin Durning-Lawrence, James R. Ferguson, Ernest G. Rose, and 'Arden' (who notes that the number 111 gives 'F. Bacon' in reverse cipher). A. E. Loosley (*Baconiana*, January 1950) remarks that the Breeches Bible gives a count of 47 words from the beginning to 'shake' and 44 from the end to 'spear'; it is only the Authorized Version which yields the useful numerical results. He adds that Bacon was the 'overall editor' of the Authorized Version, with 47 translators working under his direction; and 47 minus 1 is 46. 'If this be true, and I feel one is justified in believing it', Loosley concludes, 'a very interesting light is thrown on the keen working of Bacon's mind. The trick would be one in which he would take a keen delight.'

It is hardly necessary to dwell at length on the fatuity of the numerological 'method'. That 'signatures' are easy to find wherever one wants to find them is suggested by the incredibly wide range of sources the Baconian numerologists are able to cite. The corollary—that one should be able to find 'signatures' of the same or other authors in other works, almost at will— is noticed by Theobald in his *Shakespeare Sonnets Unmasked*; he counters the objection as follows:

> To guard against misconception Bacon usually arrived at at least two different forms of his name on the same page, so that the suggestion of coincidence might be eliminated as much as possible.... Indeed a certain number of stray signatures...must inevitably appear by the ordinary laws of probability...in order to prove intention an author would certainly use such a system as this methodically through all his works.

The 'system' Theobald refers to is, of course, no system at all, and the manipulations are so easy that one can without difficulty devise 'at least two different forms' of any name and proceed to find them on the same page, and scattered liberally through any collection of works. But it is interesting to notice this attempt to bolster the weaknesses of a 'system' with quite extraneous considerations. We have come across similar cases before: there is Owen's challenge that one could not carry a cipher story through to its completion if one 'neglected the guides', Cunningham's emphasis that a true 'cover name' must 'check through 100 per cent', and Arensberg's recourse to hints in the text which signal the acrostic 'signature'. In valid cryptography there is no need for such devices; the system itself is foolproof, and involved arguments to substantiate a correctly deciphered message are nothing to the point.

There is, of course, another fundamental drawback to numerological 'proofs': any chosen number can stand for a whole host of different names. Theobald's reply to this objection is again evasive:

Naturally...a few cases of over-lapping will be found.... The numeral 119 stands for Lodge in the Kay cipher as well as Francis Bacon in the Reverse cipher...but this does not really affect the position...we should have to find LODGE and THOMAS LODGE repeatedly and methodically on the title page and first and last page of any works now attributed to Bacon which the critic wished to claim for Lodge....

Seymour (who harboured a grudge against Theobald for his unsympathetic treatment of his, Seymour's, acrostic 'discoveries') put the case against the 'method' quite neatly by pointing out that 287, while standing for 'Fra Rosicrosse' in the 'kay cipher', can equally well be taken to represent 'Bacon Society Incorporated'; 103 (Shakespeare), can be read as 'Queen Eliza', or even 'Stutis' (the company from whom the Bacon Society were then hiring their premises).

In addition to this ambiguity we have noticed that any amount of unsystematic manipulation (addition, subtraction, reversal of digits, addition of digits, factorization, and indiscriminate separation of totals into sums of two or more numbers) is allowed, and that there is a generous range of different counting systems (simple, reversed, kay, and short count alphabets), so that any number inconvenient in one system may well yield a promising result in another.

It is perhaps surprising that the Baconian numerologists have not taken advantage of still more, and older, methods of reckoning words in terms of numbers. There are plenty of cabalist alphabets available. One of these runs:

A	B	C	D	E	F	G	H	I	L	M
1	2	3	4	5	6	7	8	9	10	20

N	O	P	Q	R	S	T	V	X	Y	Z
30	40	50	60	70	80	90	100	200	300	400

A Lutheran cabalist working on this basis produced a remarkable composition. Taking the beginning of Luke I. 39, which reads 'And Mary arose and went into the hill country', he derived the magic number 960 from the Latin text:

EXURGENS [sic]   MARIA   ABIIT   IN   MONTANA
497   + 101 + 111 + 39 +   212   = 960

and wove round it the story of Mary's visit, in good Latin verse, each line of which was equivalent in numerical value to 960. His feat illustrates the ease with which numerological computations can be handled, and the large variety of 'messages' any given number may be made to yield; and it makes the Baconians' efforts seem puny in comparison.

Indeed, 'proofs' of authorship based on this kind of operation are even easier to come by than those derived from anagrams; the method is even more flexible, and it is entirely impotent to establish anything except the gullibility of those who use it. If anyone still disputes this, we shall be content with proving that we ourselves wrote the works of Bacon and Shakespeare. In simple count 'Wm. Friedman' is represented by 100; therefore, wherever the number 100 appears (as it does frequently, according to the Baconians, since it also represents 'Francis Bacon') there exists a sign of our authorship. But in case of doubt, we have left additional clues in a different form of signature, 'Wm. & E. Friedman', which in kay cipher comes to 287 (the magic number traced so profusely as the sign of 'Fra Rosicrosse').

We are not alone in this; anyone with sufficient diligence, prepared to juggle with his name in suitable ways, and to plough through the texts of the First Folio searching for numerical clues, should be able to prove to his own satisfaction that he wrote Shakespeare's plays. As the mathematician Eric T. Bell remarks, in his treatise on *Numerology* (Baltimore, 1933), 'although numbers cannot lie, they have a positive genius for telling the truth with intention to deceive'. Reading messages in them is a fatal pastime; there are so many ways of proving so many things that in the end we see that there is really no way of proving anything at all. As cryptologists we cannot admit that there is safety in numbers.

CHAPTER XIII

THE BILITERAL CIPHER AND
ELIZABETH WELLS GALLUP

W E come last of all to the cryptographic system which marks the highest point in all these attempts to prove authorship by decipherment. We shall give our remaining chapters to a careful investigation of the system, the claims made for it and the support it has had. Of all the ciphers said to be present in the plays, the biliteral cipher is the most scientific, the most plausible, the most practical, and, because it was invented by Francis Bacon, the most appealing. Yet as Mrs Gallup asserted it was used, it is also the most difficult to evaluate. It demands approaches from various directions: not only the cryptographer but the typographer and the forensic scientist as well must testify. We have been fortunate in assembling expert evidence in these fields.

Elizabeth Wells Gallup was a well-educated woman. She was born in Paris, N.Y., in 1848; she went to school in New York, to the State Normal College in Michigan, to the Sorbonne in the other Paris, and to the University of Marburg. She taught in Michigan for twenty years or so, and became Principal of a High School. She had always been interested in literature, and particularly in Bacon; she was attracted to Dr Owen's theory, and with her sister Kate Wells she was persuaded to join in his work. She never made it clear whether she had always been convinced by Owen and his methods, or whether she gradually came to accept his point of view; it was a thing about which she was unwilling in later years to speak. But there are notable similarities between her work and his.

Her first book, *The Biliteral Cypher of Sir Francis Bacon Discovered in his Works and Deciphered by Mrs Elizabeth Wells Gallup*, came out in 1899. There was an enlarged second edition in 1900, and a third in 1901. It was not until much later that we knew her; between 1915 and 1920 we lived on the same estate (except for a period of war service). We came to know her well—her character and her work. Of her work we are about to write at length; of her character we wish to say that we had a high regard for her. She was honest, sincere, gentle, upright and devoutly religious (as was her sister). We thought her intelligent and learned; there is no doubt that she was also tireless in her efforts to have her work accepted by scholars.

Studying Dr Owen's source-material, Mrs Gallup came inevitably and repeatedly on Bacon's own remarks about ciphers. She was working, as Owen and his assistants worked, on facsimile editions; naturally she was struck by the frequent and apparently arbitrary use of different type-forms or letter-shapes: ordinary roman, italic, and what the printer calls swash italic letters (usually capitals: C, $\mathcal{J}$, $\mathcal{M}$, $\mathcal{R}$, but occasionally small letters as well ω, k, z). Equally naturally it occurred to her that here, actually in use, was Bacon's biliteral cipher.

It will be remembered that Bacon gave 'an Example of a Biliterarie Alphabet' composed of permutations of the letters *a* and *b* in groups of five (*aaaaa* is A, *aaaab* is B, *aaaba* is C and so on—see ch. III, p. 30, fig. 1). Provided that the two forms (*a* and *b* in this case) can be indicated in some covert way in the message (as for instance by different letter-shapes), anyone who has the key can arrive at the message. The exterior message must of course be five times as long as the hidden message, since every five letters of the one indicate only one letter of the other.

The use of a '*bi-literarie alphabet*', as Bacon called his combination of '*a*-forms' and '*b*-forms', implies very careful instructions to a very careful printer; otherwise the message would be garbled. Reproducing the message in type also raises subsidiary problems, which we shall deal with later. Basically they stem from the known deficiencies of English printing in the late sixteenth and early seventeenth centuries. Bacon's printers did manage it, however, in the long and ingenious example given in the *De Augmentis*.[1] The message itself is well-con-

---

[1] Although it is true that the printers of the London and the Paris editions of the *De Augmentis* did not set Bacon's examples in type (woodcuts, made to

trived: the interior coded message says exactly the opposite of the exterior text. The exterior text reads plausibly; no hint is given of the deception; yet anyone who correctly applies the key will reach the one and only solution. The system is therefore cryptologically valid.

What could be more useful? It is an argument for both sides in this controversy that printers of the time commonly used two or more founts of type indiscriminately in one book. Stratfordians might suggest that this indicates that the first printers of the Shakespeare plays meant no more by the practice than any other printers; Baconians can reply that since the use of more than one letter shape was common, the cipher could be introduced in this way without exciting attention. All that was needed was that the printer should have a suitably marked manuscript; the marks need not for that matter have come from the scribe who wrote the manuscript down. It is even arguable that they could have been inserted in the manuscripts of books by someone other than the author.

All this must have struck Mrs Gallup very forcibly; as another writer on the same topic remarked, it 'came with the same effect as does a bright light to one who has lost his way in the dark night'.[1] She had long noticed that more than one fount of type had been used in the Folio; here was the reason.

Since it is in the italic founts that the differences are most striking, she began to try to decipher the Prologue to *Troilus and Cressida*; this stands out as a page almost wholly in italic. The first task, indeed the principal task, was to assign the letters to their *a*- and *b*-forms. She spent a long time examining and comparing the letters with a magnifying glass. She found the differences between individual letters so slight and so hard to relate to each other and to codify that the task of distinguishing the two complete alphabets was enormously difficult. (It must be noted that neither she nor her defenders said it was

simulate handwritten script, were used for this purpose), the printers of some of the later editions set his examples in the ordinary way, using two slightly different founts of italics to incorporate the secret message in the apparently innocent external message. See the first of the long examples on p. 32 above.

[1] J. A. Powell in *The Greatest Work of Sir Francis Bacon* (Geneva, Illinois: The Riverbank Laboratories, 1916), p. 14.

easy; yet the difficulty, as we shall see, often offered the decipherer a chance to shift his ground and accept the 'right' answer, alleging a previous mis-identification.) J. A. Powell says of this stage:

It is not exaggerating to assert that many days of labor were required to formulate the 'alphabets' of the *a* and *b* form of each letter employed in the 'Prologue' page. Frequently a letter would be assigned during the examination to the *a* or to the *b* form only to find that such assignment resulted in a combination which was meaningless, when the group of five letters to which it belonged was compared to the key. Further examination and comparison were then of course necessitated, and a redefinition of the characteristics of the respective forms followed.

But in the end Mrs Gallup felt sure that she had made a correct classification of the letters. She produced intelligible texts with it; she was using Bacon's own key; what more could be asked? From the Prologue to *Troilus* she produced this:

Francis St Alban, descended from the mighty heroes of Troy, loving and revering these noble ancestors, hid in his writings Homer's *Iliads* and *Odyssey* (in cipher), with the *Aeneid* of the noble Virgil, prince of Latin poets, inscribing the letters to Elizabeth, R.

F. St A.

From the 'Names of the Principal Actors' she got this:

As I sometimes place rules and directions in other Ciphers, you must seek for others soone to aide in writing.   Fr. of Ve.

From 'A Catalogue of the several Comedies' she produced a more interesting avowal, more liberally sprinkled with 'Elizabethan' spellings:

Queene Elizabeth is my true mother, and I am the lawfull heire to the throne. Find the Cipher storie my bookes containe; it tells great secrets, every one of which, if imparted openly, would forfeit my life.   F. Bacon.

The reader will have noted that this theory about Bacon had been first produced by Owen. Similar statements are repeated over and over again in Mrs Gallup's large corpus of decipherments. We do not know that Mrs Gallup ever said explicitly that Owen's methods would not bear inspection; for she hardly ever spoke to us of her work with Owen; certainly she never openly commended his approach. Yet we have the feeling that all along she was trying (perhaps we should say hoping) by her more exact method to establish the truth of the statements he had first made about Bacon's birth and his voluminous works. She was in a sense trying to follow Owen, but by different paths. The only written comment she ever made on his work was in these sentences in the prefatory section of the third edition of *The Biliteral Cypher of Sir Francis Bacon*, where she praises her own cipher but slips in an ambiguous puff for Owen's:

> The Bi-literal is exact—scientific—inflexible. The translation of the Word Cipher, however, like translations from the Greek...is, within certain limitations, more elastic. There might be variation in the phrasing of two people, but the substance would be in accord from the hands of experienced cryptographers.

Her decipherments did record some observations by Bacon on the word cipher, which we discuss at the end of the next chapter, notably the claim that the 'Word Cypher [was] superiour to all others we have invented'. One's view on this statement must necessarily depend on one's opinion of the general reliability of Mrs Gallup's decipherments.

Mrs Gallup firmly adhered to Owen's theory of Bacon's birth and parentage. She believed in effect that Bacon had inserted his story and his claim in the plays in order that posterity should have its view of Elizabethan history corrected in certain important respects. During Elizabeth's life he could not say openly who he was; but since he was an expert cryptographer it occurred to him to record his life in cipher in his works of literature. When in 1623, with Elizabeth twenty years dead, he came to write the *De Augmentis*, he was free to give posterity the other necessary information—namely open instructions on how to read the cipher. According to Mrs Gallup he had already hinted at his activity in 1605; indeed while he was dropping these hints with one hand, he was with the other writing into *The Advancement* further details of his life—or so she says in the 'Explanatory Introduction' to her book:

The subject of Ciphers and Cipher-writing became, with Francis Bacon, a hobby, if not an absorbing passion, the extent of which may be judged from the voluminous and important matter being brought to light, which he enfolded in his writings.... In his work published in 1605, 'Of the Advancement of Learning', he makes a topic of Ciphers, as a branch of educational progress, and hints at, but does not explain, the bi-literal method of Cipher-writing, while he was at the same time enfolding, in the Italic letters of the book itself, portions of his own secret history....

He continued to write ciphers into his various works until 1624,[1] when, none having discovered the secret, the very success of the system seeming likely to defeat its object, and when all personal danger from a premature exposure of what he had written was past, he published in the Latin version, the *De Augmentis Scientiarum*, a clear and minute description and illustration of the cipher... fearing that nothing less would lead to its discovery and translation.

A historian would strongly doubt whether it would in fact have been safer for Bacon to disclose his system in 1623 than at any earlier time; James I would have been no more pleased than Elizabeth to have such claims advanced. Be that as it may, a number of ardent Baconians embrace the theory of his royal parentage. There are indeed one or two things which seem to support it. Nicholas Bacon died in 1579, leaving nothing to Francis, though he left much property to his other sons. The Queen is often alleged to have been amorous and even indiscreet. There is also the curious defaced inscription on one of the walls of Canonbury Tower in London, where Bacon once lived. The inscription names all the monarchs from William the Conqueror to Charles II. Between Elizabeth and James I there are certain letters which might once have been a name; all but one have been chiselled out, but the initial remaining is an F. Some Baconians would claim that it stands for Francis; but who put it there if it was not Bacon and how he knew that Bacon was 'Elizabeth's son' is another matter.

As for Bacon's 'absorbing passion' for ciphers or his practical experience of cryptology in government business, we have only the temperate reference in the *De Augmentis* to

---

[1] The first (London) edition of the *De Augmentis* actually appeared in 1623; but the Paris edition, on which Mrs Gallup was working, was published a year later.

warrant the assumption. Of writers on Bacon only one, to our knowledge, claimed that Bacon was a government-employed cryptanalyst; this writer, Charles P. Bowditch, said Bacon was 'an expert decipherer himself and was employed by the Queen in unearthing several conspiracies in which cipher abounded'. There is no evidence for this statement, other than that provided by Mrs Gallup; she produced a testimony 'by Bacon' that he had deciphered messages proving that Mary Queen of Scots was aiming at the British throne. Bacon's 'father' (the Earl of Leicester) was implicated in the plot; and it was plainly a bad moment for all four. The story is entertaining, but hardly evidence of Bacon's absorbing passion for cryptography; and it is arguing in a circle to take it as evidence.

Mrs Gallup goes on in the 'Explanatory Introduction' (in the first edition of her book) to list the writers who were masks for Bacon, as claimed by the decipherments she had made. They were Marlowe, Peele, Greene, Spenser, Jonson and Burton (*Anatomy of Melancholy* only); a remarkable echo of Owen's list. 'In all of these', she says,

are fragments of Bacon's personal history, the statement that Elizabeth was the lawful wife of the Earl of Leicester by a secret marriage, before becoming Queen; that the issue of this marriage was two sons—Francis Bacon, so-called, and Robert Devereux, afterward Earl of Essex; that Francis was at birth received by Mistress Ann Bacon and was reared and educated as the son of Nicholas Bacon. It appears that at about the age of sixteen Francis discovered the facts of his nativity through the gossip of a Court lady, and in a fit of anger the Queen acknowledged to him her motherhood and his sonship, and that he was immediately sent to France, and subsequent action was taken by which he was barred from the succession to the throne....The work hidden takes the form of a series of letters, or divisions, each being closed with a signature of Francis Bacon, or with initials or some of the titles he bore....Much space is devoted to the secret personal history of himself and his brother Robert.

The first edition of Mrs Gallup's book was based on her first decipherments; she indicated which of the works of Shakespeare, Bacon and others she had worked on. The second edition had portions covering Bacon's cipher-writings between

1590 and the end of his career. In them he emphasized the importance of finding the earlier writings of 1579–90. Accordingly Mrs Gallup and her sister went to England and laboured in the British Museum. In the third edition she added decipherments from Spenser's *Shepherd's Calendar* (1579), Peele's *Arraignment of Paris* (1584), Greene's *Mirror of Modesty* (1584), Greene's *Planetomachia* (1585), T. Bright's *Treatise of Melancholy* (1586), Greene's *Euphues-Morando* (1587), his *Perimides-Pandosto* (1588) and his *Spanish Masquerado* (1589).

In all these works the deciphered story is carried on in a kind of counterpoint; words or sentences are broken in one place, and caught up again in another, and the message completed The substance of the story is repeated many times, in different books, as if Bacon had been making sure that at least one of the sources should be stumbled on.

In the rest of Mrs Gallup's introductory matter she sets out Bacon's own explanation of the cipher, and discusses the difficulties which impeded its decipherment. Each book had its own difficulties, for the letter-shapes were different, and each was a separate study. Roman letters in italic words had to be disregarded; but where an italic letter occurred in a word in roman letters, all had to be used. She discusses mistakes in pagination and how she dealt with them; the spelling of her deciphered texts—wayward because of the 'unsettled ortho graphy' of the time; how Rawley, Bacon's literary executor, carried on the cipher story after Bacon's death (Owen's influence again), how to her astonishment she found Bacon's translation of the *Iliad* and the *Argument of the Odyssey*. The last differed very much from any known version and, as she was no classical scholar, she felt that their oddness and her ignorance was a guarantee that she could not have invented them. What she did not say in any of the editions of her book was where she began to apply the cipher method, or why she began there Did she begin with the first italic letter in the book? Did she consider the page-headings, which are almost invariably in italic? Did she include the catchwords at the foot of the page? Did she use the printer's signatures? (See the letters at the foot of every sixteenth page of this book. In the Folio the signatures were sometimes in italic.) Questions such as these are not answered. As her writings are ill-arranged, checking her methods is very difficult. But we shall do the best we can.

Publication of the book created an enormous flurry. Almost everywhere newspapers carried her 'story'; inevitably there was some pretty withering scorn as well, much of it shading into hysterical attacks and accusations of insanity. Some of it was temperate; for instance, W. H. Mallock wrote an article in the *Nineteenth Century*, stating what was a fact: that the Baconian controversy had been shifted to a new ground. When Sir Sidney Lee attacked Mrs Gallup in a letter to *The Times*, and showed incidentally that he had not understood the principles of Bacon's cipher, Mallock replied with another letter. He pointed out that he was a 'convert' to Mrs Gallup's theory only to the extent that he believed it worthwhile enough to have its truth tested. Mallock's sensible view was the point of equilibrium in a discussion that became ever more violent, either for or against. Andrew Lang sided with Lee, just as arrogantly. Certain Baconians, notably Mrs D. J. Kindersley, Henry Seymour and others, announced their allegiance; some of them even produced work-sheets corroborating Mrs Gallup's assignments of type-forms.

All this controversy was probably hateful to Mrs Gallup. But in 1902 her publishers produced a small pamphlet called *Replies to Criticisms*, which was sent free on request. An enlarged version, called *Pros and Cons of the Controversy*, was issued in 1906. The first pamphlet came out almost simultaneously with an article in the *Pall Mall Magazine*, written by cabled invitation of the editor. In it she said, mildly: 'I did not find myself a Baconian until the discovery of the Bacon Ciphers answered the questions in such a final way that controversy should end....In giving to the world the results of my researches, I have felt...that my work should be left without any attempt to influence or mould opinion in any other way.' After a discussion of ciphers in general and the biliteral in particular, she says of the latter that it would not be necessary to take the printer into the encipherer's confidence; the markings on the manuscript would give him no clue to the cipher. This is very dubious. To insert the cipher one did not merely insert roman instead of italic, one used one form of italic (the *b*-form) rather than the normal form (the *a*-form). It is underestimating the curiosity and intelligence of the compositor to suppose that he would carry out this unusual and highly specific function without wondering why. He would almost certainly have guessed he was inserting a cipher of some kind. It is, moreover, demonstrably untrue that the principles of the biliteral cipher were not known in those days (Bacon at any rate made them public, though not until the same year as the Folio was printed in London). The printer who had the marked manuscript before him would not even have to carry out the first stage of decipherment. Unlike Mrs Gallup, he would have no need to pore over the printed text to assign the letters to their *a*- and *b*-forms: it would be done for him on the manuscript. Add to all this the basic assumption that various printers in various printing-houses from 1579 to 1623 had been carefully obeying this bizarre instruction; is it not likely that suspicion would have been aroused? To a security-minded age, it seems an absurd risk to have taken. But this is by the way. Mrs Gallup concludes with a calmness which should have been a lesson to her detractors:

Surprise followed surprise as the hidden messages were disclosed, and disappointment as well was not infrequently encountered. Some of the disclosures are of a nature repugnant, in many respects, to my very soul....As a decipherer I had no choice, and I am in no way responsible for the disclosures, except as to the correctness of the transcription....[1]

The value of anything I could say upon the Bacon-Shakespeare controversy resolves itself into a question of fact—have I found a cipher, and has it been correctly applied?...Literary probabilities or improbabilities have no longer any bearing, and their discussion has become purely agitations of the air: the sole question is—what are the facts? These cannot be determined by slight and imperfect examinations, preconceived ideas, abstract contemplation, or vigour of denunciation.

---

[1] Freud might perhaps have had a comment to make on that statement.

To correspondents who told her that after some hours of study they had been unable to grasp the system in principle or detect its application, she replied in an article in *Baconiana*:

> It would be difficult and hardly to be expected that an understanding of Greek or Sanscrit could be reached with the aid of a few written lines or with a few hours study. It is equally so with the Cipher. Deciphering the Bi-literal Cipher as it appears in Bacon's works will be impossible to those who are not possessed of an eyesight of the keenest and most perfect accuracy of vision in distinguishing minute differences in form, lines, angles and curves in the printed letters. Other things absolutely essential are unlimited time and patience, and aptitude, love for overcoming puzzling difficulties, *and, I sometimes think inspiration* [our italics]. As not every one can be a poet, an artist or astronomer, or adept in other branches requiring special aptitude, so for the very same reasons, not every one will be able to master the intricacies of the cipher, for in many ways it is most intricate and puzzling, not in the system itself, but in its application, as it is found in the old books. It must not be made too plain, lest it be discovered too quickly, nor hid too deep lest it never see the light of day. . . . The idea seems to be prevalent that 'any one' should be able to do the work once the biliteral alphabet is known. This is as great a mistake as it would be to reject the translations of the character writings and hieroglyphics of older times which have been deciphered, merely because we could not in a few hours master them ourselves. Ciphers are used to hide things not to make them clear.

But once the key to the cipher is known its application should be clear in the sense that it can be followed, step by step. And the analogy with hieroglyphics does not mention that when two people who have acquired the necessary knowledge apply it to the text, their translations will be identical. No one else has been able independently to reach Mrs Gallup's conclusions.

In the controversy aroused by Mrs Gallup's book, one Baconian made extremely damaging criticisms. He was George Cox Bompas, President of the Bacon Society. He presented a paper, printed in *Baconiana* for July 1905, on her treatment of Bacon's *The History of the Reign of King Henry the Seventh* (*Henry VII* for short). He analysed a passage containing 140 letters and alleged that in a corrected version of a decipherment she had made earlier, Mrs Gallup changed her assignments for fifteen capital and forty small letters. This led him to the conclusion that 'if 55 letters out of 140 can be changed at will...the alleged cipher is plainly illusory'. In ch. xvii we shall consider this kind of statistical assessment in more detail, but we can say now that in so far as it is based on statistics this charge cannot stand. Bompas also criticized Mrs Gallup's assignments for the page-headings of twenty consecutive pages; but since his knowledge of the practice of early printers was defective his charges were still not decisive arguments.[1] He was nearer the mark when he pointed out that as far as he could see, 'there were only seven letters which existed indisputably in an *a* and *b* form in *Henry VII*'. He went on: 'But the apparently correct use (with a few exceptions) of seven letters ...affords but slender proof of the genuineness of the cipher. None at all if, as appears to be the case, the remaining capitals and small letters are used indiscriminately.' He pointed out that with seventeen letters remaining indeterminate, and only seven certainly identified, almost any message could be extracted at will. Now this is certainly a telling argument. Yet it was not this demonstration by the Society's president which led to the solemn excommunication of Mrs Gallup by British Baconians; it had in fact taken place in December 1900, very shortly after publication of her book. The Council had passed this resolution, which goes to the real centre of the argument:

That in view of the failure to produce satisfactory key-alphabets for the cipher narratives, declared by Mrs Gallup to have been inserted by Francis Bacon in various books, and the inconclusive nature of her demonstrations, the Society is unable to give any support or countenance to the alleged discovery.

It had been added that this decision did not preclude discussion of the cipher in the Society's publications. And here, five years later, the president was still arguing against the claim; proof enough that Mrs Gallup had started something that would not easily stop. In the same issue as Bompas' article, Mrs D. J. Kindersley answered his criticism. She had, it seems, sent

---

[1] Bompas' arguments are discussed in more detail on pp. 234 ff.

Mrs Gallup her copy of *Henry VII*; Mrs Gallup had confirmed that it was almost identical with her own and returned it; Mrs Kindersley had then satisfied herself (if no-one else) that Mrs Gallup's assignments were correct. Mrs Kindersley admitted a doubt: of six copies of *Henry VII* in her possession, only two were alike. What she seems not to have known was that there were two editions, both dated 1622; ignorance of a point like that makes her testimony less impressive.

Mrs Gallup herself wrote an article replying to Bompas in *Baconiana* for October 1905. When her publishers brought out *Some Pros and Cons* in 1906 only Mrs Kindersley's and her own reply were included, not Bompas' criticism; which seems to weight the scale rather in favour of the 'Pros'. By now it might seem to have become a rearguard action; at any rate the public interest was not so keen. There were still occasional articles in *Baconiana* or in newspapers and journals; Mrs Gallup's supporters in the United States were mostly Baconians of the Owenite variety, such as Dr and Mrs Prescott of Boston, who had supported Owen and now inherited Mrs Gallup. By 1906 Mrs Gallup had resumed the extraction of additional material from further books, after a lapse of some years (caused by eye-strain contracted while working in the dim light of the British Museum and, later, the need to write articles explaining and defending her discoveries). In 1910 she produced another book, *The Lost Manuscripts*. It was written early in the period when aged boatmen were bobbing about in their lavishly hired craft on the River Wye, when other strange men were prodding the floors of the smelly caverns of Chepstow Castle, and yet others trying flamboyantly to get the owner of Piercefield Park to give them access to sixty-six iron boxes somewhere on the premises. These things may be allowed to have established a trend, which Mrs Gallup was furthering. England was a lively place in the manuscript-hunting season.

The most important of the books Mrs Gallup had now examined was the London edition (1623) of the *De Augmentis Scientiarum*; an exceedingly rare book because of the small size of the edition. She spent four months peering at it; what it told her she sums up as follows:

The hidden message is largely devoted to a concise account of the circumstances of Bacon's birth, the mental condition of the Queen, his mother, and of the immediate removal of Bacon to York House in the care of Lady Anne Bacon. Owing to the birth shortly thereafter of a still-born child to Lady Anne, and the adoption of Francis in the place of her own lifeless infant, he became known thereafter as her own son.

It was not until towards the end of the book that what had long been vainly sought came out—some reference to the original manuscripts of the various writings which Bacon had claimed in the Cipher as coming from his own pen.

She quotes from the cipher:

William Rawley [to whom we were introduced by Owen] must fulfill our plann of placing certain MSS....to insure their preservation, in tombes, graves or in monuments.... With much care we shall carve upon the stones placed to mark their lowly or lofty sepulchres... such cipher instructions as must lead unto true knowledge of all we shall hide within....There cannot be found a better device than that of the stone of the Stratford Tablet...to preserve a large part of the playes....A boxe shall thereby appear much quest....

She goes on:

The importance of these astounding revelations will be apparent to every one; their verification seemed imperative for the correction of historical records of Bacon and his times, and for the establishment of the correctness of the cipher work. With such overmastering incentive, I sailed in July 1907 for England to make an effort to find, if possible, some of the manuscripts.

When she got there she found that Greene's grave was beneath a railway terminus; Marlowe's fifteen feet below the tower of St Nicholas, Deptford; Peele's could not be found. 'There remained', she said, 'the graves and monuments of Edmund Spenser, in Westminster Abbey, of Robert Burton, at Oxford, of Shakespeare, at Stratford-on-Avon, and of Francis Bacon, at St Albans.' She could not get any of the tombs opened; which was all the more frustrating in that in two cases she had what she thought was corroboration from other sources. Spenser's tombstone had crumbled away; but it was represented in an engraving in the 1679 edition of *The Faerie Queene*, and she 'deciphered' that. It said 'A small inner space at the west end contains the MS. named.' On Burton's tomb in Christ Church, Oxford, she found a biliteral cipher message: 'Take heed; in a box is MS.—F.B.' Shakespeare's tombstone, as we know, has had much ingenuity expended on it. Mrs Gallup did not bother with the substitute slab; in any case decipherings from volumes later than the *De Augmentis* of 1623 explained that plans had been changed: the manuscripts were elsewhere. Bacon's tombstone is also a late replacement of the original; she did not trouble with it.

In October 1907 she took residence in Oxford, and in the Bodleian began to study other works by Bacon so far undeciphered. They were the *Historia Ventorum* of 1622, *Apothegms* of 1625, the *Essays* of the same year, the *Miscellany Works* of 1629, *The Felicity of Queen Elizabeth* of 1651, and the *Resuscitatio* of 1657. Bacon died in 1626; according to Mrs Gallup, William Rawley, his devoted secretary and literary executor, had inserted later messages in the cipher. In the *Resuscitatio* Rawley had placed this hidden text:

Certain old panels in the double work of Canonbury Tower, and at our Countrie Manor, Gorha'bury, alone sav'd most valu'd MSS. Thus co'cealed, more closely watched, more suited to escape sub'lest inquiry, you shall find th' dramas hee wisht to hide in th' stone...in the Ch. of Stratford.

There is a pleasant clerkliness about Rawley's cipher style; he was a man of many words and at the same time of many contractions and little formalisms: the ideal lawyer's clerk. Proud to be the bearer of such a message, he continues:

Now to reach rare papers, take panell five in F.'s tower room, slide it under fifty with such force as to gird a spring. Follow a.b.c's therein. Soone will the MSS. so much vaunted, theme of F.'s many bookes, be your owne.

We have already mentioned the inscription of the names of the kings in Canonbury Tower. The Tower itself was built in the early sixteenth century. After the Dissolution of the Monasteries Henry VIII gave Canonbury House to John Dudley, father of Robert Dudley, Earl of Leicester, Elizabeth's favourite and—according to Mrs Gallup—Bacon's father.

When Mary I came to the throne, she gave the property to a rich alderman whose daughter eloped from the house in a baker's basket (cf. *The Merry Wives of Windsor*) to marry the Earl of Northampton. This couple later let the property, as records attest, to 'Sir Francis Bacon Knight, His Majs. Attorney General'. Elizabeth had visited Canonbury; a room there was known as 'The Queen's Lodge'. Later, Bacon lived at Canonbury for some years; he could perhaps have had the mysterious inscription put there, to satisfy his pride. In the Tower Room there was once a secret chamber behind 'panel five'. It was discovered when Canonbury was reconstructed at a later date, and then shut up as unsafe. All this is not independent corroboration of the decipherment; there is no reason why Mrs Gallup should not have known of it before she produced Rawley's message.

She went back to America while *The Lost Manuscripts* was in the press. There she examined two copies of the 1671 edition of *Resuscitatio*, which contained two sections not in the 1657 edition: *A Discourse touching the Office of the Lord Chancellor* by John Selden and a list of Lord Chancellors compiled by William Dugdale. Even here Mrs Gallup found messages. A practical difficulty was that Rawley died in 1667; he too must have had an executor who inserted posthumous messages for him. Mrs Gallup summed up all her work in the Preface to *The Lost Manuscripts*:

Thus tracing the bi-literal cipher through a period of 92 years—from 1579 to 1671, we find it was inserted by Bacon, Ben Jonson, Rawley, and also Rawley's 'executor'....The work has led me through 61 different books in which this cipher is printed. In the third edition of 'The Bi-literal Cipher of Francis Bacon' were published the disclosures found in 53 books—from Edmund Spenser in 1579 to *Sylva Sylvarum* by Rawley in 1635. In the present volume are translations from the *De Augmentis* 1623, through 8 books, including *Resuscitatio* 1671. The narrative is, in substance, repeated many times, those by whom it was inserted not knowing in which work it would be found, and probably not expecting that it would be followed through all the editions; the corroborations are thus numerous and complete....

The revelations briefly epitomized in the quotations given solve the mystery which has surrounded the absolute disappearance of the original manuscripts....Surmise has attributed the loss to the great fire which destroyed London....The solution is here.

Mrs Gallup points out that Canonbury is reconstructed, Gorhambury in ruins, and the tombstones on several relevant graves replaced; none the less she urges further search for the manuscripts. Her decipherments, she believes, are sufficient spur and testimony. No one doubts, she points out, that the Rosetta Stone has been correctly deciphered, yet 'how many individuals have worked it out, or can work it out to the proof?' The answer to that is, 'Not a great many, but more than one, and they all get the same answer.'

CHAPTER XIV

MRS GALLUP AND COLONEL
FABYAN

MRS KATE PRESCOTT of Boston was a kind of contact-woman of the Baconian underworld or, to vary the metaphor, the liaison agent between the American cells of international anti-Stratfordianism. She had followed Owen to England; now she was to introduce Mrs Gallup to Colonel George Fabyan. Fabyan had already spent a lot of money so that Owen might dig through twelve feet of river mud to find a small empty stone structure. He was now to finance Mrs Gallup's researches for the rest of her days.

Fabyan was a man of good family but with little formal education. He ended his schooling as a young boy by running away from home to make his fortune—which he did, in textiles. He was never in any armed service; his military title was conferred on him by the Governor of Illinois; in fact he was what in the United States is called a 'Kentucky Colonel'. He had great natural gifts of energy and dynamism. He also had the trick of parroting other people's jargon; his conversation was usually impressive—superficially, anyway. It was a maxim of his that anything could be sold by a well-planned campaign—especially if he took it up. He took up Mrs Gallup, and with her her sister, established her at the Riverbank Laboratories on his estate at Geneva, Illinois, gave her a staff, and set himself to win some measure of academic respectability for her work. It was not far from his mind that if Bacon were proved to be Shakespeare, Mrs Gallup would also be seen to be (administratively and financially) Colonel Fabyan, which would be very satisfactory.

If Mrs Gallup had not so far caught on in the scholarly world, the only reason he could conceive was that her work had not been properly presented and publicized: she needed a campaign. Prominent scholars were therefore invited to Riverbank, as to an intellectual Mecca. They travelled at Fabyan's expense, were fed, housed and entertained at his villa; they were urged to observe the students, to see their work, to confer with Mrs Gallup and to question her, and above all to keep an open mind. A well-organized lecture on Bacon's cipher, with lantern slides, was given on the first day. At intervals Fabyan produced simple visual illustrations of the biliteral method, or old books on ciphers. The more picturesque portions of the Elizabeth-Leicester-Bacon story or the Canonbury inscription were alluded to in cheerful conversation. The careful academic minds of the visitors were given an alternation of sedatives and sharp shocks: a sort of Baconian brainwashing. Certain members of the Riverbank staff, of course, had it borne in upon them that they should watch their tongues—with good reason, for they were becoming disillusioned with the whole affair.

Fabyan's creed was printed on the back of the first pamphlet on Mrs Gallup's work to be issued from Riverbank. It ran as follows:

It couldn't be done

There are thousands who'll tell you it cannot be done,
  There are thousands who prophesy failure;
There are thousands to point out to you, one by one,
  The dangers that wait to assail you.
But just buckle in with a bit of a grin,
  Then take off your coat and go to it—
Just start in to sing as you tackle the thing
  That 'cannot be done'—and you'll do it.

EDGAR A. GUEST

Fabyan in fact had just buckled in with a bit of a grin to the business of establishing Baconian authorship by hook or occasionally by crook. One of the most ingenious of his devices for publicizing Mrs Gallup's work was, in 1916, to have a legal action brought against himself. William N. Selig, a Hollywood film producer, sought an injunction before an Illinois court to restrain Fabyan from publishing material 'tending to prove' that Bacon wrote Shakespeare—for Selig was about to film some of the plays. Fabyan published a brochure couched in the form of a legal brief, and entitled:

Circuit Court In Chancery, State Of Illinois—County of Cook SS. William N. Selig vs George Fabyan et al. (In which the existence and use of the Biliteral Cipher were passed on by Judge Tuthill.) THE EVIDENCE IN THE CASE. Charles J. O'Connor, 1730 Tribune Building, Solicitor for Defendants.

At Riverbank Fabyan made no pretence of concealing that he had instigated the case for the sake of publicity. It was taken seriously by Baconians, and not discredited officially by them until 1934, when Mr Henry Seymour, then President of the Bacon Society, went to the bottom of the matter and wrote 'A Belated Publication' which appeared in *Baconiana* of January 1935. He wrote:

Referring to the legal action taken by William N. Selig against Colonel George Fabyan and others for a judicial decision that Francis Bacon was not the real author of the Plays ascribed to 'Shakespeare'. In his decision...Judge Tuthill found for... Colonel Fabyan and awarded damages to him in the sum of $5000, for restraint of publication that Francis Bacon was, in fact, the real author. This action was tried in the year 1916. The decision set a good many people, on both sides of the Atlantic, to think furiously, and the London Bacon Society issued a propagandist leaflet putting forth the particulars.

It seems that a certain Baconian, not satisfied with the regularity of the case, instituted inquiries, and obtained from the clerk of the court a letter which ended:

The Executive Committee, at the time of the entry of the decree in question...were of the opinion...that the question of the authorship of the writings attributed to William Shakespeare was not properly before the Court.

Seymour therefore announced:

Under these extraordinary circumstances, the Bacon Society takes the earliest opportunity of withdrawing its propaganda leaflet No. 1 from circulation, in the common interest of truth and fair play.

A very proper decision; yet in *Baconiana* of Autumn 1950 there is a reference to the Selig trial as if the 'findings' had been correctly interpreted.

In fact the trial did not get more than passing attention in the United States. Fabyan, as if ashamed, pursued more orthodox methods of persuasion from then on. Mrs Gallup remained at Riverbank until well into the 1920's, though her sight and health generally deteriorated. She was then pensioned by Fabyan, and died in 1934 at the age of eighty-seven. Fabyan died in 1936; his large library of cryptographia and Elizabethan and Jacobean literature was left by his widow to the Library of Congress.

Towards the end, Fabyan had modified his views considerably. In a letter of 1929 he said of his campaign: 'The so-called Baconians are interested because they expect to use the results to prove that Bacon wrote Shakespeare, and in my opinion he didn't do anything of the kind, at least not in the accepted sense of "write" today.' Whatever that means, it looks as if Fabyan was now biting the hand he had fed. In our view he would have been glad to prove the existence of the cipher, whoever put it there.

Such was the man who had adopted Mrs Gallup. What did she do in all her years at Riverbank? While she was there, Fabyan issued in his series of Riverbank publications six small items relating to the biliteral cipher. There is not a single new decipherment in them; all had appeared in her earlier publications. While we were at Riverbank we were always told that Mrs Gallup was deciphering a continuation of the *New Atlantis*. If it was finished, it was never published. She became in fact the head of a research establishment 'tending to prove' that the biliteral cipher was there to be found in all the books she had 'deciphered'. She led a team of students who never quite came up with the results expected; so she had generally speaking to do all their work again when they brought it to her for her comment.

Our own contact with Mrs Gallup's work began when in 1915 Mr Friedman and in 1916 Mrs Friedman were taken on as research workers at Geneva. Mr Friedman took up the cipher as a hobby; he had really gone to the Laboratories as a geneticist. His part in the investigation was 'phase one', Mrs Friedman's 'phase two' of the Gallup project.

For basically there were two operations to be performed; first the *a*-forms and *b*-forms of the letters had to be identified; then the identification had to be applied to the printed texts in

PLATE VII

Elizabeth Wells Gallup, *c.* 1915.

PLATE VIII

Colonel George Fabyan, *c.* 1915.

the endeavour to find messages. For the first task, what had before been done by one or two amateurs was now done on a large scale. Photographic enlargements were made of page after page of printed books where various type founts were used; the enlargements were cut up, and divided into two classifications according to the letter form. 'Alphabet classifiers' were prepared, providing master-forms for the *a*-form and the *b*-form of each capital and small letter. These could then be placed over a page so that individual letters could be checked against them. Mrs Gallup had always said that the differences, though just visible to the naked eye, were minute; but they were expected to become clear on enlargement. This was not so; rather the opposite. Indeed, the differences between letter shapes often turned out to be ascribable to what the printer calls ink-spread (where the ink is absorbed into the paper in a halo round the outline of the letter) or to imperfections in the surface of the paper, or to damaged type.

It had been a criticism of her work that she had never explained clearly or in detail the technical bases of her classifications into *a*- and *b*-forms. When challenged on a specific identification she would sometimes defend herself by invoking what she called 'dotted' and 'accented' letters. For the rest, she talked in a general way of serifs, the slope or uprightness of the letter, the position of the dot over the 'i', and so on; but never did she set out the two full alphabets with a technical description of each. (In the second edition of her book in 1900 she included one plate showing the biformed alphabet she had extracted from the *Novum Organum*; when the third edition appeared, a year later, this master alphabet was omitted.)

For lack of that plain description of visibly identifiable forms, the basis for a trial assignment to *a*- and *b*-forms would naturally have to be one of frequency. The more frequent form of a letter would, in the nature of the case, be the *a*-form; for in Bacon's biliteral key the relationship of *a*'s to *b*'s is 68 to 52, in the 120 *a*'s and *b*'s which represent his twenty-four-letter alphabet (I=both I and J; V=both U and V). Therefore if all twenty-four letters had the same chance of occurring (which is far from true) any text would tend to consist of $56\frac{2}{3}$ per cent *a*-forms and $43\frac{1}{3}$ per cent *b*-forms. But if the relative frequency of occurrence of each letter in normal English is taken into account, the ratio of *a*'s to *b*'s increases; there are 64 per cent *a*-forms and 36 per cent *b*-forms. This is because the most frequent letters in English, E, T, R, I, A, have more *a*'s than *b*'s in their biliteral equivalents (*aabaa, baaba, baaaa, abaaa, aaaaa*); the combination of frequency with the initial preponderance of *a*'s makes the difference.

So one part of the Riverbank staff was cutting up enlarged alphabets, working out frequency tests and tentatively assigning letters to *a*- and *b*-forms, and, after Mrs Gallup had selected what she considered to be master- or typical-forms, the other part was applying these assignments to the texts and trying to get messages.

Mrs Friedman was involved in the second part of the process. She had been drawn into the work by a mixture of astonishment, incredulity and curiosity and the strong persuasion of a meeting with Colonel Fabyan. She found herself one of a number of students; all keen of eye, some with a background knowledge of English literature, none with any particular preference for either Shakespeare or Bacon as candidates for authorship. The main body of students marked by eye the two forms of italic type on hundreds of pages of print. Mrs Friedman then collated their markings into a master copy; she assigned the forms as the result of a tally. The letters were then divided into groups of five. Mrs Friedman or Miss Wells (Mrs Gallup's sister) then tried to get the message. When they failed, as they invariably did, to get more than a word or two, the text was taken to Mrs Gallup, who produced extensive readings with little apparent effort. Mrs Friedman would then say, 'But you must have changed some of the assignments'; she would reply that we had all failed to see a dot or an accent which changed the assignment, not noted the position of the dot over an 'i', and so on. This happened in texts which she had not deciphered before and also in those which she had deciphered and given the students as work-sheets: she always had some explanation for failure to see what she saw. Mrs Friedman has recorded the gradual crystallization of her opinions:

I became confused and then sceptical, but I suspended judgment as long as I could. For some time my admiration was stimulated by her facility in reducing what I brought to her as wholly unintelligible successions of *a* and *b* assignments to successive groups of five, in which the *a*'s and *b*'s fitted Bacon's alphabet key and from which she readily produced intelligible messages. After months of struggling without success to see her interpretation of the founts, and to produce hidden messages of my own, my admiration for her facility turned to uneasy questioning, and then to agonizing doubt, and then to downright disbelief.

I can state categorically that neither I nor any other one of the industrious research workers at Riverbank ever succeeded in extracting a single long sentence of a hidden message; nor did one of us so much as reproduce, independently, a single complete sentence which Mrs Gallup had already deciphered and published.

It is fitting here to point out once more that in any true cryptogram any given number of decipherers must, and will, arrive at the same solution.

We both left Riverbank in 1918. After completion of cryptographic work connected with the First World War we were urged to return to Riverbank, to continue the investigation of the biliteral cipher. We agreed, but on condition that we should be allowed full freedom to prove or disprove the existence of the cipher. We left again after a year and a half, in 1920. We were not encouraged, to put the matter lightly, to reveal any of our findings.

Mrs Gallup of course remained; and Fabyan continued to be her impresario. She still became news, now and again. There was the incident concerning General Cartier, a very prominent cryptologist in the French Army, whose apparent endorsement of her methods and results set Baconians into a whirl of dizzy delight. The affair has been so misunderstood that we give it a separate chapter. There were still articles and arguments; a novel was even written round the Bacon story. As time went by, Mrs Gallup became more and more a remote figure who was assumed to have found the only valid cipher, though no one else had quite mastered it. But if no one else could reproduce her results, no one had discredited them either; she remained intellectually respectable. We are about to examine that assumption in detail. A few general remarks may be made first.

We said at one point that if the decipherments were intelligible and obeyed normal linguistic rules we could accept them without argument; that was part of our dual test. So much is true of the cryptographer's professional practice at any rate; but as an ordinary human being with an interest in what he is deciphering or checking, he has his private opinions. Here are ours, offered as such.

In many of her decipherments a large part of the message—a quarter, or even as much as a half—deals with the biliteral cipher itself; its mechanics, its difficulties, its value, the skill and astuteness necessary in a decipherer, and so on. Her very first decipherment of Bacon's secret history has about 400 words; about 140 of them go on in this vein: 'Till a discypherer finde a prepar'd, or readily discover'd alphabet, it seemeth to us a thing almost impossible, save by Divine gift and heavenly instinct, that he should bee able to read what is thus reveal'd.' Now to encipher a text is a difficult business for the originator of the message and a delicate task for the printer. Is it likely that Bacon would have been so prodigal with his own labour that he could afford to enclose these prosings, which are mainly self-congratulatory and entirely unnecessary? What is the need for phrases like 'Divine gift and heavenly instinct', which are repetitious in themselves and mere cant in any case? ('Heavenly instincts' would be the curse of any cryptographic endeavour.) Is there not something odd about the logic of 'almost impossible...to read what is thus reveal'd'. Is not 'concealed' the word required here?

According to Mrs Gallup, George Peele's *The Arraignment of Paris* contains, in biliteral cipher, an endorsement of Dr Owen; it says that the 'Word-Cyphar' is used in the same book and commends it. In the decipherments from the *Novum Organum* two more extended comments appear:

This Cyphar [the biliteral] will make the Word Cipher more plaine, and it is chiefly in ayding its deciphering that all others that have been found do give some rules. It is our most importa't Cypher, having th' complete story told therein.

And again:

Wee have sometime found our other inventions of some worth,

in our worke, and we have spente occasionall idole minutes making such maskes serve instead of the two Cyphers so much us'd, for of soe many good methods of speaking to the readers of our workes, wee must quite naturally have a preference, and we owne that the Word-Cypher seemeth to us superiour to all others wee have invented. We have, however, devis'd six which wee have us'd in a few of our bookes. These are the Bi-literall; Wordd; Capital letter; Time, or as more oft call'd Clocke; Symboll; and Anagrammaticke.

Some Baconians have taken this hint and set to work to find the other ciphers, without any valid results. Of them all, only the word cipher is explained, and this in a sequence some thousands of words long, and so flaccidly constructed that at one point the complacent author says in an aside: 'No doubt my wanderings much resemble the chatter a senseless creature of Caliban's temper and nature might give out if hee were to speak in a secret manner, but such is my design.' This sort of 'explanation' occurs often: according to Bacon, it was to ensure that one day a decipherer would stumble on one of the keys to the secret story.

The word cipher is often praised as 'th' cheefe of my inventions' and this kind of remark is not felt to be inconsistent with the other claim that the biliteral is 'My great Cipher of Ciphers'. The reader becomes weary of Bacon's confidences; all the more so because they are trivial and inconclusive. Nothing seems to get said. Over and over again the serious and open-minded examiner of Baconian theories is forced to ask himself how it can be asserted that one great genius wrote Bacon's works, and allegedly the Shakespeare plays, as mere vehicles for the fundamentally more important secret messages; yet the secret utterances, now at last deciphered, are poverty-stricken in intellectual content. As for the particular remarks about the word cipher, it is reasonable to maintain that Bacon could never have heard of it; that particular type of cipher was invented by Owen. If Bacon had heard of it, and had endorsed it, then in our opinion his rating as a writer on cryptography would sink at once to zero.

Apart from these objections, which are the province of common sense, how do Mrs Gallup's decipherments appear when subjected to our dual test?

As for the linguistic validity of the plain texts, the crypt-analyst's requirements are fairly well satisfied. The texts are in reasonable English. The faults are not of style so much as of inconsequential thought. It is true that words are used in senses which lexicographers say those words did not have when the cipher was inserted. For example, in Mrs Gallup's decipher-ments, Bacon says once that he would like to introduce crypto-graphy into the curricula of universities. Now in Bacon's time *curricula* could only mean racecourses; its use as 'courses of study' followed much later. Similarly, some events are men-tioned which happened after the death of the author of the cipher. But that is not our affair; at most it could invalidate only the portions of the cipher where the error occurred (through a misreading on Mrs Gallup's part, for instance). In the main the texts themselves will do.

Not everyone will allow that much. C. L'Estrange Ewen, himself a Baconian, in a letter to *Baconiana* of October 1937, said:

A cursory examination and comparison of the orthography of the books as printed and the transliteration of Mrs Gallup demonstrates that her abbreviations such as adoptio', ciphe', dange', th' (before consonants!), differing entirely from those of the original text, and, in fact, unparalleled elsewhere, are hers alone. Moreover, be it remembered, that in the sixteenth century (being an era of irregular orthography) the printer naturally had no hesitation in justifying his lines [making the lines of type of exactly even length] by introducing variant spellings, and for Bacon to preserve his secret history and translation unmangled, he would have had to forbid the practice. Here again a brief scrutiny shows that equalizing the length of the line of type...has actually been accomplished in the customary way, not only by the insertion of 'spaces,' but also by such occasional odd spellings as the', yee, etc., each one of which would have destroyed the continuity of a hidden message.

These are shrewd arguments. To meet them, Mrs Gallup's champions must and do insist that, since it was necessary to forbid the arbitrary variation of spellings to suit the length of line, this could have been done, and was.

But what of the validity of the key? Is it not Bacon's own? We said earlier that if any element of the key is such that it

demands a decision by the decipherer which is based on subjective considerations or slight and imponderable factors, then
it will be difficult or impossible for the decipherer to get an
incontestable answer. There is the heart of the matter, in
Mrs Gallup's case as in others. Our next chapters examine just
this question; and our basic contention, supported by technical
evidence, will be that the differences between the forms of
letters are so minute and multifarious that the assignment to
an *a*- or *b*-form is always difficult and often impossible. It
becomes an exercise of personal judgment, which cannot be
understood, communicated, checked or duplicated.

Inevitably a Baconian must reply that the distinction was
bound to be small, for the sake of concealment. That is true;
but the difference must be detectable, for the sake of decipherment; that, after all, was Bacon's purpose. If a difference is
clear enough to be seen by one, it ought to be clear enough to
be seen by others; if not, the others must take the decipherment
as not proven. Now many students—not initially scoffers—
spent hours, weeks, months, even years, trying to check
Mrs Gallup's findings. They always failed; except in one or two
limited special cases, which we shall examine. What can we
say about the decipherments and the author? She was not a
conscious fraud; we know that from personal experience. We
are equally certain that she had not found, in all the books she
examined, one application of the biliteral cipher; we shall now
try to prove our assertion.

CHAPTER XV

ELIZABETHAN PRINTING AND ITS BEARING ON THE BILITERAL CIPHER

I F the biliteral cipher had really been inserted in the works of Bacon, the plays of Shakespeare, or any of the other books examined by Mrs Gallup, it would have been done by the compositors in the printing-houses concerned. With a carefully marked manuscript before him, or with an instructor standing beside him, each compositor would have set up the text, scrupulously inserting the *b*-forms of the letters wherever the cipher required it. Printers of the time worked (as hand-compositors do today) by picking the individual pieces of type-metal from a 'case' (a kind of shallow tray divided into compartments for stocks of each letter, space, or punctuation mark) and putting them together in a 'stick' (which is again rather like a smaller framed tray which holds the letters upright in compact blocks of the required width). It is clear that if the cipher were ever to be deciphered with certainty:

(*a*) the two forms, *a* and *b*, would have to be clearly distinct. One can imagine the compositor working from *two* cases, each holding a supply of each fount of type;

(*b*) the compositor would have to pick and set the right form in each instance. He could make errors, as printers do, but not more than a certain number.[1] Common sense suggests that his text, once set, would be proofed, checked carefully against the marked manuscript and corrected before printing. For lack of such correction the cipher would almost certainly be garbled.

Both these assumptions are based on presuppositions associated with modern printing practice. It is our aim to show that in sixteenth- and seventeenth-century printing-houses both conditions would be hard to meet, and to suggest, moreover, that in the books concerned these conditions were not met at all. We

For the permissible margin of error see below, pp. 266 ff.

shall then go on to consider some further implications of early English printing practice; the arguments there will be less general in their bearing; none the less they constitute telling criticisms of Mrs Gallup's theories.

We deal first with the basic contention of all upholders of the biliteral theory; that the printed texts concerned were set in two founts of type, giving two letter-forms.

Colonel Fabyan was no fool. He must have seen that the testimony of a professional typographer would carry more weight than any amount of amateur theorizing. Some time in 1920 he commissioned the distinguished American type-designer F. W. Goudy to examine the whole question and to report to him. Any printer can tell when a 'wrong fount' appears in a proof: it is a common form of typographical error; but a designer and scholar like Goudy can also relate types to each other in families, date them with precision, and even say quite often who designed them and in what country. It was not therefore a very formidable task for Goudy to undertake. He reported, and we have seen the report. It was never published, but it probably cost Fabyan a sizable fee; so he was perhaps unwilling to destroy it. It remained in his collection of books and papers, which went to the Library of Congress. Just where one would expect the writer's name to appear there is a blank, an erasure so thorough that not a single letter can be discerned even by the established techniques of 'grazing' and ultra-violet light—and this is unusual.

We felt that it must be Goudy's work; so we compared the handwriting with his—even compared the watermark of the paper with that of other papers in the Goudy Collection in the Library of Congress. Our detections were cut short by our finding in that collection a large envelope, inscribed 'With Colonel Fabyan and Staff'; inside was another envelope bearing the legend '*Novum Organum*—commissioned but not printed by Colonel Fabyan'; it contained two carbon copies of the report we had seen. Why Fabyan did not publish it becomes quite plain when one reads it.

We need only let Goudy present his own case:

The Riverbank Laboratories has commissioned the writer to make a scientific study of the italic types in which John Bill, King's

Typographer, printed Francis Bacon's *Novum Organum* (1620), in order to establish the presence of two or more forms of each letter employed, or to show conclusively the contrary fact; if varying forms were found, to ascertain whether the two forms were regular, constant, and maintained consistently throughout the alphabet. In fact, the problem which the writer was asked to solve was whether the heterogeneity of the forms of the *Novum Organum* is an ordered result, or the result of bad press-work, poor ink, broken and distorted letters, etc., or whether due to some *essential* and *inherent variations* in the design of the types themselves of which Bacon might avail himself to constitute a biformed alphabet for use in the biliteral cipher which he presents and explains....

The heterogeneity of the type-forms is patent to any one who will give them a discriminating attention. That there is undoubtedly more than one form of some letters is too obvious to require more than a cursory examination. Whether there are two or more forms of *each* letter can only be decided by a careful study of them under conditions not always under the control of the casual reader. To bring the forms within the ken of any one interested, in such a way that he may decide for himself, the writer herewith presents enlarged drawings of each letter of the alphabet, capital and lower-case letters and their ligatures, for the accuracy of which he is prepared to accept full responsibility as to their faithful translation, both in form and spirit....

Human nature is much the same today as in Bacon's time; a designer of type would then produce forms influenced or inspired by the forms of letters with which he was familiar and as he worked to give those forms new expressions, certain features of design would call for certain sequences. The type designer today, asked to solve the same problem under similar conditions, would proceed very much as did his prototype, and produce results distinctly similar. *The designer may now project himself back, as it were, into the thought and mood of the older craftsman and decide almost with exactness just what the original must have been, and, too, with even greater assurance that his reconstruction is likely to be more near y correct than the scientist's reconstruction of some prehistoric monster from a single bone.*[1]

With no egotistic intentions the writer wishes to assure the reader that his artistic conscience will not allow him to present any dubious form for the sake of expediency, and where there is a doubt he has not attempted to coerce a letter into a varying form simply to supply

---

[1] Our italics. Goudy here implies that the type-designer can take an assortment of types, and by picking out family resemblances which his experience leads him to expect, sort them out into complete founts.

material. Neither has he attempted to decide which forms might be construed as being the 'a' or 'b' of Mrs Gallup's classification. He has, however, attempted to indicate which forms probably constituted parts of the same fonts....

After several paragraphs explaining the impossibility of making such determinations as he sought from photographic or other facsimile reproductions, Goudy tells how he made his studies from an original copy of *Novum Organum* at the Riverbank Laboratories, and made them with a *camera lucida*, 'turning the pages hundreds of times for corroborative evidence before accepting the drawings as finished enlargements'. He states that the trained eye is able to detect with ease a difference of three thousandths of an inch. He goes on:

The *Novum Organum* is not a well printed work. In England in 1620 printing was at a low degree of excellence....

Without attempting to place himself on record as to the merits or fallacy of the claims regarding the Baconian cipher, the writer is yet free to say that *if* Francis Bacon desired to conceal any message in the *Novum Organum*, the materials were immediately to hand in the possession of his printer John Bill.... Variety in forms was usual... the additional forms necessary to the cipher would not necessarily excite suspicion, a point of which Bacon would no doubt take full advantage.

As a type designer of long experience...it is quite evident (to the writer at least, who is also a practical printer) that letters from totally foreign founts have been deliberately interpolated among those that would ordinarily be required—and these strangers are indicated by the thickened impression (or a lighter impression), bad lining, different heights, etc., which occur frequently in one or more letters of a single word....

Printing in 1620 was done on hand presses of weak construction, on paper which first had to be softened by dampening, against a blanket of wool in the tympan to make the types of unusual height fairly readable—the spongy blanket serving to diffuse the pressure to all the types under standard height. The paper dried out unequally so that types on one page might vary slightly in size from those on another.... Such letters as *a*, *e*, *o*, etc. would fill with excess of ink and show a spot in the impression that might be taken for actual print from type.

After a careful explanation of his terminology, Goudy included in his report most meticulous and exact drawings of the forms of single and ligatured letters in the *Novum Organum* (Plate IX). In only a few instances was Goudy able to reduce the forms to two and only two. Among the upper-case (capital) letters he shows two forms of 'lining' A, and two forms of swash *A*; three types of capital C; three of E, I and T. With lower-case (small) letters, he shows four forms of c; four of e, i, l; three of m, four of o, r, and t; of the ligatures (linked letters, e.g. ffi) nearly all have four forms. Our plate shows the pencilled lines indicating the varying slope of the letters; it also indicates the care and skill of the draughtsman.

It is not exactly a simple matter. Goudy pointed out that types were handed on from printer to printer; John Day (the best English printer of his time) brought italic types of a high quality into use in England, and they were so much admired that they were used by others long after his death in 1584. William Blades, an English writer on early printing, points out that when types became battered and worn in use and had to be replaced, this was often done by simply 'correcting' a damaged letter with a graver, striking it into wax to make a matrix and casting further letters from it. Hence there would be a steady debasement of the quality of the letter and, more important, a myriad progressive tiny variations in shape, producing eventually something quite different. Goudy said that some of the italics in the *Novum Organum* had been in use long before Bacon's time; that some of the variations in letter-forms were due to this makeshift of the printers, and some others simply due to the motley collection of founts all used indiscriminately together. He quoted the American typographer De Vinne, who had pointed out that 'there are old-style italics in use that seem to have been made up from a haphazard collection of discarded punches and matrices, gathered from old Dutch and early English type-founders'.

In other words Goudy found not two forms, but a multitude. Bill printed the *Novum Organum* with a multiformed assembly of types. One cannot therefore talk of *a*-forms and *b*-forms, though it might be possible to talk of *a*-families of forms and *b*-families of forms: each family approximating to an *a*- or *b*-form. But this is a shift of ground; it would make the task of a decipherer incomparably more difficult; and it is not in any case supported by Goudy's evidence. Indeed Mrs Gallup insisted that, as a rule, there were only two forms; she had alphabet classifications prepared on this basis. We reproduce one such alphabet in Fig. 17; it appeared only in the second edition of her *Biliteral Cypher of Sir Francis Bacon*, and was, as we earlier remarked, silently dropped from the third edition. Her two versions are irreconcilable with Goudy's three or four. It will have been noticed that Goudy leaned over backwards to say that the biliteral was theoretically *possible*, given the assortments of type available. What he could not support was a simple two-fount mixture in the books in question. He did not commit himself to a view about the purposiveness of the use of varying founts. But the implication of his analysis is that their use is quite haphazard. It was presumably for this reason that Fabyan never published the report.

In 1953 we thought that Goudy's findings might well be supplemented by the techniques of document-examination which have been evolved since his day, particularly by the Federal Bureau of Investigation. We asked the help of Mr J. Edgar Hoover, Director of the Bureau, hoping in particular that we might get technical assistance from the staff of the F.B.I. laboratory. Mr Hoover suggested that Special Agent Fred M. Miller, who had the longest experience in document examination, might be sufficiently interested to take on the assignment in his free time. Dr Miller was interested, and very kindly undertook to examine the problem.

We gave him excellent photographs from the Folger Shakespeare Library of two passages: the 'Prologue' to *Troilus and Cressida* from the Library's copy no. 28 of the First Folio, and p. 23 of *Novum Organum*, contained in the Harmsworth copy of *Instauratio Magna*. In both cases we had in our possession copies of Mrs Gallup's assignments of the letters to their *a*- and *b*-forms. The questions we asked Dr Miller were: could he find consistency in Mrs Gallup's classification; was there a small or a large variation between the letters classified as *a* or *b*; was it possible to identify letters as from the same matrix? We asked this last question because, if an identification of that sort

ALPHABETS, NOVUM ORGANUM.			
LARGE	TYPE	SCRIPT	
FONT A.	FONT B.	A.	B.
A a	A a	A a	a
B b	B b	B	
C c c	C c c	C	
D d	D d		∂
E e	E e	e	
F ƒƒſƒ	F ƒſƒƒ	F	
G g	G g		g
H H h	H h	h.	
J J i i	I J i	J i i	J i
L l	L l	L	l
M m	M M m	m m	m m
N N n	N N N n	N n	
O o o	O o	o	
P p	P p	p	p
Q Q q	Q q		
R R r	R r r	R r	R
S S ſſſſ s	S ſſſſſ s s	s	S
T T t t ta	T i T t t	t	
V v u	U v u	u	u
NO W. IN LATIN	NO W. IN LATIN		
X x	X x		
Y y		y	y
Z z		z	
&	&		

Fig. 17. Mrs Gallup's biformed alphabet applicable to the letters of the *Novum Organum* (1620).

were possible, Mrs Gallup's assignments could be checked in successive instances. One would see at once if she had been consistent or merely arbitrary by checking her treatment of letters which, coming from the same matrix, must have been identical in shape.

Dr Miller summarized his findings in four sentences:

1. An analysis of the type disclosed the existence of a wide variation among those letters classified as *a*-font as well as among those classified as *b*-font.
2. No characteristics were found which support the classification into two fonts, such as *a*-font and *b*-font.
3. Greater similarities were found between individual letters of the different fonts than between various letters within the same font.
4. No two letters were found among either of the two fonts which can be identified as having originated from the same matrix.

Dr Miller supported these statements with diagrams, of which we reproduce one (Plate X). The first line in each group of letters gives *a*-forms, the second *b*-forms, according to Mrs Gallup's classifications. The reader can be left to judge them for himself.

At this stage of our discussion we can state quite firmly that the biliteral thesis in any *strict* sense is invalid; it is just not true that the printer used two and only two letter-forms which can be identified as *a*- and *b*-forms and deciphered. The most an ardent upholder of the Gallup thesis could maintain is that the manifold letter forms might perhaps fall into two categories or families; within each category the characteristics of the several members might be roughly similar. It would be a matter of *a*-type or *b*-type. There are two obvious corollaries; one that the business of decipherment is made immensely more difficult, unless electronic equipment or a staff of F.B.I. agents is brought to bear; two, that by Dr Miller's testimony Mrs Gallup did not herself make a successful distinction between the kinds (see his point 3). It should also be pointed out that Dr Miller's use of the words 'the two different fonts' does not mean that he himself accepted the distinction into two founts, but that for the purpose of the investigation he was accepting Mrs Gallup's assignments as something 'given'. The whole tendency of his findings is that the assignments she made are not mutually consistent.

We know, of course, that Mrs Gertrude Horsford Fiske in America and Mrs Henry Pott, Mr Henry Seymour and Mrs D. J. Kindersley in England all maintained that they too had arrived at Mrs Gallup's decipherments. Mrs Fiske, to be sure, found others as well; we gave some examples in ch. VI. Seymour often stated that he had deciphered *Henry VII* without consultation with Mrs Gallup, and that his reading differed from hers by only a few words. What he did not say was whether he had *seen* Mrs Gallup's messages before producing his own; we think he had. And of all these decipherers we are bound to say that they had long been Baconians, familiar with the kind of message elicited from the works, and (to our minds) apt to produce from them the same sort of thing—even if they were not consciously dominated by a wish to confirm Baconian findings. Both Mrs Fiske and Mrs Kindersley worked under the direct influence—even the eye—of Mrs Gallup or Miss Wells. It was a Baconian who said it is not satisfactory to claim that one has checked Mrs Gallup if a supporter, already convinced of her work, does so with her decipherment before him.[1]

One of Mrs Gallup's first violent critics became later a no less ardent defender. This was James Phinney Baxter, who in 1915 produced *The Greatest of Literary Problems: the Authorship of the Shakespeare Works*. He subtitled the book 'An exposition of all points at issue, from their inception to the present moment'. His ch. 16 brings us to ciphers, where he gives most attention to Mrs Gallup's work on the biliteral cipher. He tells of a test he once made, using the 'I.M.' poem in the First Folio:

> It occurred to us that the best test of Mrs Gallup's trustworthiness as a decipherer would be to enfold in the body of the 'I.M. poem' a combination of German words and submit it to her. We therefore had a photograph, many times enlarged, made of the poem, from which the letters were cut, and an alphabet made of the two fonts of

[1] W. L. Eagle in *Baconiana*, April 1949.

PLATE IX

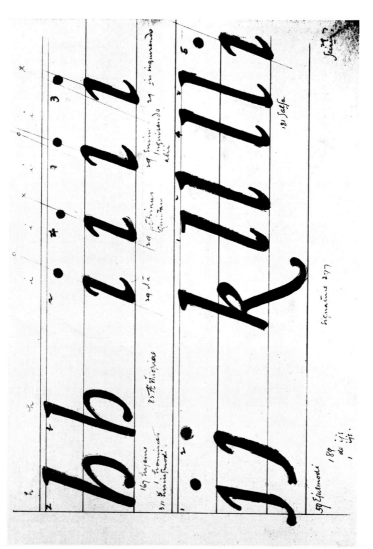

F. W. Goudy's drawings of letters in the *Novum Organum* (1620).

PLATE X

Dr Miller's analysis of type-founts in the 'Prologue' to *Troilus and Cressida*, First Folio. The first lines of each group of letters are the *a*-fount, the second the *b*-fount.

type in which it was printed. Though time and patience had been devoted to distinguishing between the letters *t, n, e, o, w,* and *r,* the proper ones were selected as nearly as possible, pasted upon a large sheet of cardboard, and then photographed down to the original size in the Folio. This we mailed to Mrs Gallup, requesting her to favour us by deciphering it.

She sent him her decipherment; but it differed a little from his original message. He then found, he says, that he had made some errors; he corrected them, sent the poem to her again, and she replied with a correct decipherment.

Baxter then devised another test. He wanted to prove that the founts in the Second Folio were also classifiable into biliteral alphabets. As before, he photographed a poem (this time the one by Leonard Digges), and again he abstracted and drew up alphabets containing *typical* forms of each letter, based on Mrs Gallup's own decipherments. This time, instead of reconstituting the Digges text with a secret message, he used his master alphabets to set out Sonnets XXXII, XXXVI and XXXVIII, enclosing in the open text a poem of his own. Mrs Gallup deciphered this at once, and returned the secret message by return of post.

Baxter was tremendously impressed, to the point where his critical faculty was completely swamped. Opposite p. 635 of his book he prints a 'Note to Bibliography' in italic, saying that it has a secret message in it from him, but the letters are facsimiles of Bacon's own alphabets as given in the *De Augmentis.* He goes on: 'The fact that the letters in which this Note is printed are facsimiles of those used by Bacon himself, to illustrate his Biliteral Cipher, proves beyond question its employment by him.' This is patently absurd. All it proves is that Bacon used the cipher in his demonstration of the cipher—which is not surprising. It proves nothing else.

A more rational view was expressed by George B. Curtis of Lehigh University in *Baconiana* of January 1939. He told how he had performed a test with members of his university, using Baxter's Second Folio experiment. Curtis photographed Baxter's version of the three Sonnets, showed them to three people who were not Baconians; gave them also Bacon's own explanation of the cipher, and left them to work it out for themselves. All three deciphered the message. Curtis thought this more remarkable as a test than the first two tests tried on Mrs Gallup by Baxter—particularly her extraction of the message from Baxter's rearrangement of the 'I.M.' poem. This, thought Curtis, was no great feat at all, for 'all she had to do was to note the transposition of the letters within the passage—a task not very difficult for her or for any one familiar with her solution of the original'. Curtis pointed out that Baxter had never stated in plain words what it was that he sent Mrs Gallup and that she deciphered—namely, a truly biliteral message, made up entirely of *only two* letter-forms. This of course is in flagrant contrast with the printing of the late sixteenth and early seventeenth centuries, which was, as Goudy and Dr Miller showed, multi-literal or multi-formed.

The thoughtful Baxter had, it seems clear, made the task easy by selecting two easily distinguishable forms from the multitude, producing as many copies of each as he needed, and using them consistently. Mrs Gallup's speed in deciphering the text is a tribute only to his skill in abstracting and using two master-forms. He did for her what seventeenth-century printers could never have done. What is more, he left unchanged the first and last two words of her own decipherment of the same text. Thus she had a crib of useful length.

Tests of Baxter's kind are fairly easy to prepare, and prove nothing essential to the main question. No one has ever denied the validity of the cipher, or the possibility of inserting it; the questions are: is it there, and did Mrs Gallup find it in the particular works discussed? Yet she herself was about as pleased with her performance as Baxter. She used the tests as a sample study for her Riverbank pupils. Not very remarkably, this was the one thing they could always do to her satisfaction, the one decipherment they could corroborate. It gave them a fleeting sense of pride and achievement, and went some way towards convincing them that the cipher was not a mirage, but they never got any further. The tests were also demonstrated to visitors to Riverbank, and no doubt had some effect. It could hardly be expected that a stranger to the topic should see at once the serious flaw in Baxter's tests and their essential irrelevance to the central point at issue.

So much then for our point (*a*) (p. 216) about the two forms. Our point (*b*) was that careful setting by a compositor who knew what he was doing, followed by careful proof-reading and correction before printing, were essential if the message were not to be garbled by errors. It follows also that all copies of the works bearing the cipher must be identical; so that only one right message could be extracted by the decipherer, whatever copy (among all the copies in the edition) he used.

Again, this is plainly not the case. In the Folger Shakespeare Library at Washington there is the world's largest collection—some eighty copies—of the First Folio. Letter by letter, these copies are being collated by Prof. Charlton Hinman, of Johns Hopkins University, aided by a grant from the Old Dominion Foundation and an ingenious electrical collating machine of his own design. The aim is to ascertain the measure of similarity and the extent of the differences. It is already clear that there may not even be two copies which are identical throughout all 454 leaves (900-odd pages of two columns). This is not news to bibliographers, for there are in all probability no two identical copies of any book of the time; printing methods precluded it.

We have looked through the eye-pieces of Prof. Hinman's machine to confirm by ocular demonstration what, for the sake of the simple or the obdurate, Prof. Hinman kindly set down for us in the form of a categorical statement:

> In any given copy of the First Folio of Shakespeare, there is no full page of the text which is without letters that are so different in appearance from the corresponding letters in other copies that they seem to have been, though they were not, printed from different types. Inking variations are doubtless the commonest cause of these differences, but many other agencies could have, and in various instances unquestionably did, contribute to the result.
>
> (Signed) CHARLTON HINMAN
> 20 *February* 1954

The 'other agencies' are indicated in a paper by Prof. Hinman on 'Variant readings in the First Folio of Shakespeare' in the

Shakespeare Quarterly of July 1953. We italicize some portions which most concern our argument:

It is perhaps not yet fully appreciated that 'the First Folio text' is, strictly speaking, only an abstraction, since individual copies of the First Folio in fact present us with a great variety of different texts. This should not be surprising. For more than two centuries the commonly employed methods of press-correction were such that *different copies of the edition of a given text could not fail to be variant.* The first impressions or pulls from a 'forme' (the letterpress for one side of a full, unfolded sheet: two type-pages, of course, in folio printing) were used as proof-sheets; *but printing was continued all the while the proof-reading was going on,* about three pulls a minute being made from the still uncorrected forme. As proof-reading would take time, a good many copies of the 'first state' of the forme were produced before the marked proof was ready, presswork was interrupted, and the changes required by the proof-reader were at last effected. Only now could the press begin to print from the corrected state of the forme. *Since, moreover, both paper and presswork were commodities too precious to be wasted, the uncorrected copies hitherto wrought off were destroyed only if thought to contain serious, perhaps dangerous, errors.* Ordinarily they were preserved and eventually found their way, just as if corrected, into some copies of the finished volume. Nor did the uncorrected states of the successive formes making up the whole book go regularly into the *same* copies.... Different copies of (the First Folio) show all conceivable mixtures of early and late, of corrected and uncorrected formes.... *The statements so far made about the stop-press correction that characterized the printing of the First Folio (and of many other books of the period) do not rest upon inference and supposition, but are matters of demonstrable fact....* The Folio unquestionably does contain *large numbers* of variant readings. The collation of eighty copies throughout the eighteen *Othello* formes shows that nine of these—a full 50 per cent—are variant.... 51 of the 163 formes that make up the Tragedies have already been found variant, some in more than two states....Hundreds of individual variants have already been discovered; many more are sure to turn up...but the evidence already in hand firmly establishes two general principles. It demonstrates clearly: (1) that *no two copies of the First Folio selected at random should ever be supposed textually identical throughout*; and (2) that no single copy is likely to preserve anything that can properly be considered '*the* First Folio text'.

Let the reader try to imagine the difficulty of the printer in keeping in mind—if not under control—the corrections to be made, and using the *a*- and *b*-forms correctly in the changes. It is almost inconceivable. Is it not also clear that every copy of the First Folio would give a slightly different deciphered message as a result of the correction? Yet Mrs Gallup never even thought of this. She did not even bother to work from a true copy of the First Folio, but from a facsimile—made at a time when facsimiles were not good.

It is fairly plain what this implies for the biliteral cipher, but we shall ram the argument home:

(i) The whole trend of general printing practice militates against its use; but

(ii) it would have been possible if the printer of the First Folio had changed from his usual methods. After all, the cipher *was* inserted in the *De Augmentis* illustration in certain editions after the 1623, 1624 and 1640 (Gilbert Wats) editions;[1] yet

(iii) Prof. Hinman shows that the First Folio conforms to the normal proof-reading and printing practice of the time.

This, together with the testimony of Goudy and Dr Miller seems *a priori* to demolish arguments for the presence of the cipher in the books in which Mrs Gallup claimed she found it. We shall continue the discussion in our next chapter, where we consider some more specific objections to Mrs Gallup's decipherments.

[1] See p. 189, footnote.

CHAPTER XVI

A STUDY OF THE GALLUP
DECIPHERMENTS

A NUMBER of Mrs Gallup's critics predicted that at some point in her voluminous decipherments (in all about 150,000 words) she would overlook some small technical matter and this small error or oversight would provide the starting-point of arguments demolishing her whole thesis.

Among these writers was C. L'Estrange Ewen; he was a Baconian, but felt that her decipherments were a poor support for the theory which in general he accepted. In an article called 'The Gallup Decipher' in *Baconiana* of October 1935, he found a weakness in her method. In her book she had recorded decipherments from certain works which existed in two editions. In some cases they are genuinely distinct editions (i.e. separate settings of type providing a slightly different text), but in one case the two 'editions' were, at any rate in part, only successive impressions from the same type. When the editions differ substantially—particularly in the arrangement of italic type—one would expect Mrs Gallup to produce differing decipherments; when they are from the same type, her decipherments ought to be identical. If they are not, one is entitled to doubt her methods.

Ewen studied Robert Greene's *The Spanish Masquerado*, of which there were two editions in 1589. He indicated the significance of his findings in a later article (in *Baconiana*, January 1937): 'Mrs Gallup operated on the safest possible grounds in claiming to see what others could not. Her greatest danger lay in using the same passage twice. That I submit she did unwittingly in the case of *The Spanish Masquerado* and thereby made the fallacy of her work demonstrable.' He did in fact find two different decipherments; and for certain parts of the book it was his contention that these decipherments were extracted from two successive impressions of the same pieces of type, which had not been distributed after the first impression but kept 'standing', as printers call it, and then incorporated with the type of the second edition.

Mrs Gallup had naturally noticed that parts of the two editions were identical. The title-pages were the same, for instance, and the first sixty letters of her decipherment (rendering the 300 italic letters in the original title-page) are the same. But from the sixty-first letter, her decipherments are entirely different. Hence the italic letters in the printed text *ought* from that point to be correspondingly different. But Ewen contended that while most of the pages were printed from different type-settings, some were not; so that in both decipherments those particular passages should be identically rendered. Very often they were not.

The clearest case of this kind was signature A, p. 2 verso, which gives a sonnet by Thomas Lodge in 247 italic letters. Here Mrs Gallup produced two decipherments, while Ewen held that the type in both cases was the same. He says:

A count shows that in deciphering 247 italic letters twice over Mrs Gallup has failed to repeat her symbols in 111 cases, thus revealing 45 per cent inaccuracy, a proportion which...would absolutely debar her from interpreting any message even if one were hidden.

Any reader desiring to test the soundness of the conclusions now presented...should first satisfy himself that [A 2 verso] is identical in both...editions...and secondly that two readings cannot come from one passage by way of the Bacon symbols. These Mrs Gallup has given us, and it can be said without hesitation that from that fact alone her decipher is completely discredited.

This dismaying charge was made in the very number in which Mrs Gallup's death was recorded. It was discussed (in the same issue) by Mr Henry Seymour, then Honorary Secretary of the Bacon Society, and the very man who had claimed to have independently deciphered *Henry VII* (see p. 224). Seymour wrote:

The editors are bound to preserve an attitude of impartiality in the matter, since the accuracy or otherwise of Mrs Gallup's deciphering does not affect the Baconian position. The Society has never officially committed itself to her claims, but, on the contrary, did, many years ago, reject them as unproven. It is unfortunate that Mrs Gallup is not able any longer to defend herself. The matter must therefore be left for our readers to form their own conclusions.

They did so, and were glad to express them, but the only counter-attack of any serious worth came from G. B. Curtis, whom we have mentioned above (p. 225). Curtis was a fervent Baconian, but by no means an uncritical one. He had rejected every cryptographic argument for Baconian authorship until he began to study Mrs Gallup's work. He was impressed, and made meticulous efforts to verify her conclusions, studying type-forms, and making experiments with his colleagues at Lehigh. If therefore he defended Mrs Gallup against Ewen's charge, it was as the result of a mature conviction, fortified by experiment, that even if Mrs Gallup was not proved right it would take a lot to prove that she was wrong.[1] Four years after Ewen's article Curtis wrote 'A Study in Elizabethan Typography' in *Baconiana* of January 1939. He stated that Ewen's allegation that Mrs Gallup had made 111 discrepant assignments of letters was based on Ewen's own transliteration; he (Curtis) had been able to work from Mrs Gallup's work sheets. Thus Ewen had been wrong to include the roman letters A and TO in the dedication page, for 'it was never Mrs Gallup's practice to decipher signatures and catchwords'. The inclusion of these letters made Ewen's transliteration incorrect from that point on. Curtis then showed Mrs Gallup's actual assignments, and showed that there were only eighty-four differences, not 111, between the two renderings. Nor did he accept that the type was entirely identical for both editions.

Ewen, while insisting that the decipherment would be invalid if the assignments were not 96 per cent correct, had accused Mrs Gallup of 45 per cent error. Curtis now reduced the percentage to 34 per cent. As Mrs Gallup's more rational supporters had only claimed a maximum accuracy of 60–70 per cent in her identification of the two forms, Curtis's intervention

---

[1] We knew Mr Curtis. In the last few years of his life he rejected Mrs Gallup's deciperments. He still believed in the existence of a cipher in the First Folio, but thought that the key had still to be found.

in the argument was thus support for them. And indeed, in going twice over what were now admitted to be in part the same type-characters, Mrs Gallup had produced identical readings in about two-thirds of the letters.

This argument therefore resolves itself into a discussion of the amount of permissible error. Ewen allowed only 4 per cent, saying that if more than that proportion of letters were incorrectly assigned, the message would be garbled beyond hope. Curtis felt that a 25–30 per cent error was permissible. Neither of the disputants was a cryptographer, and both were wrong. It is not the percentage of doubtful letters which alone determines intelligibility in the deciphered message: at times 2–5 per cent of doubtful letters would cloud the result impossibly, while at others 20–40 per cent of doubtful assignments would not impede a correct decipherment. There have been cases of more than 50 per cent error: that is, cases where the letters of the text had been incorrectly enciphered in the first place or garbled in transmission, so that more than half of the message was unintelligible on first trial. Yet persistence and a knowledge of the kind of error made by cipher clerks and telegraph operators have produced the right result. Nowadays of course it is possible to ask for a retransmission, as a check. Bacon could only do that originally by issuing another printing of the same book. He is now in any case beyond appeal; but if more than one cryptanalyst were to get the same result, that would be as good as a retransmission. That has not happened. In the meantime we can only say that more important than the proportion of doubtfully assigned letters to the total is their distribution between *a*- and *b*-forms, the nature of the text itself, and the concentration or scattering of the errors. If they fell in large groups in a few places, those passages might be entirely lost (though they might also be indicated by the context) and the remainder of the message would be unaffected. If the errors were spread through the text, it might prove impossible to arrive at a result that was demonstrably correct; it would depend on the number of errors. And if we are asked, 'Well, *how* many?', we have to say there is no answer. We made an experiment in which 50 per cent of the letters were not classified but were well distributed through the text. It was reconstructed without too much work. This experiment is described on pp. 266 ff.

That particular argument, between Ewen and Curtis, was not entirely conclusive either way, though it did show an appreciation of the real issues involved and was in itself damaging to Mrs Gallup's alleged sharp sight and scientific method. Let us return to the decipherment of Bacon's *The History of the Reign of King Henry the Seventh*. We mentioned this, and Bompas' attempted inquiry, on p. 198. Here again there were two impressions of the book, both made in 1622; this had not been realized by Mrs Kindersley, who claimed to have corroborated Mrs Gallup's findings. Henry Seymour made the same claim. Mrs Gallup had worked on only one of the impressions, though it is not certain that both her supporters used the same one. The kind of charge levelled against her by Ewen cannot be made in this case. But Bompas' criticism—that she had given different assignments to letters of the page-headings when these were in fact repeated uses of the same pieces of type—is closely related: basically it means that even when working with only one of the impressions she failed to note the repeated use of 'standing' type (type moved en bloc from one page to another). Bompas' own accusation was based on an error; he thought all the headings on the left would be printed from one line of type, and all the headings on the right from a second. In fact, according to the format of the book, four, eight or twelve pages were printed at once, all the type for those pages being held in a rectangular frame called a forme. Type would only be lifted and inserted from forme to forme, i.e. from p. 1 to p. 5, 9, or 13 and so on, and not from page to page. This is the elementary ignorance of printing practice on which Bompas' case falls down. He was, however, right in thinking that type was lifted from heading to heading. In practice Mrs Gallup recognized this in some cases. This is a sign, if it were needed, that she was not working entirely arbitrarily; her eye was sharp enough to recognize identities, her practice was consistent enough to assign these to the same form, *a* or *b*.

But let us see just how sharp-eyed and consistent she was. It may be that this study will be more conclusive than Ewen's. We have studied the copy of the book which Mrs Gallup used, for it is still in the Fabyan Collection in the Library of Congress.

We begin with a table of identical headings in the first hundred pages (pp. 2–99 in actual fact). This shows that the left-hand page heading was set six times and each setting repeated from six to ten times; the right-hand page heading was set seven times and each setting repeated two to nine times.

LEFT-HAND PAGES						RIGHT-HAND PAGES						
Setting						Setting						
1	2	3	4	5	6	1	2	3	4	5	6	7
Page						Page						
2	4	6	8	12	14	3	5	11	13	19	21	73
10	16	22	20	38	30	7	9	27	35	25	29	99
18	24	32	28	46	34	15	17	39	43	47	33	—
26	36	42	40	50	54	23	37	51	55	69	41	—
44	56	68	48	58	64	31	49	57	63	75	53	—
60	70	78	52	72	66	45	67	71	65	95	59	—
74	82	90	62	84	—	61	87	83	81	—	77	—
—	94	—	76	88	—	79	91	89	85	—	93	—
—	—	—	92	—	—	—	—	—	97	—	—	—
—	—	—	98	—	—	—	—	—	—	—	—	—

In the transcription of twenty-one pages which Mrs Gallup sent Bompas, she made identical assignments for four left-hand headings (THE HISTORIE OF THE RAIGNE OF on pp. 4 and 16, 10 and 18) and three right-hand headings (KING [HENRY] THE SEUENTH on pp. 3, 7, 15). Thus she recognized the identities in the settings for seven out of twenty-one pages, but she did not notice that the heading of p. 2 is identical with pp. 10 and 18, or that pp. 8 and 20, and pp. 5, 9 and 17 are also identical.

What about other cases of lifted type in headings? Did she, having recognized some instances, consistently assign to their a- and b-forms the letters in other repeated settings? Her defenders said she had a keener eye for such things than anyone else; we should therefore expect an unerring recognition of these cases. We decided to check Mrs Gallup's work for ourselves; we shall now give a brief description of how it was done.

The number of italic letters on a page can vary. Each page-heading therefore might start with its first letter falling any-where in the group of five which corresponds to a letter of the message. The combinations for a left-hand heading would be:

1.	THEHI	STORI	EOFTH	ERAIG	NEOF.
2.	....T	HEHIS	TORIE	OFTHE	RAIGN	EOF..
3.	...TH	EHIST	ORIEO	FTHER	AIGNE	OF...
4.	..THE	HISTO	RIEOF	THERA	IGNEO	F....
5.	.THEH	ISTOR	IEOFT	HERAI	GNEOF	.....

On these groupings, and the way the two founts are disposed in them, will depend the plain text which emerges from them. But once the assignments to *a*- and *b*-forms made by Mrs Gallup are accepted, it becomes clear that the number of possibilities is greatly reduced; for where identical type is being deciphered, the assignments must always be the same.

As an example let us take the headings for pp. 2, 10, 18, 26, etc., where one setting is repeated. We have records of Mrs Gallup's assignments for p. 2; they are:

THEHISTORIEOFTHERAIGNEOF
a a a b a a b a a a a a b a a b a a b a a b a b

According to the five possible divisions listed above, the biliteral readings for this line must be:

1.		C / I / E / T / L or M
2.		E / R / K / E / W, X, Y or Z
3.	A, E, I, N, R, W / K / A / T / K / and any letter from I to Q
4.	A, I, R / T / B / E / T / and any letter from R to Z
5.	B or S / E / C / K / F /

Now if Mrs Gallup has made no mistakes in her decipherments, the message extracted from this repeated heading, on pp. 2, 10, 18, 26 and so on, must *always* reveal a plain text composed of one of these five series of letters.

Let us make the same experiment with the heading repeated on pp. 3, 7, 15, 23, 31, 45, 61, 79. The heading has only three italic words; the name HENRY is in roman capitals.

Mrs Gallup's assignment could therefore only give two plain-text letters and a part of the preceding or following one:

KING[...]THE SEUENTH
abab ... aab   *abaabba*

According to our five divisions, this gives the following possibilities:

1.   L / L / N or O
2.   A, C, E, G, I–J, L, N, P, R, T, W, Y / W / W / (no group be-
                                         gins with two
                                         b's)
3.   B, F, K, O, S, X / K / K / and any letter
                                         from R to Z
4.   C, L, T / T / U or V / and any letter
                                         from A to Q
5.   F or X / F / G

The same process can be repeated for the headings on pp. 4 and 5; and these combinations can be used to check the deciphered text for each repetition of these headings.

Having now assembled the possibilities for the settings on pp. 2, 3, 4, 5, 7, 9, 10, 15, 16, 17, 18, and so on we examined Mrs Gallup's decipherments of the page-headings in detail. We made on one tape a careful letter-by-letter copy of the italic words in the first sixty pages of *Henry VII*, and on another a copy of her corresponding decipherments, with the letters five spaces apart. It then became a matter of matching one tape against the other, and finding the points of correspondence between them.

To find the fit between the two tapes, we first counted the number of italic letters before the heading of p. 2; there were 510. Dividing this by five, the expected number of plain-text letters comes to 102; so we should expect Mrs Gallup's decipherment of the heading on p. 2 to show itself after about 100 letters of plain text.

The decipherment reads as follows:

As you are beginning now to decypher a most interesting play, a portion of which doth concern my history, you get in a newe maner keyes, or signes, anie eye not blinde will only too truly note: or indeed, not a newe Ciphe' but th' first modified. I will, however, as much change my newe, for what be most oft observ'd doff greatlie the ayde and protection, reall and known, o' unfamiliaritie.

Marke *t, f, c* and *e*. See that in no place have th' accents on *k* at midle of th' front where this joyneth t' th' uprighte, yet overturn'd it. Th' letter hath still only such a use, in our modell or forme, as it might in or by vertue of its form. But we do contrive t' make most peculiar, artfull shiftes, that so much shelter our most evident pretensions, it is a subtler or swifter mind can followe us then most men do possesse. Take care for all of our accented letters, and do not baffle us. That I, by curious, noteworthie skill, so hide this secret, it fullie proveth t' everybody of just temper, somewhat better than by words, how much greate' valew the' inne' portions possesse then th' part seene. Bacon is to many only a great autho', quick with his writi'g. . . .

Round about the hundredth letter we expect to find:

		W		A				
		X		E		A		
CIET ^L_M	or	ERKEY	or	IKATK	or	ITBET	or	^B_SECKF
		Z		N		R		
				R				
				W				

which are our possible readings. The only match is the second one; letters 102 onwards of Mrs Gallup's decipherment are ERKEY. We are on the right road.

Our second division (. . . .T HEHIS TORIE OFTHE RAIGN EOF. .) is therefore the one which fits; the first T is the last letter in the last group of five of the preceding page. There are 163 other italic letters on p. 2; which will give $32\frac{3}{5}$ hidden letters. Therefore about thirty letters on from our first match we should find as the plain text of the heading

	C	
		U
LL ^N_O	or	LT ^U_V
	T	

followed by any letter from A to Q. The other three possibilities (?WW, or ?KK, or ^F_XFG) can be discarded because they are plainly unlikely in English—or any language. After thirty-two letters we in fact find LLO in the words WILL ONLY. This confirms that we have discovered the 'fit' for our two tapes.

It was now possible to begin the more accurate checking we required. On each page we began by matching the heading against Mrs Gallup's plain text, having first seen what her assignments ought to be. For example, on p. 10 the heading of p. 2 is repeated; the grouping, according to a count along the tape, is

TH EHIST ORIEO FTHER AIGNE OF...

and the assignments (corresponding with those for p. 2) should be:

...*aa abaab aaaaa baaba abaab ab*...

giving a plain text:

A		I
E		.
I	KATK	.
N		.
R		.
W		Q

(any letter from I to Q)

In this case we found that Mrs Gallup made a wrong assignment for the n of 'Raigne', making the fifth group *ababb*. Her fourth plain-text letter was therefore an M instead of a K, and her decipherment read 'accents on *k* at midle'.

Having adjusted the grouping of each page heading as this was necessitated by the decipherments, we counted the intervening italic letters as far as the next heading, divided by five, and moved a corresponding number of letters along the decipherment to begin a new page. We continued this study for sixty page headings. We found that Mrs Gallup frequently changed her assignments, and frequently 'added' or 'subtracted' letters to or from the cover text to suit her purpose.

We ended with one whole page, p. 59; chosen because Henry Seymour also chose to print and publish his examination of Mrs Gallup's decipherment of it, in *Baconiana* of June 1922. The page happens to be almost entirely in italic; and we assumed he would choose a page which he thought she had done perfectly.

But in fact, even Seymour admitted that there 'are several errors' in her decipherment of this page alone. Two capital letters, which have what one would think were unmistakable characteristics, must be considered wrongly assigned; so must a number of lower-case letters. Two italic letters have been dropped from the cover text, so that in two cases groups of six letters produce a letter each of the hidden text. Seymour himself failed to notice another case of an omitted letter: *Force*, the last word in the twelfth line, appears in his transcript as 'Fore'. Thus in one page three separate cases occur when an italic letter must be omitted to suit the demands of the hidden text. But when these adjustments had been made, and we checked the next heading, on p. 60, the letters produced by the cipher were just the ones required to agree with the decipherment of the identical heading on pp. 10 and 18. Thus the Seymour-Gallup decipherment occasionally reaches the 'right' result by somewhat devious methods.

According to our analysis of the page headings, that on p. 59 is identical with p. 21. Seymour's transcription starts with one letter from the bottom of p. 58 used to make up the first group in the heading of p. 59:

.KING	THESE	UENTH	WILLS	AUETH	EBLOU	DINTH
.aaba	*abaab*	*babaa*	*aabbb*	*aabaa*	*baaaa*	*aabaa*
C	K	W	H	E	R	E

ECITI	ENORT
abaaa	*abbaa*
I	N

The heading for p. 21 had earlier caused us a good deal of puzzlement; it was difficult to find a fit for it. Given this information, however, we tried again. The heading on p. 20 had been identified; there are 164 intervening italic letters, giving a count of 32⅘ letters in the decipherment. This means that the K of the heading on p. 21 should be joined by the last four italic letters on p. 20 to form the first group. Thus Mrs Gallup's assignments for the heading, if the letters are correctly counted and grouped, should read:

....K	INGTH	ESEUE	NTH..		
....a	*abaab*	*aabba*	*baa..*		
K	N	R, S, T	or	U/V	

But her decipherments in fact read C K W at this point; in other words she had chosen the same grouping as that on p. 59. To achieve this, she must silently have ignored three of the italic letters in the cover text on p. 20.

Here are the details of our check on Mrs Gallup's rendering of the headings of the first twenty-one pages of the Folio only:

Italic letters added	23
Italic letters dropped	8
Changed assignments	10
Identical headings recognized	7
Identical headings unrecognized	8

The number of letters added or dropped varies from one to seven per page. The changed assignments (what Mrs Gallup called 'wrong-font letters') are not so serious; in all cryptograms errors in transmission or decipherment of individual letters must be expected and a few may even be added or dropped. They can be checked in normal practice by retransmission. That is impossible here; and it should be pointed out that the additions or deletions, errors small in themselves, have cumulative effects. In any case, if in twenty-one pages so many allowances of this kind must be made in the page-headings themselves, what must one expect in the bulk of the volume (which has 78,537 italic letters, covering a hidden text which, as Mrs Gallup deciphered it, ran to fourteen printed pages)? Must not our confidence be shaken?

Seymour himself tried to restore this confidence. He pointed out that Mrs Gallup had always said that *Henry VII* was the most baffling of all the books she deciphered (though he claimed that he had deciphered it himself; one may be inclined to doubt this). He went on: 'There are 78,537 italic letters in *Henry VII*. On counting the letters in Mrs Gallup's deciphered epistle, which by the rule should numerically equal one-fifth of the italic letters, I find a considerable discrepancy.' This is not surprising, in view of what we have said above. But it is interesting to see how Seymour explains it. Mrs Gallup had omitted to use 417 letters, he found, and this was explained by:

1. Omission of the italic letters in a marginal note on p. 154.

2. Omission of the italic letters in 'Faults Escaped' (the printer's list of errors; which should have been a warning in other ways).

3. Omission of a few letters after Bacon's signature on the last page.

4. Omission of catchwords in italics.

5. Omission of 'seven letters in as many errors of wrong assignments or wrong grouping (or possibly tricks) which occur throughout the book'.

These 'tricks' were, according to Mrs Gallup and Seymour, places where 'it behooves the investigator to be on guard against the obvious'. If the long italic *C* was obviously a *b*-form, it should be marked '*a*'; it was deliberately inserted to confuse, because 'ciphers are made to hide things, not discover them'. This is the thin end of another disturbing wedge; obviously it could be a convenient weapon in an emergency. We have noted that the dots which Mrs Gallup also claimed as authority for changing assignments were genuine characteristics of certain pieces of type. Dots were noticeable wherever those pieces appeared, and not only in the few cases where she needed to change the assignment, and invoked their assistance.

Seymour claimed that the omissions set out above accounted for all 417 missing letters. He claimed in effect that 410 of them were deliberate omissions, seven only being due to wrong groupings. What are we to say of this when we have counted three on his transcription of p. 59 alone? In the twenty-one pages first examined, we found in all eight letters dropped and twenty-three added; add these to the three on p. 59, and we have a total discrepancy of thirty-four for twenty-two pages, or over one-and-a-half per page.

One last point about headings: Mrs Gallup also uses them in her decipherments of the First Folio; and, indeed, one message from the 'I.M. Poem' said 'Search for keyes, the headings of the comedies'.[1] Mrs Gallup actually dealt with the headings of the Comedies, the Histories, and the Tragedies as separate studies, and she extracted lengthy messages from them. Now the fact is that these headings also contain lifted type. Dr E. E. Willoughby says in his bibliographical study, *The Printing of the First Folio of Shakespeare*, 'Jaggard's journeymen,

---

[1] According to the *Oxford English Dictionary* the word 'heading' was first used in this sense in 1849.

when composing the running titles [the page-headings] of the
First Folio, by introducing necessary changes, used the same
setting of type and quad [space] to print the headlines of
successive plays '. After a long analysis of the individual pages
Dr Willoughby repeats this assertion:

To sum up, we have shown that...Jaggard's journeymen in
composing the running titles of the plays of the First Folio used,
with a minimum number of alterations, the same setting of type to
print the headlines of successive pages. In determining cases in
which we can say with certainty that this method was employed, we
are forced to rely almost entirely upon the testimony of damaged
letters. This evidence is not easy to find, and the fact that it yields
such a comparative abundance of instances proves almost with
certainty that this labour-saving device was employed whenever
practicable.

Mrs Gallup did not know this, and her decipherments do not
take account of it. Moreover, if Bacon had indeed wanted to
use these headings as a cover text, his scope would have been
greatly restricted and his task impossibly complicated by the
need to take account of the printer's practice in lifting type
in general, and in this book in particular.

The aim of this chapter and the preceding one has been to
show that the implementation of the biliteral cipher has
technical implications. The discussion shows that printing
conditions of the time made an extended use of the cipher
virtually impossible; it shows also that the books in which
Mrs Gallup believed ciphers to exist conform to the normal
practice of the day and do not show signs of that extra care
which insertion of the cipher would have made necessary. It
shows in the third place that experts like Goudy and Dr Miller
cannot accept the existence of a true biliteral cipher composed
of only two founts, nor can they detect signs of purposive use
of the many founts actually employed. In the fourth place it
shows a disabling ignorance of printing practice on the part
of Mrs Gallup. Certainly she worked at a time before bibliographical knowledge had reached its present state; but in fact,
the biliteral, if it existed and were consistently enciphered by

Bacon and consistently deciphered by her, should of itself have enabled her to deduce certain printing practices. For instance a consistent decipherment of the headings would have led her to realize that they were in many cases from identical type. Finally, our examination of certain passages deciphered by her shows a margin of error and arbitrariness which throughout a whole deciphered book would be of dismaying proportions. What more need be said? A great deal, unfortunately, and we shall go on to say some of it.

We cannot hope that by the time we have finished our examination the last echo of the controversy will respectfully die away. It is of the nature of the Gallup case that new and old adherents will always be attracted or comforted by its appearance of credibility and the volume of its support. This is all the more so when an eminent cryptographer like General Cartier gives it his approval. So General Cartier must now have turned on him a co-professional eye.

CHAPTER XVII

GENERAL CARTIER AND THE BILITERAL CIPHER

PEOPLE who are not themselves experts in some particular
study are almost bound to accept the pronouncements of
those who are. It has been a source of satisfaction to many
Baconians that the biliteral cipher has had the explicit printed
blessing of a distinguished cryptologist. Mrs Gallup's own
decipherments were a boon to them. Believing Bacon to be the
author of the plays, they needed something which justified his
failure simply to say he was; Owen's and Mrs Gallup's theories
provided him with a distinguished parentage and at the same
time explained why he wrote the plays—to conceal his life
history. This is no reason, really, why he should not have put
his name to them if he could to his other works, but it gives
the whole deception some point. If one accepts his authorship
and kingship, it becomes necessary to have some official
backing for the cipher which disclosed them. When General
Cartier supplied this he closed the circle.

It is this which in part explains the extreme tenacity of
Mrs Gallup's theories. She was in a way excommunicated by
the Bacon Society almost as soon as she published her work.
But in 1927, more than a quarter of a century afterwards, the
President of the Society, Sir John Cockburn, could note sadly
in an article in *Baconiana* that 'a great portion of the official
journal of the Society, *Baconiana*, has been taken up by the
question of the biliteral cipher, although no one, even after
patient study and desire to be convinced, has been able independently to follow it'. In the very same issue the dauntless
Mr Henry Seymour replied for the Gallup party. His arguments
are the ones which concern us in this chapter. He said:

The *onus probandi* is certainly on the shoulders of those who affirm
the reality of Mrs Gallup's deciphering, and as far as I know there
is no attempt to shirk its responsibility. The whole question resolves

itself into a necessity for the strictly experimental examination of Mrs Gallup's classification of symbols....This method has never been attempted so far by the Bacon Society, in spite of the unctuous resolution [not to give her its endorsement]...and that is why it is felt by many of us that it is high time to put this work to a thoroughly impartial scientific investigation.

What an admirable spirit and determination shine through those words! What an admirable resolve they show—and how we agree with it! What a pity therefore that Seymour allows himself to be convinced that examination is no longer necessary. His grammar goes to pieces with his resolution:

The fact that Sir John or anyone else have [*sic*] not yet been able, independently, to follow it is no evidence of its unreality. On the other hand [trump card coming] those who can claim to have some skill in the art of cyphers, such as the experts of the Riverbank Laboratory and General Cartier (head of the Cryptographic Department of the French Army during the late war), are convinced that Mrs Gallup's deciphering is genuine.

This sort of confidence had its effect. In 1936 the then President of the Bacon Society wrote in *Baconiana*:

In his articles in the *Mercure de France*, September 1922, General Cartier, chief of the cryptographical staff of the Allies in the Great War, stated, *inter alia* (I translate his French): 'We think it right to insist on the fact that from the standpoint of cryptography we have personally undertaken the work of checking a considerable number of passages, and that we are of opinion that the discussion should leave on one side the cryptographical point of view, which seems to us unassailable.'

In another article...General Cartier stated...'I consider the decipherings accomplished by Mrs Gallup and verified by the cryptographers of Riverbank Laboratories under the direction of Colonel Fabyan to be authentic.'

In view of these and other considerations my own opinion is... that no case has been made out for distrusting Mrs Gallup's work as a whole.

This is a very different conclusion from the one the Society came to in 1901. The reader has before his eyes an example of myth-making, or the moulding of public opinion. He will have noticed a certain up-grading process: General Cartier has been promoted from head of the Cryptographic Department of the French Army (Seymour's version), to 'chief of the crypto-graphical staff of the Allies'. Colonel Fabyan has taken on a military status, and is understood to have directed a staff of loyal experts in the verification of the decipherments. Here is the myth in its latest, ripest stage, taken from a book called *The Marriage of Elizabeth Tudor* by Alfred Dodd, published in England in 1940:

> A very casual examination of italic letters shows us that the cypher exists.... The heads of the Secret Services of America, England and France in the Great War have declared there is a genuine cypher which could neither have been fabricated nor imagined by Mrs Gallup. No amount of denial by literary men, who know nothing about Cyphers and Codes...will abrogate the truth.... Cypher experts like General Cartier, late head of the French Secret Service, have not only declared the cypher exists, but it has on the whole been correctly interpreted.

Where did all these heads come from? General Cartier is identified. We are forced to conclude that Colonel Fabyan has been promoted head of the 'American Secret Service'. The Englishman, mysterious figure (as befits his post) was almost certainly the literary apotheosis of a certain Major Stevenson. He was brought to the notice of readers of *American Baconiana* in November 1923 by a letter from Parker Woodward. He draws attention to what he calls 'a confirmation of the biliteral cypher' which was printed in *Cassell's Weekly* in May 1923. It was by a 'Major Stevenson, head of the British Department of Deciphering'. The issue of *Cassell's Weekly* does contain an article on the cipher by Stevenson: rather a poor effort. It does not mention Mrs Gallup, and speaks in very general terms; but in those terms it commends the cipher. The editor of the *Weekly* wrote this note on the author of the article:

> Major Stevenson...is an expert of high standing on all questions of codes. He was a well-known, mysterious and ubiquitous figure at G.H.Q. and over the whole front in France throughout the war, being known as the 'Hush Hush' man—the deciphering of enemy messages being regarded necessarily as ultra secret....Major Stevenson had triumphs of far-reaching importance, although

known only to a handful of higher Staff Officers. In the early days he was pitted against a galaxy of German professors, and at the time of the first Zeppelin raids Lord Kitchener himself took the keenest interest in this struggle of wits. A scholar, a cousin of R.L.S., it is not necessary further to emphasize both his interest in literature and his authority when discussing ciphers.

Major Stevenson should sell his film-rights. We cannot vouch for his ubiquity, but he is mysterious all right, and by no means well known. It must have been a very small 'handful of higher Staff Officers' who knew him; we have tried all the ones we know—mostly cryptographers—without result, and his name is unknown in the literature of the subject. We are willing to commit ourselves to the statements that Major Stevenson is or was an amateur in cryptography, and that he was not competent to discuss the cipher. Nor does he discuss it; he endorses it without examination because the biliteral is a valid cipher and because Elizabethan books are printed in a variety of type-forms.

That knocks out the heads of the British and American 'Secret Services' (a betraying phrase; no one would use it who had any experience of the work). General Cartier remains. He was a French Army reservist who became head of the crypto-logical service of the Deuxième Bureau (G-2) of the French Army General Staff in the war of 1914–18. We were given an appreciatory note of him, prepared specifically for us in May 1954 by Lt.-Col. Arnaud, head of the Cipher Section of the Secretariat of the French Armed Forces, and we quote from it with his permission:

General Cartier was early attracted to cryptographic studies. From 1900 to 1912 he was Secretary and also the most active member of the Commission for Military Cryptography headed successively by Generals Penel, Berthaut and de Castelnau. In 1912 he was appointed Head of the Cipher Section at the Ministry of War, and he remained in this position until 1921.

It was during that period, and primarily during the war of 1914–1918, that his great competence and the distinguished record of the group of cryptologists inspired by him brought his name into prominence and gave him a fame which spread beyond the frontiers of France.

The name of General Cartier is destined to remain in the roll of first-rate cryptologists in the history of national and international cryptography, as much for the direction and impetus which he gave to cryptographical research as for the invaluable successes scored under his leadership.

The 'experts' directed by Colonel Fabyan derive in part from Cartier's own writings about the cipher. Cartier was under a genuine misapprehension, which Fabyan did nothing to remove. The General, like Seymour, had the impression, as he once wrote, that Mrs Gallup's decipherments were produced and authenticated by a group of experts 'under the direction of Colonel George Fabyan of the American Army'. Fabyan was never in the army; the only campaigns he took part in were sales campaigns. All that Cartier knew was that certain publications on cryptographical studies were published as a series (*The Riverbank Laboratories Publications on Cryptography*) emanating from Fabyan's establishment. Those of the series which he had seen he respected; indeed he went so far as to have one of them translated forthwith for the Cipher Bureau of the French Army. This was *The Index of Coincidence and its Applications in Cryptography*, which, like most of the other general cryptographical studies in the series, was by William F. Friedman. Cartier in fact had this translated and printed before the English version appeared; and as *L'Indice du Coincidence et ses Applications en Cryptographie* it was often assumed to be by Cartier himself.

Of the publications in general we should point out that they were in two categories. One was the sort that Cartier knew and valued; it comprised fifteen papers with titles like *Methods for the Solution of Running-Key Ciphers, Synoptic Tables for the Solution of Ciphers, An Application of the Science of Statistics to Cryptography* (also translated into French) and so on. All these, though we say it ourselves (Mrs Friedman also collaborated in one, *Methods for the Reconstruction of Primary Alphabets*) would have given Cartier over in France reason to respect the work of the Laboratories. What he would not have realized was the complete dichotomy between these works, which had no direct bearing on Mrs Gallup, and those few other publications which had. There were five of them; four dealing with what was called 'The Greatest Work of Sir Francis Bacon', and one called *Ciphers for the Little Folks*. Cartier would not have seen them, and if he had he probably would not have respected them.

The other thing which Cartier would not have known was that all Mrs Gallup's published decipherments were made a dozen years or more before she came to Riverbank. After her removal to Riverbank not a single new decipherment was published. We have already pointed out that the research staff was not able to confirm any of her findings, though its primary function was to examine and carry on her work. Cartier therefore had a totally false impression of what had been achieved at the Laboratories and of the attitude of the experts to her work.

This is pardonable; he never visited Riverbank. We know it has been said, for instance in *Baconiana* for June 1923, that 'General Cartier having been impressed by the internal evidence of the alleged decipherings, lost no time in paying a visit to the Fabyan Laboratory to investigate further and judge for himself the scientific accuracy of the work'. This is not true.

At the end of 1920 we left Riverbank for government employment; we were not there at the time of the alleged visit. But we have the testimony of Mrs Cora Jensen Tyzzer, who was there until Fabyan died in 1936, that Cartier never came. In any case Cartier said himself that his projected visit never took place.[1] Hence all relations between Cartier and Riverbank were by letter. It was Fabyan who wrote originally; he requested that Cartier should give the cipher his attention. In our opinion it was also Fabyan who either allowed Cartier to form an inexact conception of the work going on at Riverbank or deliberately misled him. What this all boils down to is that the only 'experts' at Riverbank who reported any satisfaction with the decipherments were Mrs Gallup and Miss Wells, and they were the experts who happened to have produced them.

When this is said, it remains that Cartier did subject the cipher to some kind of examination and pronounced himself satisfied with it. It is this which Gallupian Baconians have

[1] Prefatory remarks, p. 10, of *Un Problème de Cryptographie et d'Histoire*.

chiefly in mind when they invoke his name. Take for instance this statement by the current (1956) editor of *Baconiana*, writing in January 1952:

> The most brilliant exposition of these [ciphers concerning Bacon's life] perhaps is demonstrated by Gen. Cartier, chief of the Cipher Department of the French Army in the first World War of 1914–1918, in his work 'Un problème de Cryptographie d'Histoire' [*sic*], 1938....Bacon's opponents can only meet this evidence by flouts and sneers or by ignoring these ciphers.

It behoves us therefore to offer, not flouts and sneers, but an examination of Cartier's findings. We are sorry to report that it will be a destructive examination but, if we may say so, it is itself evidence which is not to be met with flouts or sneers, nor to be ignored.

Cartier first published his findings as a series of occasional articles called 'Un problème d'histoire et de cryptographie' in the *Mercure de France*, from December 1921 until 1923. They were collected and republished in 1938 in a book called *Un Problème de Cryptographie et d'Histoire*; there may be some significance in the change of order in the title. We shall deal here with the book and with another article which he published in 1923 in an obscure and now defunct periodical called *Fly Leaves of the Ladies' Guild of Saint Albans*. This article, by the way, contains the statement that Mrs Gallup's decipherments had been verified by the cryptologists of the Riverbank Laboratories under the direction of Fabyan, in one of a set of statements in which Cartier summarized his findings. We translate them here:

1. There is a cryptographic system which was invented by Bacon between 1576 and 1579 and was first described by him in his work *The Advancement of Learning*, published in London in 1605.
2. Printing establishments in Bacon's time had the assortments of types needed to apply the system in order to encipher secrets to be hidden in any external text.
3. Nobody, at least to my knowledge, has discovered any document (manuscript notes or correspondence of some sort) clearly indicating an application of Bacon's system in printed or other works.

4. I consider the decipherments made by Mrs Gallup and verified by the cryptologists of the Riverbank Laboratories under the direction of Colonel Fabyan to be valid.

5. I have no opinion whatever with regard to any other decipherments made by that lady, whose integrity appears to me to be beyond suspicion.

6. I disclaim any competence as regards the conclusions to be drawn from the enciphered biography of Francis Bacon.

Now points 1, 2 and 3 are all perfectly reasonable—even if they are so general in their application as to be entirely neutral in the argument we are about to conduct. Point 4 we have discussed and, we believe, explained. The first part of point 5 is mere fence-sitting; the second part we endorse entirely. Point 6 is fence-sitting again.

The technical part of Cartier's examination, both in the *Fly Leaves* article and the book, concerns a 'test' he made of Mrs Gallup's decipherment of p. 192 of Bacon's *Novum Organum*. This is the real core of the argument. In the *Fly Leaves* article he explained how he began his investigation:

I took one of the photographs [of a few pages of the *Novum Organum* on which the *a*- and *b*-forms had been determined by Mrs Gallup] which Colonel Fabyan had sent me; I numbered the letters by indicating the line number followed by the letter number in the line. I cut all the letters apart and grouped all the a's, all the b's and so on, which gave me 24 groups of letters. In each of these groups I selected two letters very clearly different from each other; I compared all the other letters with these two letters and I managed thus to divide each group into three subgroups, one (the most numerous) which I called the *a* group, another which I called the *b* group and lastly the third, which comprised the letters of doubtful classification.

My classification for the majority of the letters agreed with that of Mrs Gallup; there was disagreement to the extent of about 10 per cent of the letters; as to the letters which I had considered to be of doubtful form I decided I was in error and adopted Mrs Gallup's classification for them. However that may be, and despite the differences there were between my classifications and those of Mrs Gallup, my decipherment agreed with hers save for a few words.

Note the sentence we have italicized. Cartier found a 10 per cent discrepancy between his *positive* identifications and

Mrs Gallup's. But, in addition, for the whole category of letters which he first thought doubtful, he merely decided to adopt her classification. He does not say how many letters were originally doubtful; but they plainly increase the discrepancy beyond 10 per cent, and to an unknown extent. This whole operation is at the outset enough to disqualify all his subsequent reasoning, but it is not his only blunder.

To proceed: as a result of this dubious transaction Cartier had—to take one letter as an example—sixty-one lower-case italic a's divided into forty a-forms and twenty-one b-forms. This assignment, as he pointed out, was based on frequency; he assumed that a-forms would automatically be more frequent than b-forms. Again this is an excessively simple-minded argument; it is complicated by his first error: for of the doubtful cases how many did he assign to a's and how many to b's; how did he decide to adjust the relationship? It is particularly important to have the answer to this question for the letters of high frequency—lower-case e, i and u. But Cartier is entirely uninformative: all we know is that he followed Mrs Gallup. In doing this he did what he tended to do throughout his investigation: to accept as correct what he was supposed to be trying to check.

His rough rule that a-forms would be more frequent than b-forms would lead him into further error. It would be very difficult to decide on frequency considerations alone which form was involved with letters almost equally divided between the two forms—in this particular text b, c, f, g, h, j, n, o, q, v, x and &. Out of the total cover-text of 575 letters, this accounts for 119 letters or some 20 per cent as a start. That is to say that among these letters, the ones classified on the basis of frequency as a-form might with equal likelihood have been b-form. And for lower-case c's Cartier would in fact have been wrong (according to Mrs Gallup's assignment) if he took the most frequent form as the a-form; the same is true of g and v.

Cartier now got down to the decipherment of p. 192 of *Novum Organum*. Part of Mrs Gallup's plain text is: 'If he shall publish what is conceal'd herein let him winnowe it well. If he doe this not, the booke must displease which should afford pleasure.' The five-letter groups for this extract begin with the n of 'in', the third word in the first line. The cover-text, transliteration and decipherment begin as follows:

nseru	dimen	taqua	edame	xilis	Calor	ishab	etlic
abaaa	aabab	aabbb	aabaa	baaab	aabbb	aaaaa	ababa
I	F	H	E	S	H	A	L

etnon	hucus	quevt	adtac	tumpe	rcipi	aturN
ababa	abbba	baabb	aaaab	ababa	abaaa	baaab
L	P	U	B	L	I	S

This is reproduced on p. 55 of *Un Problème* from Mrs Gallup's work. Starting his examination, Cartier rather surprisingly invokes a well-known Baconian, Frank Woodward, who claimed that after working under Mrs Gallup's direction he reached 70–80 per cent accuracy in his assignments to *a*- and *b*-forms, and William Rawley, who 'said' he had always failed to identify with certainty b, i, l, m, n, p, s and z. Taking these statements as the basis of an experiment, Cartier took some of the five-letter groups in Mrs Gallup's transliteration, and assumed that all the letters had been correctly assigned except those letters which Rawley had difficulty with. These he chose to regard as indeterminate: that is he allowed that whenever b, i, l, m, n, p, s or z occurred in the external text it should be taken as either *a*- or *b*-form. This, then, gives the following groups:

1	2	3	4	5	6	7	8
nseru	dimen	taqua	edame	xilis	Calor	ishab	etlic
??aaa	a??a?	aabbb	aab?a	b????	aa?bb	??aaa	ab?b?

9	10	11	12	13	14	15
etnon	hucus	quevt	adtac	tumpe	rcipi	aturN
ab?b?	abbb?	baabb	aaaab	ab??a	ab???	baaa?

Those at any rate are the first fifteen out of twenty groups transliterated by Cartier. As a matter of fact there are two errors already: group 7 should be *??aa?* and not *??aaa*; group 8 should be *ab??a* and not *ab?b?*.

Let us note here in parenthesis that these are not the only cases of careless error. On pp. 38–9 of Cartier's book there is a facsimile of p. 192 of *Novum Organum*. The sixth word in the first line is *quadam*, which is not good Latin, and which is in any case a peculiarity or aberrancy of the copy Cartier reproduced. But Cartier's transcription (p. 55 of *Un Problème*) gives the word as *quaedam*, which is correct Latin and the norm for the edition. He transliterates accordingly. But he ought to have noticed and drawn attention to the discrepancy; all the more so in that the addition or deletion of a single letter in the external text in the biliteral cipher results in a change in the five-letter groupings from that point on. This is a striking example of carelessness on Cartier's part; and an appropriate example of the kind of proof-reading and printing practice discussed in ch. xv and of the results which errors in the setting *ought* to produce in the cipher. In fact, Cartier avoided the consequences by overlooking the error.

But to proceed; Cartier had now to list all the alternative values which might be indicated, according as the doubtful letters were made *a-* or *b-*forms. He pointed out that the first group, *??aaa* can be:

> *aaaaa* which gives A
> *abaaa* which gives I
> *baaaa* which gives R

No group in Bacon's alphabet begins with *bb*, so the possibilities end there. In the second group, *a??a?*, Cartier made another bad and careless error. He listed the possibilities A, E, N, B, F, O, but omitted I and K.

For the first two groups, Cartier now announced that he had the following possibilities:

> AA, AE, AN, AB, AF, AO
> IA, IE, IN, IB, IF, IO
> RA, RE, RN, RB, RF, RO

In fact he had these additional possible readings:

> AI, AK, II, IK, RI, RK

Cartier continued his argument by saying that certain of these possibilities could be overlooked—he assumed (for no good reason) that he was dealing with the first two letters of the first word of a message in English; hence he could discount AA, AE, AO, IA, IE, IB, IO, RN, RB, RF.

Even granted his initial assumption, this is not correct. Since I and J are interchangeable, IA, IE and IO remain possibilities. However, Cartier had now, to his own satisfaction, reduced the possibilities to AN, AB, AF, IN, IF, RA, RI, RO.

Here is another mistake. RI has appeared from nowhere, and RE has disappeared equally mysteriously, though as an initial digraph (two letters) it is the fifth most frequent in English. Even in French it is very frequent; so this is a disgraceful piece of carelessness.

Cartier continues. The third group is an H without doubt. The fourth can be E or G. This now gives us, for the first four groups, these possibilities (according to Cartier):

ANHE, ABHE, AFHE, INHE, IFHE
RAHE, RIHE, ROHE
ANHG, ABHG, AFHG, INHG, IFHG
RAHG, RIHG, ROHG

Cartier reduces this number to ANHE, ABHE, INHE and IFHE, because he thinks they are the only likely candidates (why ABHE, one wonders?), and concludes triumphantly 'The last, IFHE, is evidently the most plausible.' Why? ANHE is synonymous with IFHE in Elizabethan English; INHE is a possible beginning for a number of words. The whole trouble obviously is that Cartier is just a little too eager to reach Mrs Gallup's conclusions, and so accepts all her assumptions.

These assumptions are:

(i) the enciphered text is in English. Why not Latin, the language of the open text, and a double safeguard against discovery? Mrs Gallup never considered this possibility— perhaps she was no good at Latin.

(ii) that the sentence to be deciphered begins in the middle of a two-letter word ('in'), the third word in the first sentence in the first paragraph on p. 192.[1] This is a very large and quite unwarranted assumption. It impels Cartier to look for initial digraphs, which he then chooses on the basis of their likelihood as such. If the message does not begin in this place his whole

---

[1] The paragraph is numbered '7' by Bacon.

chain of reasoning collapses; all of his possible candidates have to be reconsidered on an entirely different basis.

Having made this short cut to his 'initial tetragram', he ceases to think of groups and concentrates on individual letters. The fifth group *b????* can be R, S, T, U or V, W, X, Y, Z. The sixth can be D or H; the seventh A, I or R. Another error here, which we have already noted: the group should be rendered *??aa?*, not *??aaa*. The possibilities are therefore A, B, I, K, R, S: six possibilities for Cartier's three.

Groups 8 and 9 he thought could both be L, M, P, Q. Wrong again. The eighth group should be transliterated *ab??a*; which gives as possibilities I, L, N, P.

Having established the possibilities for twelve groups (but not realizing that he had made the errors we have noted) Cartier set them out in columns:

I	2	3	4	5	6	7	8	9	10	11	12
A	N	H	E	R	D	A	L	L	P	U, V	B
A	B	—	—	S	H	I	M	M	Q	—	—
I	N	—	—	T	—	R	P	P	—	—	—
I	F	—	—	U, V	—	—	Q	Q	—	—	—
—	—	—	—	W	—	—	—	—	—	—	—
—	—	—	—	X	—	—	—	—	—	—	—
—	—	—	—	Y	—	—	—	—	—	—	—
—	—	—	—	Z	—	—	—	—	—	—	—

These are the possibilities as he established them, not the correct ones. Taking a letter from each column, he got the text IF HE SHALL PUB. He continued:

The last trigram suggests the word PUBLISH, which is possible, the letters LISH being possible correspondences

L *ababa* for the 13th group *ab??a*
I *abaaa* for the 14th group *ab???*
S *baaab* for the 15th group *baaa?*
H *aabbb* for the 16th group *a??bb*

The decipherment is completed in this same manner, advancing progressively and judiciously, *the letters and the words already deter-mined permitting the limitation of the number of trials that remain for suggesting letters and words likely to follow* [our italics]. Erroneous identifications can of course complicate the work and will sometimes suggest incorrect words. But the errors, as well as the indeterminate cases, eliminate themselves progressively, and it can be estimated that as soon as the correct identifications reach 60 to 70 per cent of the letters, the correct reconstruction of the plain text can be counted on without much difficulty.

However it is necessary to recognize that in exceptional cases some wrong words could be substituted for the correct ones, especially if they have the same number of letters and some letters in common, and if the meaning of the sentence does not permit the error to be recognized.

Cartier ends his discussion by inviting the reader to examine all the solutions grammatically possible which the columns of his diagram provide. We accepted this invitation, and found, with some dismay, this:

IN HER DAMP PUB[ES]

which is Jacobean in its directness if not in its terminology. If one refuses to accept the assumption that this decipherment should begin with the first complete word of a sentence, one can say that the letters in column 1 and 2 are the final letters of a word ending in AN or IN, the last word of the previous sentence. The decipherment could then begin a new sentence with these words: HER HAPP[INESS].

If we correct Cartier's errors, the columns are changed to:

1	2	3	4	5	6	7	8	9	10	11	12
A	A	H	E	R	D	A	I	L	P	U, V	B
I	B	—	G	S	H	B	L	M	Q	—	—
R	E	—	—	T	—	I	N	P	—	—	—
—	F	—	—	U, V	—	K	P	Q	—	—	—
—	I	—	—	W	—	R	—	—	—	—	—
—	K	—	—	X	—	S	—	—	—	—	—
—	N	—	—	Y	—	—	—	—	—	—	—
—	O	—	—	Z	—	—	—	—	—	—	—

This produces IF HE THIN[K], if in the ninth letter we assume that the fourth letter, O, of the five-letter group in the cover text was a doubtful case, and the group could therefore be read as *ab???*, giving I, K, L, M, N, O, P, Q as possible readings. By the same kind of process, the U in the third group in the cover text might be indeterminate, making the group *aab?b* and the possible readings F and H. In this case the enciphered text could be REFER DAIL[Y]. In these two instances one single case of indeterminacy produces an entire change in the possible decipherment. These changes were always possible, in Mrs Gallup's practice. If we make them in Cartier's set of possible values as corrected, and assume a mere five additional cases of indeterminate forms (one each in the third, eighth, ninth, tenth and twelfth groups, giving the additional possibilities marked with an asterisk below) we have:

1	2	3	4	5	6	7	8	9	10	11	12
A	A	F*	E	R	D	A	I	L	N*	U, V	B
I	B	H	G	S	H	B	K*	M	O*	—	S*
R	E	—	—	T	—	I	L	P	P	—	—
—	F	—	—	U, V	—	K	M*	Q	Q	—	—
—	I	—	—	W	—	R	N	T*	—	—	—
—	K	—	—	X	—	S	O*	U, V*	—	—	—
—	N	—	—	Y	—	—	P	Y*	—	—	—
—	O	—	—	Z	—	—	Q*	Z*	—	—	—

This gives REFER HIM TO US; a completely different text produced by five changed assignments in sixty letters of the cover text. This demolishes entirely Cartier's argument that 'as soon as the correct identifications reach 60–70 per cent of the letters, the correct reconstruction of the plain text can be counted on without much difficulty'. Cartier had dealt closely with sixty letters. He assumed that eighteen, or 30 per cent, were indeterminate, and with this margin of latitude and some errors of his own he had been able to arrive at Mrs Gallup's text. We got a different message (of a sort) from his readings, and a second message from his corrected readings. By adding another five indeterminates (to make a total of 38 per cent) we obtained a totally different plain text, with no correspondence at all between it and Mrs Gallup's. So an 8 per cent variation in readings can produce a complete change in the deciphered text. It should also be remembered that if Cartier had chosen to begin to decipher from a different and no less arbitrary point he would again have been able, with the same range of indeterminate readings, to have produced a totally different decipherment.

Now the percentage of indeterminate forms in this sample analysis may be taken to be below the normal in Mrs Gallup's chosen open texts. There are in fact relatively few instances— mostly capital letters—where the forms are quite distinct. It has by now become abundantly obvious that what is at the heart of the whole problem of the Gallup decipherments is this very difficulty of determining two forms of each letter and assigning all instances without doubt to one or the other form. The difficulty is found in nearly every letter; certainly the great majority. If to the natural difficulty of assigning multi-formed type to two families is added the further indeterminacy pro- duced by bad impression, battered type, worn type, poor inking, irregular shrinkage in the paper as it dried, flaws in the surface of the paper, and so on, at what point do we lose confidence (if we ever had it)? As the indeterminacy approaches 50 per cent, confidence should begin to forsake us—at any rate if half the letters are indeterminate and are well scattered through the text the number of alternative readings may permit a multitude of decipherments, all equally plausible. This is an argument to which we must return. Let us first finish with Cartier.

In his whole book he deals only with 575 letters of the text. We have examined his one close analysis, which is of a mere sixty letters. He does not say how many more of the 575 he examined with the same care (if that is the word). None the less 575 letters is a slight basis on which to make an assessment of Mrs Gallup's work; and in the examination we have made we have found so many errors that it is plain that Cartier's evidence is worthless as well as slight. He made errors of reasoning and judgment, mechanical errors of transcription and the extraction of possible readings, and throughout he showed a quite un- scientific inability to base his experiment on sound assumptions (or even to see what they were).

What is one to say of his naïve acceptance of Woodward's claims as a working assumption? Or of his admission that in cases of doubt he accepted Mrs Gallup's findings—i.e. accepted what he was supposed to be checking? Or the statistical vagueness of his assignment of doubtful forms? What about his grossest naïveté: the acceptance of Rawley's 'statement'? Where did that statement come from, if not from a decipherment by Mrs Gallup? Is it then to be used as an argument in the discussion of Mrs Gallup's decipherments? How circular can your arguments get?

There is no need to analyse further the various errors which we pointed out as we proceeded. Let us merely revert to the quotation from *Un Problème*, p. 217: 'The decipherment is completed in this same manner, advancing progressively and judiciously, the letters and words already determined permitting the limitation of the number of trials that remain for suggesting letters and words likely to follow.' It is hard to say what that word 'judiciously' is doing in the sentence. Cartier has done two things here; he has given himself away, and he has probably given Mrs Gallup away as well. As Prof. Georges Connes once pointed out (in his book *Le mystère Shakespearien*) Mrs Gallup probably worked by a species of auto-suggestion. To some extent she betrayed herself; she pointed out that it was very difficult to assign the letters to *a-* or *b-*forms 'the books being old, stained, and poorly printed', and she stated that it was necessary to educate the eyes to the degree required to recognize them. What this meant, in all probability, was that in any given case the sense of the message as it unfolded itself would dictate whether a letter should be assigned to an *a-* or a *b-*form; indeed the mere requirements of intelligibility—or such degree of intelligibility as she attained—would determine her choice. And here Cartier shows himself to have done the same thing in her wake, only instead of following (as she did) a sense of what in general the message might be expected to say, he had merely to duplicate her results. We should perhaps be grateful to him for supplying a clear-cut corroboration of our own account of the mystery of Mrs Gallup's decipherments. At all events his examination of her work is worthless. Quite apart from the numerous flaws in his reasoning, he is careless to a degree not permissible in serious cryptological work.

It is painful to have to expose what can only be accounted as unprofessionally sloppy work in a professional cryptologist of such eminence. In extenuation of the General's poor showing, the super-salesmanship of Colonel Fabyan seems to have gained in him a convert of great influence, although it failed to gain a single convert among the many persons brought to Riverbank to look into Mrs Gallup's work at first hand. For that matter, no one working independently has ever been able to duplicate Mrs Gallup's findings. It is true that a few of her disciples claim to have done so; but in every case the disciple was already convinced of the validity of Mrs Gallup's work. Whatever test was made was merely 'confirmatory'; it was not an independent experiment made without the decipherer either having a copy of Mrs Gallup's decipherment before him or a knowledge of the results she claimed to have obtained.

CHAPTER XVIII

THE BILITERAL CIPHER:
EXPERIMENTS AND DEDUCTIONS

L ET us at this point summarize our case against the possible use of the biliteral cipher in the books examined and 'deciphered' by Mrs Gallup. Various experts on typographical matters gave important testimony against the cipher. It would have required a change in the printer's method of proof-correction, and there is no evidence to suggest this was done. In its 'pure' state it required the careful setting of two distinct founts, and we have impressive evidence that this was not done; the books were set in a variegated assembly of types which are virtually impossible to separate into two families. Indeed, as our chapter on General Cartier showed, the most that Mrs Gallup could have done (and Cartier did exactly the same) was to establish as a- and b-forms for each letter the shapes which were least like each other, and then to go through the texts assigning to the two categories all the individual instances which fell somewhere between these two extremes. Plainly, somewhere in the middle there would be a range of cases where the differences would be slight and the assignment perilous. Here the real difficulty lies, and here the case for the Gallup cipher is eventually decided. Dr Miller showed that in Mrs Gallup's assignments there was more variation between some forms within each category than there was between forms in different categories. Our examination of Mrs Gallup's decipherments of repeated uses of the same pieces of type showed that she did not always recognize such repetitions or repeat exactly her former assignments. Our examination of Cartier's work showed among other things the kind of error which can be made; it also showed that the indeterminacy involved in the assignment of indistinguishable forms can be sufficient to falsify the results completely. It is fairly plain by now that we consider that Goudy, Dr Miller and Prof. Hinman show it to be impossible that the cipher was used, that the examination of Cartier's work shows his support to be worthless (that it is even evidence *against* the cipher), and that Mrs Gallup's own practice was in any case inconsistent and subjective. We hinted in our last chapter that since there was not enough difference between the type-forms to support the assignment to either the *a*- or *b*-form in almost every case, and since she had herself pointed out that it was often possible to change the assignments anyway, she could go through the texts extracting from them what she unconsciously wished to see in them. The doubtfulness of assignment enabled her without doing violence to the 'rules' to see an *a*- or *b*-form whenever the intelligibility of the message (such as it was) required it. With each successive letter deciphered she had a choice— limited but definite—of possibilities; and so, as she went on, there would be a kind of collaboration between the decipherer and the text, each influencing the other. Hence perhaps the curious maundering wordy character of the extracted messages, very like the communications of the spirit world: with some sense but no real mind behind them, just a sort of drifting intention, taking occasional sudden whimsical turns when the text momentarily mastered the decipherer. It did this to us, for instance, in the message from the mental underworld which we were presented with on p. 258. This is the kind of message which, if Mrs Gallup had come upon it, she would have accepted, though it was repugnant in many respects to her very soul, as she once said.

For she was, as we have said before, a sincere and honourable woman, and no fraud. When we first met her more than a quarter of a century ago, we felt then as we do now, that she found in her texts what she wanted to find, and by methods which might almost have been deliberately devised to assist her. It is easy to see that the biliteral cipher, in the only way in which it would still be possible to claim it was used,[1] was in fact the perfect trap for the searcher not elaborately on his guard

---

[1] That is, by the 'family' argument: that the extremely varied type-forms do eventually fall into two broad categories. We do not believe this to be so; nor did Mrs Gallup, for she did not realize the essential multiplicity of the forms in use.

against its deceptions. Once we had reached this possible explanation of Mrs Gallup's case, it was not hard to devise experiments to test it.

A typical incident once happened to Mr Friedman. He was preparing material for a talk on the cipher, and found a worked example which he had made himself years before and forgotten. It was a message in a biformed alphabet based on the design of the Spanish type-designer and calligrapher Francisco Lucas in 1577. Having forgotten the solution, but having the key, Mr Friedman set about deciphering it. The first ten letters came out as

A ALPHABET L

As 'alphabet' emerged it seemed the natural and right solution. But usage would suggest 'an' not 'a' alphabet; there must be some mistake. It was then late at night; he stopped work, and came fresh to the task next morning. On the second trial he got

ALL THAT GLI

At this point, of course, the mind makes its own leap ahead: it must be 'all that glisters is not gold'. And now, knowing what text was to be found, it was easy to make the assignments.

As a matter of interest, he went back to his first effort to see where he had gone wrong. The first ten letters represented fifty in the cover text; and only eleven were now seen to be wrongly assigned; that is, about one in five. But what a difference they made to the final decipherment! And just as when he got to 'gli...' he saw that the word must be 'glisters', so when he got to 'alp' he felt the word must be 'alphabet'. One mental leap was right and the other was wrong. Yet how plausible the wrong one was, considering the circumstances! Here was a case of honest self-deception. Since he was a professional (as Mrs Gallup was not) certain checks and mental reservations were brought into play, and the process restarted when an error seemed probable. This is what Mrs Gallup did not do. And in Mr Friedman's case he had inserted the message himself, and eventually remembered it when he got on to the right track. It was in the nature of Mrs Gallup's case that she could not do so. She was therefore at the mercy of the promptings of her expectant mind.

In the light of this experience consider now the following passage from Mrs Kate Prescott's *Reminiscences of a Baconian*, telling the story of Mrs Gallup's first 'discovery':

She decided to make her trial on the Prologue to *Troilus and Cressida* part I, because this was where Dr. Owen found his start... and partly because this prologue is printed entirely in italic type and the letters are slightly larger than elsewhere in the Folio. It was first necessary to study each letter and find the variants of each. She made drawings of both forms, accentuating the distinguishing differences for reference. When she tested her work the result was 'pi'. This was discouraging. In looking it over to find some light on the trouble, she noticed near the end of the piece a group of letters: ELIZ.B..H. As this was probably meant to be 'Elizabeth', she studied the wrong letters and found that by changing the font of a single letter, a 'y', she would get the correct A, E and T. She then went back and changed this single wrong 'y' all the way through and got a connected, smoothly running story.

In different circumstances this would not necessarily be a damaging admission. Any cryptographic system suitable for practical use must allow for a certain degree of error; it must not at any rate be seriously hindered by one or two mistakes. The extent to which a system will remain readable without excessive work and constant retransmission varies. In this particular system (as we saw in examining Cartier's work) there is the additional problem of differences between the letter shapes so minute that the decipherer cannot decide whether to call them *a*- or *b*-forms; how many cases of indeterminacy can be tolerated?

In what follows we make the basic assumption that all the letters are reducible immediately or eventually to two categories. The questions to be answered are: (i) How many cases could remain indeterminate; that is, how many times could Mrs Gallup be quite uncertain whether an *a*-fount or *b*-fount letter was involved, without making the system unworkable? (ii) How many genuine errors could she make; that is, how many *a*-fount letters could she classify as *b*-fount without again making the system unworkable?

Our first experiment was meant to decide whether, if 50 per cent of the letters in a message were indeterminate, the message would be extremely hard or impossible to decipher.

A text of good literary English, 100 letters long, was transliterated into Bacon's five-letter groups, giving a sequence of
500 *a*'s and *b*'s. This sequence was divided into five sections of
100 characters. Next a set of 100 numbers from 00 to 99 was
written on identical slips of paper, put in a box, and thoroughly
shaken. Fifty of the slips were drawn out at random, and the
numbers thus given (as for instance 66, 60, 20, 39, 93 ...) were
used to cross off in the first section of 100 *a*'s and *b*'s the
corresponding letters (the 66th, 60th, 20th, 39th, 93rd ...).
Each deletion signified that the corresponding letter in the
cover text was considered indeterminate. The process was
repeated for the next sequence of 100 characters; a fresh set of
fifty numbers was drawn at random and the corresponding
characters rendered indeterminate; and so on for all five
sections. Thus 250 *a*'s and *b*'s were made indeterminate.

The next step was to set down under each sequence of *a*'s
and *b*'s all the renderings now made possible by this degree of
indeterminacy. Thus in the first five-letter group, it turned out
that all but the first character were indeterminate. To use the
conventions we used in the examination of Cartier's work,
this group read: *b?????*. This meant that it could represent R,
S, T, U (or V), W, X, Y or Z, according as it was rendered *baaaa,
baaab, baaba, baabb, babaa, babab, babba, babbb*. The second group
could have been D, H, M, Q. Hence the first two letters of the
text (and of course it is a great advantage to *know*, as we did
under the terms of the experiment, that the message started
here and was in English) could have been selected from all the
possible 'good' digraphs contained in the two columns

	R	D
	S	H
	T	M
U, V	Q
	W	—
	X	—
	Y	—
	Z	—

The likely candidates are SH, SM, SQ, TH, WH. At the risk of
dismaying the reader, we now set out the possibilities for the
whole message:

R | | | | | |
A B C · · · N
I–J N | | | | |
E F N O W X | |
E F N O | | | |

15
A B I–J K R S | |
E W | | | | | |
R S T U–V W X Y Z
A B E F | | | |
G H P Q Y Z | |

10
R S T U–V W X Y Z
E N | | | | | |
K M O Q | | | |
S X | | | | | |
S U X Z | | | |

5
A C E G | | | |
C D G H L M P Q
A E I N | | | |
D H M Q | | | |

1
R S T U–V W X Y Z

40
A B C D E F G H | | | |
C D G H L M P Q | | | |
A B C D I–J K L M | | |
E F G H W X Y Z | | |
C T | | | | | | | | |

35
A E I–J N | | | | | |
E F | | | | | | | |
A B C D I–J K L M R S T U–V
L M P Q | | | | | | |
E F G H N O P Q | | | |

30
S U–V X Z | | | | | | |
A B I–J K | | | | | | |
A E I–J N R W | | | | |
I–J L N P | | | | | | |
D H U–V Z | | | | | | |

25
A B E F I–J K N O R S W X
C D G H L M P Q T U–V Y Z
N | | | | | | | | | | |
A A I–J | | | | | | | | |
A C E G I–J L N P R T W Y

60
B D F H K
A C E G I
E F G H I
A I–J R | |
C T | | |

55
A E I–J N R
I–J K L M N
R T | | |
A B I–J K R
A B E F |

50
G H P Q Y
T Y | | |
B F K O S
T U–V Y Z N
E G W Y |

45
E G N P W
A B E F I–J
B D F H |
R T W Y |
F H O Q X

```
  O  80 R           100 O
  Q     R T              T Y
  S     A B I–J K        W Y
  U–V   A B C · · · · · · · · · · · · · · N   L
  X     E G N P W Y      L
  Z  75 I L           95 A I–J
  P     N O P Q          D U–V
  Q     L M              D
        A B E F I–J K N O    A I–J
        C                 A R
     70 F W            90 G P Y
        N O P Q           G P Y
        A R               U–V Z
        A B C D E F G H I–J K L M N O P Q   C G
        D U–V             I–J N
     65 R W            85 A I
  N     B F K O           B D D K M
  O     C D G H L M P Q T U–V Y Z    A C I–J L
  R     A B E F I–J K N O    E N W
  S     A B C · · · · · · · · · · · · · · N   C G L P T Y
  W
  X
```

Columns 19, 61 and 77 may be any letter from A to Z.

All these steps were carried out by Mr Friedman; he then handed the sequence of possible letters to Mrs Friedman, with no clue to the nature of the plain text. Within an hour she had reconstructed it (in case any readers wish to try, the message is printed on p. 278 at the end of this chapter).

Now this suggests that in the biliteral cipher 50 per cent of the letters of the cover text can be indeterminate without preventing an accurate decipherment. Plainly Ewen was wrong when he claimed that 96 per cent accuracy is required. But before Baconians leap in to claim this experiment as impressive testimony on behalf of the cipher, let us point out:

(i) that the remaining 50 per cent of the letters are taken as absolutely certain,

(ii) that under the conditions of the experiment no doubt can be cast on the way the groups are divided (i.e. each set of letters, in the divisions here given, stands with absolute certainty for a letter in the cover text). A mistake in the grouping would invalidate all the decipherment from that point on.

(iii) The overriding and all-important assumption is that the letters of the cover text *can* be divided into two founts.

(iv) In the indeterminate cases in the experiment the decipherer knows just which they are. In these cases he has only to bear in mind a number of possible solutions rather than a unique solution. It is therefore only a matter of sifting a greater number of possibilities, most of which are quite easily eliminated on grounds of probability. The complication, to an experienced cryptographer, is not as great as it seems. In Mrs Gallup's case there are very few letters, if any, which are more or less determinate than any others, yet we see no evidence in her work that she believed that any of them could be indeterminate. In other words, for each letter she found only one possible rendering.

The conditions of the experiment certainly do not obtain for Mrs Gallup's decipherments. The implication of the experiment therefore is a narrow one: that where the cipher exists and is consistently applied, and where the decipherer has correctly grouped the letters of the cover text (and this means knowing exactly where to start),[1] then the decipherer can afford to be uncertain in a known 50 per cent of the cases whether to assign the letters to the *a*- or *b*-form.

The experiment suggests a further one. It stems from the blunt question: can even 50 per cent of the letters in Elizabethan italic type be assigned with certainty to the two forms? Suppose one could not assume (as our experiment did) that none of the remaining letters was wrongly assigned? We made a further test, to see what would happen when the decipherer, in addition to the indeterminate characters (cases, that is, of honest doubt), has to contend with definite errors of assignment. It is in the nature of the case that he should not know which assignments are wrong.

In this case a passage of 212 letters of good English was chosen and transliterated into *a*'s and *b*'s. By random selection 10 per cent of these were changed; these were to represent errors in assignment but were not indicated in any way. In addition 10 per cent were replaced by a query, to indicate that they were indeterminate; the possible letters were then ascertained and written down where they belonged. Note the very modest percentage in both cases. The sequence of possible letters was then given to Mrs Friedman. It ran:

1	2	3	4	5	6	7	8	9	10	11	12	13
C	Z	E	S	P	I–J	N	I	R	H	D	A	F
T	—	W	—	Q	L	W	—	S	—	M	—	X

14	15	16	17	18	19	20	21	22	23	24	25	26
G	U–V	E	E	A	T	N	A	S	I–J	P	O	P
H	—	—	—	B	—	O	—	—	L	Y	—	Q

27	28	29	30	31	32	33	34	35	36	37	38	39
A	L	Y	L	R	A	I–J	T	G	C	G	N	T
—	—	—	P	S	R	N	—	—	D	Y	—	—
—	—	—	—	—	—	—	—	—	G	—	—	—
—	—	—	—	—	—	—	—	—	H	—	—	—

---

[1] In Mrs Gallup's case it would also mean knowing where to go on, which words and letters to include in the cover text. In a mixed text made up of roman and italic this is a complicated business.

40	41	42	43	44	45	46	47	48	49	50	51	52
T	L	A	Q	U–V	A	T	D	N	M	E	F	L
–	–	R	–	–	–	U–V	U–V	O	–	P	–	M
–	–	–	–	–	–	–	–	–	–	–	–	P
–	–	–	–	–	–	–	–	–	–	–	–	Q

53	54	55	56	57	58	59	60	61	62	63	64	65
T	E	S	H	I–J	F	T	Z	F	R	B	M	C
U–V	–	–	–	N	–	–	–	O	–	–	–	T

66	67	68	69	70	71	72	73	74	75	76	77	78
H	E	L	R	A	S	S	N	B	D	O	N	E
–	G	–	–	C	–	–	O	F	–	–	–	–
–	–	–	–	E	–	–	–	–	–	–	–	–
–	–	–	–	G	–	–	–	–	–	–	–	–
–	–	–	–	R	–	–	–	–	–	–	–	–
–	–	–	–	T	–	–	–	–	–	–	–	–
–	–	–	–	W	–	–	–	–	–	–	–	–
–	–	–	–	Y	–	–	–	–	–	–	–	–

79	80	81	82	83	84	85	86	87	88	89	90	91
T	R	I–J	U–V	B	Q	E	N	A	S	O	E	E
Y	–	K	–	S	–	–	P	I–J	–	–	–	G
–	–	–	–	–	–	–	W	–	–	–	–	–
–	–	–	–	–	–	–	Y	–	–	–	–	–

92	93	94	95	96	97	98	99	100	101	102	103	104
G	E	T	H	E	N	O	O	R	W	S	T	A
N	F	–	–	–	–	X	Q	–	X	–	Y	–
–	–	–	–	–	–	–	–	–	Y	–	–	–
–	–	–	–	–	–	–	–	–	Z	–	–	–

105	106	107	108	109	110	111	112	113	114	115	116	117
N	A	P	M	O	S	A	A	L	C	C	P	E
–	–	–	Q	X	–	–	–	M	L	–	Q	–
–	–	–	–	–	–	–	–	–	T	–	–	–

118	119	120	121	122	123	124	125	126	127	128	129	130
R	F	E	U–V	A	B	K	B	T	H	A	T	W
–	–	N	–	E	–	–	D	U–V	–	–	–	–
–	–	–	–	I–J	–	–	–	–	–	–	–	–
–	–	–	–	N	–	–	–	–	–	–	–	–
–	–	–	–	R	–	–	–	–	–	–	–	–
–	–	–	–	W	–	–	–	–	–	–	–	–

131	132	133	134	135	136	137	138	139	140	141	142	143
O	R	D	B	F	C	Y	A	P	T	I–J	N	U–V
–	S	–	F	–	–	–	R	–	Y	L	–	Z
–	–	–	–	–	–	–	–	–	–	N	–	–
–	–	–	–	–	–	–	–	–	–	P	–	–
–	–	–	–	–	–	–	–	–	–	R	–	–
–	–	–	–	–	–	–	–	–	–	T	–	–
–	–	–	–	–	–	–	–	–	–	V	–	–

144	145	146	147	148	149	150	151	152	153	154	155	156
E	L	S	I	O	L	Q	O	D	O	F	A	I–J
–	T	–	–	–	–	–	–	–	X	X	–	L
–	–	–	–	–	–	–	–	–	–	–	–	N
–	–	–	–	–	–	–	–	–	–	–	–	P

157	158	159	160	161	162	163	164	165	166	167	168	169
C	H	E	M	A	B	T	F	O	R	E	N	D
D	–	–	–	C	–	–	–	–	S	F	P	H
–	–	–	–	–	–	–	–	–	T	–	–	–
–	–	–	–	–	–	–	–	–	U–V	–	–	–

170	171	172	173	174	175	176	177	178	179	180	181	182
A	U–V	E	B	B	A	N	E	B	K	U–V	R	C
C	–	F	S	–	–	–	–	S	–	–	W	–

183	184	185	186	187	188	189	190	191	192	193	194	195
E	O	G	C	N	P	A	E	W	N	Y	O	G
F	–	–	–	–	–	–	–	–	–	–	–	H

196	197	198	199	200	201	202	203	204	205	206	207	208
I–J	B	A	R	O	T	X	I–J	R	P	R	N	N
K	–	R	–	–	–	Z	–	T	–	–	–	–
L	–	–	–	–	–	–	–	W	–	–	–	–
M	–	–	–	–	–	–	–	Y	–	–	–	–

209	210	211	212
L	N	R	K
M	–	–	–
T	–	–	–
U–V	–	–	–

Mrs Friedman picked out THE as the probable first word—
indicated by one error and two possibilities. Then her eye was
caught by the 15th, 16th and 17th letters, UEE; the plain text

was probably QUEEN. Building on these assumptions she got: THE...MAD QUEEN TO A SLY ORAL ARRANGEMENT. Many a Baconian would have been glad to get so much sense; but since the words intervening and succeeding could not fall into place, she went back to the start. Almost at once the word SPANISH seemed to leap from the page. This suggested the third word, MASQUERADO, which had previously been MAD QUEEN TO. More of the first sentence came quite easily: 'The Spanish Masquerado is a poorly printed little quarto of five sheets from the press of....' She was able to look up the printer's name (Roger Ward) in our library. So she had eighteen words, or eighty-three letters in all.

For some reason she now got bogged down, and the steersman who had supplied 'the mad queen' now took over in earnest. She dredged up twenty-six more words from what Ewen called the 'subliminal storage', to complete the message after four hours' work as:

The Spanish Masquerado is a poorly printed little Quarto of five sheets from the press of Roger Ward fifteen eighty nine an entirely false legend about his work has grown up but the use of biformed type was common practice among sixteenth century printers.

The letters in italic are the ones she was unsure of. Now this is a good sensible message; the only trouble is that only one word is right from the eighteenth onwards. She tried again for two hours and twenty minutes, and produced the following text, saying that 'the sense is not too good'. The words in italic now are those which she felt to be completely certain.

The Spanish Masquerado is a poorly printed little Quarto of five sheets from the press of Roger Ward. The pages *of the* book are all

$$
\left\{
\begin{array}{l}
\text{as a whole so} \\
\text{totally imperfect} \\
\text{an almost} \\
\text{almost wholly}
\end{array}
\right\} \text{even for Ward } of \text{ all}
$$

printers in London and he must often have been a severe pain to many *Elizabethan printers.*

But intuition and reality do not always coincide. Mr Friedman told her which words in the second sentence were right; she then struggled for another two hours. At the end she found the whole passage except for four words which were rendered by a synonymous expression of the same length.

Let us examine the implications of this experiment. The assignment to *a*- and *b*-forms cannot always be made with certainty; and it is known that there are: (i) indeterminate letters—which cannot be assigned with certainty to the *a*- or *b*-form; and (ii) erroneous assignments. If we now take the first few possible letters in our sample text:

C Z E S P I–J N I R H
T   W   Q L W   S

it will be seen that we have for the purpose of the experiment arbitrarily limited the number of possibilities. The first letter is indeterminate; it can be C or T. Now suppose it had been erroneously classified; it would have introduced another range of possibilities. The second letter is an error; it happens here to come out as Z, so it draws attention to itself and can be discounted. Suppose it had been something more plausible? And so on; all that the decipherer—even in this artificially conditioned experiment—can hope for is that the possibilities set down may be sufficient to help him to hit upon a probable plain-text word—as Mrs Friedman did first with QUEEN and then, when she had recognized her error, with THE SPANISH. These two cases show that the suggested word may be plausible but wrong. How is one to know? One cannot; one can only continue to build up further assumed probable words before and after the one first found. Once Mrs Friedman found THE SPANISH, she had taken an immense step towards the goal. But she had a long way to go, and she was able to consult someone who knew the correct text.

How does all this compare with Mrs Gallup's method of decipherment? We believe it provides an exact parallel to her work. Though she did not use the term, she tacitly admitted the existence of a certain number of indeterminate letters: that a letter might very well be either an *a*- or *b*-form is suggested by the occasions when she alleged the existence of a dot or some similar indication as a justification for changing the assignment. That she also made errors we know very well—though she would strenuously have denied it: anyone who takes the trouble to compare her assignments with her 'master-forms' will see many cases where the assignment is wrong. Seymour for instance noted errors in her treatment of the capital C's and P's on p. 59 of *Henry VII* (see pp. 239 ff. above).

It will already have been noticed that one extremely important condition of our second experiment was that Mr Friedman, who knew what the enciphered text was, was there to be consulted. Mrs Friedman could therefore be told when she had extracted a partial solution and where she had gone wrong. The alleged encipherer of Mrs Gallup's texts was not there beside her; Mrs Gallup had therefore only her own sense of certainty to assure her that the message she had deciphered was the correct one.

If Mr Friedman had not been there, Mrs Friedman would have taken her first message as the correct one: as she pointed out, it was not only plausible and sensible but, to her mind, more so than the true message. Here are the two together,[1] Mrs Friedman's uppermost:

THE . SPANISH . MASQUERADO . IS . A . POORLY . PRINTED . LITTLE .
THE . SPANISH . MASQUERADO . IS . A . POORLY . PRINTED . LITTLE .

QUARTO . OF . FIVE . SHEETS . FROM . THE . PRESS . OF . ROGER . WARD .
QUARTO . OF . FIVE . SHEETS . FROM . THE . PRESS . OF . ROGER . WARD .

FI FTE EN . E IG HTY . NINE . AN . ENT IRELY . F ALS E . LE GE
HE . WAS . O*N* *E* . OF . THE . POOR ES T . IN . ALMOS T . *ALL* . T H*E* . S*E*

ND . A B OU T . HIS . WORK . HA S . GR OWN . UP . BUT . TH E . USE . O
*N*S E S . OF . *T* HAT . *WORD* . OF . T HE . PRI NT ERS . OF . L OND *O*

F . BIF OR MED . T YPE . WA S . COM MON . P R ACT ICE . AM ONG
N . AND . HE . *MU*S *T* . OFT EN . H AVE . BEE N . A . SOUR*CE* . OF . CON

. S IXT EE NTH . CENTURY . PRINTERS .
CERN . TO . HIS . BRO*THER* . *PRINTERS* .

[1] The correct text is the first two sentences of a paper by L. M. Oliver, 'The Spanish Masquerado: A problem in double edition' from *The Library*, June 1947, pp. 14–19.

There are similarities between Mrs Prescott's account of Mrs Gallup's first decipherment and Mrs Friedman's efforts in the experiment. Mrs Gallup picked out the word ELIZABETH, or an approximation to it; to make it exactly ELIZABETH she changed an assignment and repeated the change throughout. Mrs Friedman found QUEEN first (a wrong guess) and then T.E SP.NISH, which was right. Assuming that THE SPANISH MASQUERADO was the phrase in question she selected the necessary possibilities, and changed others where required (assuming an error in these cases). Mrs Gallup had only ELIZABETH to work with—a word which gives little indication of the context. As it happened, Mrs Gallup had Owenite-Baconian views about Elizabeth, and so produced an Owenite-Baconian message (which is bound to look suspicious to an outsider). Mrs Friedman assumed a bibliographical message was involved, and rightly; none the less she went completely wrong when she tried FIFTEEN EIGHTY NINE on the message —the date is right, but it just is not there. It so happened that a new sentence, a new line of thought, begins here, and this increases the element of conjecture. In fact the whole business of finding the likely word should have been reopened; and this would only happen if one realized another sentence had begun. Fortunately Mr Friedman could indicate that a fresh start was needed.

But Bacon could give no help to Mrs Gallup, unless she were a spiritualist as well as a Baconian. She, therefore, was always satisfied with her first decipherment.

To sum up the results of the experiment: in a message in which each letter may possibly be wrong—for the decipherer knew that a certain percentage was wrong without knowing which particular letters were concerned—it is possible to extract more than one intelligible and plausible plain text. If it be assumed to be true that Bacon or anyone else did indeed insert biliteral cipher messages in the italic type of the books concerned, we have already shown that the type-forms are so multitudinous and unsystematically varied that it is most unlikely that two or more rational investigators working independently will produce assignments which are the same or even almost the same. The discrepancy would certainly be more than the 10 per cent allowed in our experiment and might exceed 50 per cent. In fact it could vary widely with the number of investigators. If all the alternative assignments so produced were regarded as equally likely to be either right or wrong, and if the resulting plain text were deduced by the natural method of finding a probable word and building a message round it, then more than one plain text could be produced. And each text produced would have as much chance as the others of being correct—but mathematically the probability of its being correct is extremely low. What this means is that to the cryptologist no such solution can have any validity at all.

Nothing short of an instruction sheet to the printer of the First Folio, and an instruction which can be shown to have existed in 1623, could possibly *prove* that biliteral cipher messages were actually intended to be inserted in any book other than the ones which set out Bacon's demonstration of the cipher. Even documentary proof of an intention or a desire to insert the cipher cannot prove its successful insertion on a large scale. Printing conditions and methods simply did not permit it.

Proof is out of the question. Nor can one *infer* the existence of the cipher from Mrs Gallup's alleged decipherment of it. One could only accept a decipherment as testimony if it were demonstrable that the plain text was reached by the systematic and undeviating application of a genuine key. Mrs Gallup applied her key so arbitrarily that her results only show what it was she was determined to find.

The biliteral cipher is a good and interesting one. As cryptologists we regret being unable to find that it had been used. But that is the case; and what is more, we are willing to state (and in this bibliographers will add their support to cryptographers) that it is and always will be impossible on evidence derived from the study of type-forms to assert the existence of a cipher in any printed book of the period.

The message in the first experiment is:

The lessons have been arranged in a sequence according to their increasing order of complexity leading up gradually to . . .

CHAPTER XIX

CONCLUSION

THE techniques of the anti-Shakespearean cryptologists can be divided into three categories, as a result of our assessment by the twofold test which we suggested in ch. II.

First, there are those which are invalid, by our standards, because the crypto-system or the specific keys concerned are either not valid in themselves or are not rigorously applied. In this category fall all the systems described in chs. III–V and VIII–XII. Some of these systems could equally well be placed in our third category, and are mentioned there specifically.

Second, there are those which are unacceptable because the alleged plain text is so far from plain that to the outsider it seems nonsense. At best, it does not conform to accepted standards of significance or linguistic usage. In this category the most notable worker was Mrs Gertrude Horsford Fiske. She used the biliteral cipher and, as far as one can judge, she applied it as systematically as the type-forms permit: in consequence the messages she produced are gibberish, with the exception of a phrase here and there.

In the third category the cryptologists fail on both counts: their technique is inconsistent or faulty and their messages do not make sense either, by any strict standard. This group is the most numerous: it includes Hugh Black, Edgar Gordon Clark, Melchior's alleged decipherment—and for that matter all other alleged decipherments of the tombstone (ch. IV); Natalie Rice Clark (ch. VI), and Joseph Martin Feely (ch. VI); Sir Edwin Durning-Lawrence and all other decipherers of the long word (ch. VIII); and William Stone Booth (ch. IX).

If it is hoped that we are about to go on to a fourth category —of crypto-systems which pass our twofold test—we have to announce a disappointment: none does. Disappointing for us too, in a sense, since there would be a certain *réclame* to be gained by whoever settled the contest and could point at last to a decisive winner. But there it is; we have merely to incur the odium of a negative conclusion. We confess that we have contented ourselves with examining the claims of others; we have not ourselves attempted to find some other and valid cipher in the works commonly attributed to Shakespeare. This is in keeping with our unwillingness to be partisan about it all. Whoever seeks actively for a cipher usually believes one to be there. And yet on the other hand we shall not hesitate to confess this measure of scepticism: before we start looking for ciphers we need to be assured that there is some likelihood of there being one. There is some onus of proof, or at any rate of suspicion, which anti-Stratfordians need to meet, unless one is merely to doubt on principle that any author really wrote the works commonly attributed to him. As to the main issue—we are left where we were: unable to state positively who wrote the plays. But as far as the suppliers of cryptographic evidence are concerned, we neither respect their methods nor accept their conclusions.

In case it may be helpful to Baconian cryptologists who wish to try again, or to the general reader who would like some observations on the whole topic, we add these concluding remarks, which dot the most relevant i's and cross the more important t's.

Our first category contains many a cryptologist who no doubt started off with at least a professed intention of being rigorous in the application of an equally rigorous method. To put it crudely, he meant to play fair. As a result, his method permitted him to produce certain results, but they were obviously semantically bizarre, grammatically weak, decrepit in spelling, or just odd altogether. Here a temptation presents itself which the professional cryptologist regards as the great betrayal: exceptions are made to the rules, and these permit the 'right' kind of messages to be extracted. This tactic is accept-able to the professional cryptologist only if the exceptions do not exceed a certain maximum. If necessary he could derive the permitted incidence of exceptions mathematically. In the cases dealt with in this book (with the exception of Mrs Gallup) this has never been necessary—the self-deception on the part of the amateur cryptologist is obvious. Apart from himself, it deceives only those who wish to be deceived. Our first category thus contains many systems where the exponent finds himself forced, if he is honest, to come forward to 'explain' deviations. When he is not so honest, we have noted his deviations for him. Mrs Gallup had the neatest argument for exceptions—that ciphers are meant to hide things, not to make them clear. True: but ciphers are also meant to be deciphered, or no one would use them; and even their tricks and blinds must be logically derived, or no one would ever find his way through them. Indeed, true cryptography is rich in these deceptions and changes of method; and it is consequently all the easier for the professional to see through devices which are only invoked to help the decipherer out of a hole.

There is also perhaps a lesson to be derived from the solitary pre-eminence of Mrs Fiske in category two. She was one of those rare investigators who conscientiously applied a trusted method and accepted whatever results it gave her. The results are not encouraging, indeed they lead to a plain inference—that, in this instance at any rate, the cipher in question was not used. Not that it would have been much use saying so to Mrs Fiske or those few others who accepted her work and emulated it.

Our third category is the most numerous. This leads to the conclusion that, if so many investigators fail on both elementary counts, it must be because none of them has understood their absolute necessity. Their work was doomed from the outset because they did not have either the necessary technical knowledge or what one can only call the right basic attitude. One notes in fact a readiness to reach previously posited conclusions by pseudo-cryptography.

In most cases the system adopted is a defective one, such as could never be proposed by a true cryptographer. One does not need to be a professional—only an uncommitted observer —to note further that in these cases the messages produced are only such messages as the method will permit. This sounds a paradox: it is best explained by a specific example. You will only get, by anagramming honorificabilitudinitatibus, such rearrangements as that assembly of letters will make. The best that can be done with it we have seen; and we can only say that if Bacon had inserted the word in the plays meaning any one of those messages to be extracted, he was a trifler.

The whole point is that the originator of a so-called 'concealment cipher' starts with a message and enciphers it. The cover text which emerges is determined by the cryptogram. The decipherer works backwards and should reproduce the plain text. But if he applies a given method to a 'cover text' which in fact conceals nothing, he will only get the decipherment permitted by the fortuitous conjunction of method and text—which is likely to be nonsense. If then he permits himself deviations from his rules, he can work just as close to a desired message as the three circumstances—method, text and deviations—permit. If he has very strong preconceptions, we have displayed fairly ample evidence that he will choose deviations and exceptions which allow him to produce a preconceived text—for instance, a Baconian one. Unless he is absolutely unscrupulous, however, the text is likely to retain that slightly bizarre mixture of aptness, strangeness, and occasionally total inconsequence imposed by its origin. Sometimes the decipherer will be in control, sometimes the subliminal storage will take over.[1]

It needs also to be pointed out that some of the investigators we have discussed have absolutely no conception of mathematical probability—not even that sound guide usually provided by common sense. To go back to the point about the method determining the results; it is pretty plain that if the anti-Shakespearean cryptologist used a really formidable and genuine method on a cover text which concealed no cipher, he would produce complete gibberish (he would be with Mrs Fiske in category two, in fact). This situation is avoided by choosing a key

[1] There is a strong parallel with messages from the 'spirit world', especially those produced by mechanical means like planchettes, which permit unconscious or subconscious direction from the manipulator. The ordinary person is inclined in the one case to feel that 'if that is the after-life, let me be annihilated', in the other that 'if that is the best Bacon can do he's been wasting our time'. To put it strongly, there is the same mixture of triviality and some things even worse. What kind of mind produced the phantasies of incest and strange parentage in chs. x and xi?

which lends itself to filing down. The extreme examples are Donnelly and Cunningham. Donnelly's 'roots', 'modifiers', and so on, were so numerous and could be so readily diluted that they gave him absolute certainty of singling out any word he wanted (provided it was there) and justifying his choice by a few fairly simple arithmetical dodges. Cunningham's method could be used, as we showed in our letter to Colonel Roosevelt, to produce any desired message.

A parallel case is provided by those systems using anagrams loosely, as Arensberg used them. One can only repeat that short signatures like 'Bacon' can be found by these methods in any book of any length. Their incidence in the Folio proves absolutely nothing. Anagramming the long word is in a sense a more rigorous pastime, since one has an absolutely determined number and range of letters. It is none the less a highly academic and unprofitable pursuit.

Basically, one is forced to choose between two broad general conclusions if one wishes to adhere to a belief in the presence of a cipher in the plays.

First, one may believe that the plays were written to conceal a cipher of some magnitude (e.g. the theory that the whole canon of Baconian writings—and more besides—incorporates a long single narrative). Now the message to be deciphered determines the form of the cover text. It is therefore quite beside the point for Stratfordians to admire the beauty, the profundity or the eloquence of the plays; they are mere vehicles for a message; and their elements are merely those required by the message. In a sense it is fortunate that the plays make dramatic, or any sense at all, given the difficulty of reconciling the needs of the cipher with those of the plausible deception of the world at large. One must confess an inherent improbability. However, if it *did* happen, and Bacon managed to produce such a dazzling cover text that no one for many years suspected the presence of a cipher, his genius was all the greater.

Second, if one does not hold this extreme view, one must believe instead that Bacon wrote the plays as plays, and was conscious of their worth, but felt all the more obliged to assert his authorship in hints here and there—short snatches of *sotto voce* meant to put him right with posterity. Hence all the signatures and other anagrams.

The initial difficulty with the first alternative is its improbability. The difficulty with the second is that all the messages produced could so easily have happened by chance: one needs to be already a Baconian (and rather a naïve one) to believe that they occurred by design. If one is not a Baconian but, say, an Oxfordian, one can find other appropriate anagrams of equal implausibility. Those committed to neither side will draw the only moral: that none of the 'signatures' was inserted by design. But one may well wonder if reasoned argument is going to carry much weight with investigators who are so constantly moved by the providential ordering of the merely coincidental.

If it is stretching the bounds of credibility to conceive the plays as mere vehicles for a cipher, *a fortiori* it is more unlikely that they are so to speak honeycombed with ciphers—a great structure built up of the intertwined complexities of several concurrent systems. Yet we are asked to believe this. Mrs Gallup for instance said at one point that Bacon had confessed to inserting six. Mrs Gallup's 'revelation' may well have been the trigger which set off the investigations of others who later claimed to have found those particular ciphers. If her 'revelation' itself does not stand up under investigation—and it does not—then the others must collapse when this keystone is removed.

If their existence be admitted to be possible quite independently of the biliteral, they must be added to the multitude of ciphers claiming attention. If their claims to consideration are admitted to be equal, and if all are taken as valid, then the plays are indeed so riddled with ciphers that the uncommitted observer must feel that the whole case is becoming absurd. He may naturally be inclined to dismiss them all, on the grounds of probability alone, without scrutinizing any.

We have not so dismissed them because we wished not to succumb to the hasty dogmatism of some Shakespeareans. Moreover, it was important that we should be *seen* to have given each representative system a careful examination. We felt the need to conduct an inquiry of which it could not be said that it was a mere huff-and-puff dismissal of the whole question by persons committed to the opposing point of view—persons who might gain a living by expounding orthodox Shakespeare scholarship, or who might have some emotional stake in the question. So there one is, with very many ciphers competing for attention, and the exponents of each claiming that theirs is the only true one. It may be noted that if heat is generated in exchanges between Stratfordians and anti-Stratfordians, no more charity is shown between supporters of different anti-Stratfordian theories. New theorists sniff at the old, and say flatly that everyone else is wrong. In Arensberg's case, even his own early theories are admittedly abandoned as the product of an unilluminated fancy.

This does not shake the outsider so much; he may be willing to concede that all the others have been wrong. The perpetual question is—Is the new one right? If it is a matter of cryptology we have indicated tests and standards which may be invoked. It will have occurred to the reader that these are in fact the principles of common sense writ large, or more exactly the principles of logic and scientific method. These are the principles on which a true cryptographer proceeds, and they are the principles on which cryptological 'solutions' must be judged. Basically it is by misunderstanding or misuse of these principles and methods that the devisers of the systems we have investigated fail.

Nor are invalid cryptological 'solutions' confined to anti-Stratfordian theses. In ch. x we cited Rossetti and Arensberg, both believing there are ciphers in Dante. One of the most notable cases is that of the centuries-old *Voynich Manuscript*, discovered in 1912, a small volume by an unknown author consisting entirely of cryptic writing and mysterious drawings; three different 'solutions' of this manuscript have been published. The late William Romaine Newbold, Professor of Philosophy at the University of Pennsylvania, spent the last dozen years of his life on that manuscript and claimed to have found the key to its decipherment; but his solution is purely subjective. So is that of Prof. Leonell Strong, of the Medical

School Faculty of Yale University; and so also is that of Joseph Martin Feely, mentioned in another connection in an earlier chapter.

The cryptologist must discipline himself to follow certain procedures and submit to certain checks. Like the experimental scientist he is observing phenomena or occurrences to determine what they are, to discover whether they are random or systematic, and if systematic how they work—what principle can be detected in them. His method must be one of scrupulous analysis; he must be clear just what it is he observes, and what circumstances limit it or determine it. His analysis must be followed by a strict process of inference, and here he must be on his guard against introducing false steps in his argument. Indeed, if he has not conditioned himself to a mental attitude of unprejudiced receptiveness, if he allows preconceptions or unsupported inferences to pervert his argument, he is lost. He is trying to formulate an exact statement about the phenomenon before him, and a statement which will either account for all its characteristics or not conflict with any of them. He does not do this by forcing on it an interpretation which he is anxious that it should bear. Who expressed it better than Bacon? The experimental scientist has 'a mind nimble and versatile enough to catch the resemblances of things (which is the chief point), and at the same time, steady enough to fix and distinguish their subtle differences;...endowed by nature with the desire to seek, the patience to doubt, fondness to meditate, slowness to assert, readiness to reconsider, carefulness to dispose and set in order; and...neither affecting what is new, nor admiring what is old, and hating every kind of imposture'.[1]

Here is the nub of the whole matter. Cryptology is an application of scientific method: it is therefore nothing to the point for certain anti-Stratfordians—notably Mrs Gallup—to remark that the decipherment of Bacon's alleged messages is an 'art' as well as a science. All they do here is to cloud the issue. They are using the word 'art' in the sense of an applied skill. It certainly is that; the skilled cryptanalyst has a flair or a knack or an instinct—call it what you will—that the unskilled person

[1] From the Proemium to the *De Interpretatione Naturae*.

cannot have. His knowledge is so readily available to him that it can prompt his procedures quicker than thought—or so it seems. This does not alter the undoubted fact that the same skilled cryptanalyst, having seemingly arrived at his result by ellipses in his chain of reasoning, can go back and indicate the omitted steps. The chain itself is firm; it can be followed by those to whom it is explained; others can independently reach the same results; and the result itself is intelligible. It is also true that the cryptanalyst, having determined by his analysis what a crypto-system is *not*, discovers by empirical testing what it *is*: he applies a key to the cryptogram as a chemist might apply litmus paper or some other reagent to a substance. There is an 'art' if you like in selecting the appropriate reagent without running through the whole range of possibilities, but it is none the less a scientific procedure, and the deductions which follow the testing must be just as rigorous as those in any other science.

If there had been any of Mrs Gallup's team at Riverbank who could—haltingly at first, but more and more quickly as they acquired her 'art'—apply their knowledge of the biliteral cipher to the decipherment of the texts, and if they had duplicated her results, she would have had a powerful case. None could. It was not for lack of honest trying. Does this not suggest that her whole case was based on subjective intuitions, on self-persuasion? What Colonel Fabyan failed to realize, throughout his campaign to 'sell' Mrs Gallup's decipherments, was that no demonstration, however good, can take the place of experiments which can be repeated and will produce identical results.

It must be remembered that the biliteral cipher is the one reputable system among all those proposed so far in support of anti-Stratfordian theories—that is, it is the only cipher which the professional cryptologist could admit as a valid system in itself. Yet we think we have shown decisively that it was not used. As for the others, not only were they not used; they were not usable, nor even credible. We suggest that those who wish to dispute the authorship of the Shakespeare plays should not in future resort to cryptographic evidence, unless they show themselves in some way competent to do so. They must do better than their predecessors. We urge that they should acquaint themselves at least with the basic principles of the subject, and that they conduct their arguments with some standards of rigour. Before they add to the very large corpus of writings on the subject, they might also consider subjecting their findings to the inspection of a professional who has no strong leaning to either side of the dispute. If all this is done the argument will be raised to a higher plane. There is even the possibility that it would cease altogether.

INDEX

a- and *b*-type forms. *See* Biliteral cipher (technical)
acronymy, 94, 95
acrostic(s): acrotelestic, 128, 142, 149; anagrammatic, 137, 140–51; authentic examples of, 95–100; compound anagrammatic —, 137, 142; cross-gartered —, 143, 144, 147; gallows or potence, 128; history and derivation, 92, 94–5; kinds of, 97, 128; length a determining factor, 128, 139, 140, 145, 147; mesostic, 128; — method: term incorrectly used by Booth, 114–17; popular in Elizabethan literature, 99; progressive simple telestic, 97, 147; — signatures: Booth's method for locating, 114–15; — — found by Theobald, 177–8; simple, 97, 128; simple telestic, 97; used to convey prophecies, 95; — — establish authorship, 92; what makes authentic, 98–9, 100
Addison: derides acrostics and anagrams, 96
Address to the Reader, 1611 Bible: Bacon seal in, 182
Advancement of Learning, The: Bacon's rule of concealment for ciphers, 26; message found in, by Gallup, 193; 1605 edition, 28, 70, 170, 251; translation of 1623 Latin edition (London), 28, 141, 142, 171, 177; 1624 Latin edition (Paris), 189, 193 n.
Aldus Manutius, 95
Allen, Charles (*Notes on the Bacon-Shakespeare Question,* 1939), vii
Allen, Percy: contact with spirit world, 9; Oxford *v.* Bacon debates, 7, 14
Allusion Books, The Shakespeare, 12
Alphabet(s): bi-formed, Bacon's cipher, 31, 189; biliterary, Bacon's key, 29, 189; classifiers, 209, 221; Hebrew, 182; numerical, 170, 171, 180, 186
Amboise, Pierre, author *Histoire Naturelle,* 176
American Baconiana. See Baconiana
Amoretti and *Epithalamion*: Oxford signature in, 132

Amorosa Visione: Boccaccio acrostic in, 95–6
anachronisms in cipher messages, 160 n., 168, 214, 242 n.
anagram(s): a paradox, 281; authentic examples of, 93–4, 111; defined, 18, 92, 138; Donnelly's epitaph cipher, 54–6; Dryden's opinion of, 93
anagrammatic acrotelestic (Arensberg term), 142, 149
anagrammatic ciphers: Arden, 85–7; Arensberg, 141–4, 283; critique of, 113; Cunningham and Bauer, 156–8; Johnson, 83–5; the long word, 102–7
Anagrammatic Code: term used by Bauer, 164–8 *passim*
Anagrammatic Cypher, a Bacon invention?, 213
Anatomy of Melancholy (Burton), 65, 173, 194
Andrewes, Lancelot: a group author, 9, 156
Angelical Salutation (*Ave Maria*): anagrammed, 110–11
Anglo-phonetics (E. G. Clark), 54
anti-Stratfordians: belief concerning other authors than Shakespeare, 9; change of their methods, 285; double aim of, xv; each scoffs at others, 285; seize on arguments of Stratfordians, 13–14
Antiquities of Warwickshire: account of Shakespeare epitaph, 62
Apothegms: cipher placed in by Rawley?, 202
Arcadia (Sidney): source of Owen's King's Move cipher, 70, 71
Arden: his anagrammatic cipher, 85–7; — the authors' refutation of, 87; numerical signatures, 184
Arensberg, Walter Conrad: art collection, 137; change of method, 152; cipher in Dante, 137, 147; compared to Gabriele Rossetti, 154; finds Bacon signatures, 141–51; loose use of terms, 283; validity of methods, 153; visit to the authors, 150–1; 117, 156, 185, 283, 285
Argenis (Barclay), 109

cover name, a Cunningham term, 158–9, 162, 166, 185

cover text (Bacon's 'infolding writing'), 29, 158, 167, 189, 190, 239, 265, 267, 271 n.; determined by hidden text, 282, 283

cross-gartered acrostic (Arensberg term), 143–5

cryptanalysis: an application of scientific method, 21; art and skill in, 286, 287; defined, 15. *See also* cipher systems; cryptography; cryptology

cryptic legend in English parish church, 88

Cryptogram Puzzle Book, The, 23

cryptograms: capable of proof, xv, xvii; do keys exist for, in Shakespeare works?, 25–6; puzzles masked as, 23; solution of, *see* cryptologic validity; twofold requirement for validity of, 26; uses of, 16

cryptography: defined, 15; Bacon treatise on, xv

Cryptography of Shakespeare (Arensberg), 137, 139, 146–52

Cryptography of Dante (Arensberg), 137, 147

cryptologic validity: bifold tests for, 26, 279; categories of invalid methods, 279; correct solution only solution, 24, 25, 26, 113, 227; infallible test of, 23, 25, 74, 204, 211, 233, 287; length of message a factor, 22–3, 62, 100, 140, 145, 147–8; linguistic tests for, 26, 214, 279, 282; of anagrammatic methods, 107, 112, 113; of Arensberg methods, 143–54 *passim*, 283; of authentic acrostics, 100; of Bacon's Biliteral Cipher, 189–90; of Booth and followers, 120, 121, 123, 127, 129, 130, 134; of Cunningham and Bauer, 158, 159, 162, 166, 168, 279; of Donnelly, 45–50 *passim*, 279–83; of Gallup and followers, 213–15, 266, 277–8, 279; of numerical seals, 184–7; of Owen, 65, 68–9; summary of invalid methods, 279

cryptology: age of, xv; an application of scientific method, 286–7; defined, 15; is certain ground, 14; principles based on common sense, 15, 285;

use of, in sixteenth century, xv. *See also* cipher systems; cryptography; cryptologic validity

Cryptomenytices et Cryptographiæ (Selenus), 117, 181

cryptosystems. *See* cipher systems

Cunningham, Granville C.: follower of Arensberg, 151

Cunningham, Wallace McCook: a case history, 156–62; held group theory, 8; multiplicity of keys, 283; 185

Curiosities of Literature (D'Israeli), 93 n.

curricula: word found by Gallup in cipher, 214

Curtis, Dr George B.: assesses Baxter tests, 226; dispute with Ewen *re* Gallup, 232–4; his ultimate opinion, 232 n.; tests of biliteral cipher, 225

Cymbeline: signature in, 121

da Genova, Giovanni: author Latin Grammar (1460), 107

Daniel, Samuel: a group author, 8

Dante: in anagram of long word, 106; signatures, 137, 147

d'Aquino, Maria: immortalized by Boccaccio's acrostic, 95–6

Darnley, Henry: in Duncan, 166

Davies, John: copyist and scrivener, 102; maker of acrostics, 96; seals in, 176

Dawson, Dr Giles E., xvi

Day, John: foremost Elizabethan printer, 220

de Astorga, Marques: name anagrammatized, 93

De Augmentis Scientiarum: bi-formed type in, 189; wherein Bacon gives full explanation of his cipher, 28–32, 192; 34, 193, 200, 202, 225, 229

decipherer: Bacon's 'Letter to the—', 63–4; Gallup as —, 197; how to know he is right, 18, 20, 21

Defoe, Daniel: as author of the Plays, 7; seal of *Crusoe*, 181

De Interpretatione Naturae (Bacon), 286 n.

Dekker, Thomas: a group author, 8

Demblon, Celestin: nominated Roger Manners, Earl of Rutland, as author, 6